Yankee
ROCK & ICE

A History of Climbing in the
Northeastern United States

Laura and Guy Waterman
S. Peter Lewis—Photography

STACKPOLE
BOOKS

To Molly and Brad

Copyright © 1993 by Laura and Guy Waterman

Published by
STACKPOLE BOOKS
Cameron and Kelker Streets
P.O. Box 1831
Harrisburg, PA 17105

Photographs collected by S. Peter Lewis.

Printed in the United States of America

10 9 8 7 6 5 4 3 2 1

First Edition

Library of Congress Cataloging-in-Publication Data

Waterman, Laura.
 Yankee rock and ice : a history of climbing in the
Northeastern United States / Laura and Guy Waterman.
       p.   cm.
 Includes bibliographical references and index.
 ISBN 0-8117-1633-3
 1. Rock climbing—Northeastern States—History.
 2. Snow and ice climbing—Northeastern States—History.
 I. Waterman, Guy.   II. Title.
 GV199.42.N68W38   1993
 796.5'223'0974—dc20   92-26562
                                                      CIP

Contents

Preface

ERNEST THOMPSON SETON tells a fable about a peddler who sold his wares all day in a village where the villagers paid him with lies instead of money. So the peddler collected all the lies in a large black bag. At the end of the day the bag was full and bulging with all the lies inside. The peddler gave the bag a hearty shake, whereupon it seemed to have less inside. Repeatedly the peddler shook the bag until it had less and less in it and finally appeared to be almost empty. Then the peddler reached inside and removed all that was left: a small bar of pure gold. The astonished villagers cried: "Are you a magician?" The peddler replied: "No, I'm a historian."

We thought this a fine fable, and we told it to William B. Willcox, who was Yale's best ice climber in 1930 and by 1982 was a distinguished retired historian and editor of the Benjamin Franklin Papers. Willcox sent us a note later: "I'm still cherishing your fable about the historian (but the gold is never pure)." We wrote back: "If the gold is never pure, is that not then but one more lie?" He responded:

> Impure gold isn't a lie; it's just not 100 percent the real thing. The old idea that we can know the past in all its fullness as it actually was, *wie es eigentlich gewesen,* is pretty well discarded; all we can get is an approximation of the truth, which is what I meant by impure.

Still later, we recounted this exchange to Robert E. Spiller, then in his late eighties and revered dean of American literary historians. Spiller's old eyes lit up and he told us that, no, the gold is not pure truth, but it is far more important than truth. It is the creative act of the historian to assemble what remains of the past and to impose on it his or her own creative imagination, so as to produce generalization and conclusion, which is what distinguishes history from mere chronology. Done well, mused Spiller, doubtless recalling the golden years of his own achievements, the results are indeed pure gold.

Still another font of wisdom for us—for thirty-five years for one of us—has been the distinguished Southern literary critic Louis D. Rubin; and he once put it this way:

> Neither in memory, nor in the interpretation of its meaning for the present, does the truth of our experience lie. It is in the shaping of the lineaments of memory into patterns that will reveal their own meaning that experience becomes real. The way to possess it is to make it into a story that will be authentic because so much did not happen that way at all.

The gold is never pure . . . nonetheless, it *is* gold.

We have been collecting—lies? well, let's call them recollections and reminiscences—of northeastern climbers for more than ten years. We have shaken our black bag of notes many, many times and out have fallen not one but two bars of . . . substance far less pure than gold. These gems of impurity we humbly lay at the feet of our readers.

Our research began in 1979 as an effort to assemble, in one book, a comprehensive history of hiking, climbing, and the whole story of emerging northeastern mountain recreation since the Pilgrims first bouldered on Plymouth Rock. Near the end of this project, we had to concede that rock and ice climbers tend to be a breed apart from other mountain recreationists. So we separated out the nontechnical climbing, or hikers' history, and published that separately (*Forest and Crag: A History of Hiking, Trail Blazing and Adventure in the Northeast Mountains,* Boston, AMC Books, 1989).

For the climbers' history presented here, we were exceptionally fortunate that we started just in time. That is, the founding fathers of the 1920s were still around during the early 1980s. We had opportunity to talk at length with them all, and many have since died—Robert Underhill, John Case, Hassler Whitney, and Fritz Wiessner, to mention a quartet of giants among the elders of the tribe. They were a hardy bunch, having lived vigorously into their eighties and nineties, all of them gracious and generous about sharing their memories and their perspectives on the development of the sport.

For more recent years, we attempted to talk with everyone who we were told might have useful perspective. We talked with 156 climbers by our count and had useful correspondence with another 29. Again, almost everyone was extremely helpful, although among this diverse population we encountered some who were surly or even declined to help. Their view of our effort may perhaps be correct: that no one can write objectively about so recent a past. Historians should have at least twenty-five years, if not fifty, to form a balanced view of events. Our observations and generalizations about the years since 1960 (half the book!) should therefore be regarded as tentative and exploratory. Future historians will modify and correct our generalizations—and current readers will doubtless be eager to begin that process.

Besides talking and corresponding with many climbers, we also tried to gain firsthand acquaintance with climbing areas and routes of historical significance. We are greatly indebted to a number of climbers who, like Dave and Debbie Duncanson, introduced us to areas we had never climbed before, such as Maine's Mount Desert and many of the Boston area crags; and others who, like Jack Taylor and Hassler Whitney, steered us up early routes that few can find today, such as the original lines on the Pinnacle and Willard in New Hampshire and Whitney's own routes on Connecticut's Sleeping Giant; and others who, like John Dunn or Molly Burns, helped us find long-forgotten variants such as the 1929 ascent of *Damnation Gully* (fourteen years before its recorded "first" ascent) or the seventeen-pitch version of the *Whitney-Gilman,* reconstructed from a copy of Underhill's notes made in 1930. Our ability to experience firsthand the more recent routes ran up against a barrier we regret: our own limitations in that rapidly expanding world beyond 5.9, what today's Washington pundits might call double-digit fifth-class climbing. On ice, we got up some of the dead-vertical stuff they climb these days at Lake Willoughby but only because of the strong rope and stronger arms of Mike Young, who kindly led (pulled) us up. But we tried to keep our historical research from being purely theoretical.

We were fortunate in having a rich fund of written accounts to draw from. Northeastern climbing history is blessed by Robert Underhill's having been editor of *Appalachia* beginning in 1926, in time to record rock climbing news during the next eventful years. Other published sources of great value are the early guidebooks that noted first ascent data. For these, history is indebted to Art Gran and Dick Williams, Sam Streibert and John Reppy, Willy Crowther, Trudy Healy, and Joe Cote. Their modern successors have carried forth admirably. Other major contributions have been the historical essays in recent guidebooks, among which the work of Al Rubin is especially distinguished.

For the benefit of interested readers and future researchers, we have deposited all our notes and source material with the Special Collections of Dartmouth College Library, Hanover, New Hampshire. In this book, we list the chief sources of information in a "Reference Note" at the end of each chapter. Specific sources for each quotation and detailed piece of information are recorded in a sixty-six-page paper on file with all our other notes at Dartmouth. We did not wish to encumber the general reader with an imposing array of footnotes, but we hope the interested researcher will find all the references he or she could desire at Dartmouth.

In our opinion, this history is greatly enriched by the photography and illustrations, all of which were gathered and prepared for this book by S. Peter Lewis of Fryeburg, Maine, who is clearly the best climbing photographer operating in the northeast over the past ten years. We are also grateful to many climbers, past and present, who generously permitted inclusion of some of their treasured shots. Especially helpful were Henry Barber, Gerry Bloch, Ken and Betty Henderson, Don Mellor, Ken Nichols, Dick Williams, Rick Wilcox, and Joe Muir of The Black and White Image. We are particularly fortunate in having had the run of Walter Howe's magnificent photo collection, which is now deposited at Dartmouth along with all our material. We are greatly indebted to the Mountaineering Committee of the Boston Chapter of the Appalachian Mountain Club for their making this material available to us and to future students of climbing history.

As these notes suggest, we have much help to acknowledge. Besides all of the foregoing, and the specific acknowledgments for each chapter, we'd like especially to thank Bradley J. Snyder, who edited the first draft of everything we wrote; Jonathan Waterman, who read the entire manuscript and commented perceptively; Dick Williams, who reviewed the chapters on the Shawangunks and made many useful suggestions; S. Peter Lewis, whose work on the photography was both indispensable and admirable; and Judith Schnell of Stackpole Books, whose editorial direction, professional expertise, and heartening encouragement were gratefully appreciated.

A note on style may be helpful. We have generally italicized route names. But in some cases where a mountain feature becomes a route, it's not always easy to say when it is one and when it's the other. For example, the Pinnacle is a topographical feature on Mount Washington that became a rock route only after it was climbed in 1928. The Black Dike is a geological phenomenon found on Cannon Mountain, but it became one of the Northeast's more significant ice routes in 1971. We have tried to apply italics only when we were clearly talking about a climber's route, not a mountain feature, but we may not have been as consistent as we should have. Indeed, for all the generous help that we have acknowledged here, errors that remain should be regarded as strictly the responsibility of the authors. ■

Acknowledgments

G RATEFUL ACKNOWLEDGMENT IS also extended to the following individuals and publishers for permission to use in the following excerpts:
Chapter 1. Quotation of Henry Van Hoevenberg: Henry Van Hoevenberg, "The Legend of Indian Pass," reprinted in *Adirondac*, July–August 1958, pp. 81–84; the original appeared in *Stoddard's Northern Monthly*, August 1906, pp. 1–3. Reprinted with permission from the Adirondack Mountain Club. Quotation about Mel Hathaway: Tithonus [author], "Washing a Shirt on the Gothics," *High Spots*, January 1932, pp. 20–21. Reprinted with permission from the Adirondack Mountain Club. Quotation of H. L. Emerson: H. L. Emerson, "A Rock Climb in Southern New Hampshire," *Appalachia*, June 1917, pp. 154–157. Reprinted with permission from the Appalachian Mountain Club.

Chapter 3. Quotation of Robert Underhill: Robert L. M. Underhill, "Hazard on Mt. Willard," *Appalachia*, December 1945, pp. 539–540. Reprinted with permission from the Appalachian Mountain Club. Quotation of Will Allis: letter from Will Allis to L&GW, May 1, 1982. Reprinted with permission from Will Allis.

Chapter 4. Quotations of Percy Olton: Percy Olton, "New York Rock Climbs," *Appalachia*, June 1938, pp. 12–26. Reprinted with permission from the Appalachian Mountain Club. Quotations of Miriam Underhill: Miriam Underhill, "Ironmongery Then and Now," *Yearbook of the Ladies Alpine Club* (London), 1957, pp. 27–29. Reprinted with permission from the Alpine Club Library. Quotation from Dartmouth Mountaineering Club: William B. Rotch, "Introducing the Dartmouth Mountaineering Club, Hanover, NH," *Appalachia*, December 1937, p. 532. Reprinted with permission from the Appalachian Mountain Club. Quotation of Kenneth Henderson: letter from Kenneth A. Henderson to L&GW, June 26, 1982. Reprinted with permission from Kenneth A. Henderson. Quotation of British climber: letter from George A. R. Spence to Walter Howe, undated (postmarked June 5, 1936), in Walter Howe Papers, Dartmouth College Library. Reprinted with permission from Dartmouth College Library.

Chapter 6. Quotations of Julian Whittlesey: letters from Julian Whittlesey to L&GW, December 2, 1980, and December 21, 1980. Reprinted with permission from Julian Whittlesey.

Interlude/Anniversary Waltz in Pinnacle Gully: Four Climbing Generations on Huntington Ravine's Classic Route: Adapted from Guy Waterman's article of the same name in *Appalachia,* December 1990, pp. 8–17. Reprinted with permission from the Appalachian Mountain Club. Quotation of Michael Young: letter from Michael Young to L&GW, date unknown, ca. 1989. Reprinted with permission from Michael Young.

Chapter 7. Quotations of Percy Olton: Percy Olton, "New York Rock Climbs," *Appalachia,* June 1938, pp. 12–26. Reprinted with permission from the Appalachian Mountain Club. Quotation of Ken Nichols: Ken Nichols, "Historically Significant Climbs and Events in Connecticut," notes supplied to L&GW. (Undated.) Reprinted with permission from Ken Nichols. Quotations about *Madame Grunnebaum's Wulst:* anecdote circulated widely at the Shawangunks. Quoted words are from a version in a letter to L&GW, early 1980s, reprinted with permission from its author.

Chapter 8. Quotation about Irvin Davis: letter from Herb and Jan Conn to L&GW, September 16, 1991. Reprinted with permission from Herb and Jan Conn. Quotation by Walter Howe: Walter Howe Papers, Dartmouth College Library: Howe's Journal for April 19, 1938. Reprinted with permission from Dartmouth College Library. Quotation of Ray Garner: letter from Ray Garner to L&GW, December 10, 1987. Reprinted with permission from Virginia K. Garner. Quotation from Irvin Davis: Irvin M. Davis, "Last Will and Testament of the Chairman of the Rock Climbing Committee," quoted in Notes on "Rock Climbing," *Appalachia,* June 1944, pp. 114–116. Reprinted with permission from the Appalachian Mountain Club.

Chapter 9. Quotations of Beckett Howorth: Beckett Howorth, "Rock Climbing in the Shawangunks," *Appalachia,* December 1940, pp. 245–248. Reprinted with permission from the Appalachian Mountain Club.

Chapter 10. Quotation of British climber: Dick Sale, "Mountaineering's Real Values," *Mountain* 58, November-December 1977, p. 42. Reprinted with permission of *Mountain.*

Chapter 11. Quotation from Arnold Wexler: Arnold Wexler, "The Theory of Belaying," *American Alpine Journal,* 1950, pp. 378–405. Reprinted with permission from the American Alpine Club. Quotations of Safety Code: mimeographed list of pointers for beginners, "Safety Code," distributed by the Rock Climbing Committee of the New York Chapter, Appalachian Mountain Club, 1953; copy in archives of this committee. Reprinted with permission from the New York Chapter, Appalachian Mountain Club. "Safety Code" in Archives, Mountaineering Committee, New York Chapter, Appalachian Mountain Club. Reprinted with permission from the New York Chapter, Appalachian Mountain Club. Quotation of Barry Corbet: unidentified memorandum, dated 1958, by J. Barry Corbet, in Dartmouth Mountaineering Club folders, Dartmouth Outing Club archives. Reprinted with permission from Dartmouth College Library.

Chapter 13. Quotation of Earl Mosberg: letter from Earl R. Mosberg to Norton Smithe, April 21, 1952, in Archives, New York Chapter Mountaineering Committee, Appalachian Mountain Club. Reprinted with permission from the New York Chapter, Appalachian Mountain Club. Quotation of J. B. Gardner: letter from J. B. Gardner to Norton Smithe, July 1, 1952, in Archives, New York AMC Mountaineering Committee. Reprinted with permission from the New York Chapter, Appalachian Mountain Club. Quotation about Lester Germer: minutes of Qualifications Committee meeting in 1953, Archives, New York Chapter AMC Mountaineering Committee. Reprinted with permission from the New York Chapter, Appalachian Mountain Club. Quotation of Larsen motion: minutes of Qualifications Committee meeting, October 17, 1957, Archives, New York AMC Mountaineering Committee. Reprinted with permission from the New York Chapter, Appalachian Mountain Club. Quotation about Lester Germer: comment by Ruth Tallan, in a memorandum recording many comments on the Safety Program, dated December 29, 1953, Archives, New York AMC Mountaineering Committee. Reprinted with permission from the New York Chapter, Appalachian Mountain Club. Quotation of Robert Kruszyna: letter from Robert Kruszyna to William Lowell Putnam III, May 10, 1960. Reprinted with permission from Robert Kruszyna. Quotation of John E. Taylor: letter from John E. Taylor to William Lowell Putnam III, May 15, 1960. Reprinted with permission from John E. Taylor.

Interlude/Chasing Ghosts on the Armadillo: Adapted from John DeLeo, Kendall Query, and Laura and Guy Waterman, "The Armadillo Revisited: Chasing Ghosts in the South Basin of Katahdin," *Appalachia,* Summer 1986, pp. 18–27. Reprinted with permission from the Appalachian Mountain Club.

Chapter 14: Quotation of James P. McCarthy: letter from James P. McCarthy to L&GW, March 6, 1989. Reprinted with permission from James P. McCarthy. Quotations of John Turner: letter from John Turner to L&GW, May 20, 1980. Reprinted with permission from John Turner.

Chapter 15: Quotation about *Coexistence:* letter from John Stannard to Paul Piana, April 4, 1977, in collections of the Mohonk Preserve. Reprinted with permission of the Mohonk Preserve. Quotation about siege tactics: letter from John Stannard to Derek Ellis, November 8, 1972, in collections of the Mohonk Preserve. Reprinted with permission from the Mohonk Preserve. Quotation from Ed Webster: letter from Ed Webster to L&GW, October 28, 1981. Reprinted with permission from Ed Webster.

Chapter 16: Quotation of Royal Robbins: letter from Royal Robbins to L&GW, June 2, 1981. Reprinted with permission from Royal Robbins. Quotation about "hard" steel pitons: David B. Ingalls, comment on a questionnaire addressed to The Mohonk Trust, March 1972, in collections of the Mohonk Preserve. Reprinted with permission from the Mohonk Preserve. Quotation of John Stannard: letter from John Stannard to Hal Murray, January 12, 1972, in collections of the Mohonk Preserve. Reprinted with permission from the Mohonk Preserve. Quotation of Fritz Wiessner: letter from Fritz Wiessner to John Stannard, undated but apparently early 1973, in collections of the Mohonk Preserve. Reprinted with permission from the Mohonk Preserve.

Chapter 17: Quotations of Herb and Jan Conn: letters from Herb and Jan Conn to L&GW, May 25, 1980, and August 28, 1991. Reprinted with permission from Herb and Jan Conn. Quotation of Joe Cote: quoted in Tom Eastman, "Rock Climbing in the Early Years," *The Mountain Ear,* September 5, 1980, p. 13. Reprinted with permission from *The Mountain Ear.* Quotations of John Turner: letter from John Turner to L&GW, May 20, 1980. Reprinted with permission from John Turner.

Chapter 20: Quotation of Ed Webster: letter from Ed Webster to L&GW, October 28, 1981. Reprinted with permission from Ed Webster. Quotation of Robert B. Hall: letter from Robert B. Hall to Howard Peterson, undated (ca. 1974), in the possession of Peterson. Reprinted with permission from Robert B. Hall. Quotation of Geoff Childs: Geoffrey Childs, "By the Sea, By the Sea . . . A Brief History of Rock Climbing on Mount Desert Island, Maine," *Climbing,* April 1977, pp. 30–32. Reprinted with permission of *Climbing.*

Chapter 21: Quotations of Ed Webster: letter from Ed Webster to L&GW, October 28, 1981. Reprinted with permission from Ed Webster. Quotation of S. Peter Lewis: S. Peter Lewis, "Ice in the Granite State," *Climbing,* December 1983, pp. 14–18, 22–25. Reprinted with permission of *Climbing.* Quotation of John Bouchard: John Bouchard, "Black Dike First Ascent," *Climbing,* December 1983, p. 19. Reprinted with permission from *Climbing.*

Chapter 22: Quotation of *Climbing* magazine: Roger Briggs, "Rock Climbing: Where It Is Going," *Climbing,* October 1983, pp. 20–23. Reprinted with permission from *Climbing.* Quotation of Ken Nichols: Ken Nichols,

"Tied-off Hook Protection," unpublished typescript in the possession of the authors, ca. 1985, p. 1. Reprinted with permission from Ken Nichols. Quotation of Ron Gower: Ron Gower, "Some Brief Aspects of Rock-Climbing," *Bulletin* of the Potomac Appalachian Trail Club, July 1934, p. 46. Reprinted with permission of the Potomac Appalachian Trail Club. Quotations about Kevin Bein: Alison Osius, "'Mayor of the Gunks' Killed on Matterhorn," *Climbing*, October 1988, p. 38. Reprinted with permission from *Climbing*.

Chapter 23: Much of the material in Chapter 23 (Restoring Parity: The Reemergence of Women in the 1980s) appeared previously in *Rock and Roses: An Anthology of Mountaineering Essays by Some of the Best Climbers in the World*, edited by Mikel Vause, Mountain N' Air Books, La Crescenta, California, 1990. The authors acknowledge with appreciation the willingness of Mountain N' Air Books to have this chapter closely follow the account in *Rock and Roses*. Quotation of Alison Osius: David Roberts, "Alison Osius: Rocks and Other Hard Places," *Outside*, August 1985, p. 51. Reprinted with permission from *Outside* magazine. Copyright ©1985, Mariah Publications Corporation. Quotation of Rosie Andrews: Rosie Andrews, "No Spare Rib," *Mountain* 97, May-June, 1984, p. 29. Reprinted with permission from *Mountain*.

Interlude/Can Women Lead on Ice: Quotation from Emily Dickinson: From *The Complete Poems of Emily Dickinson* edited by Thomas H. Johnson. Copyright © 1935 by Martha Dickinson Bianchi; copyright renewed in 1963 by Mary L. Hampson. By permission of Little, Brown and Company. We especially thank Little, Brown and Company for this permission.

Chapter 24: Quotation from Ed Webster: letter from Ed Webster to L&GW, October 28, 1981. Reprinted with permission from Ed Webster. Quotation of Ken Nichols: letter from Ken Nichols to L&GW, June 9, 1989. Reprinted with permission from Ken Nichols.

Chapter 25: Quotation about John Tremblay: S. Peter Lewis, "Profile: Master of Ice," *Climbing*, April 1987, p. 20. Reprinted with permission from *Climbing*.

Chapter 26: Quotation of Mark Robinson: Mark Robinson, "Pox in Vulgaria: The Profit of Impurism," *Climbing*, May-June 1979, pp. 8–12. Reprinted with permission from *Climbing*. Quotation of Christian Griffiths: letter to the editor from Christian Griffiths, *Mountain* 107, January-February 1986, p. 43. Reprinted with permission from *Mountain*. Quotation of Mark Wilford: letter to the editor from Mark Wilford, *Mountain* 108, March-April 1986, p. 46. Reprinted with permission from *Mountain*. Quotation of S. Peter Lewis: S. Peter Lewis, "Basecamp: New Hampshire," *Climbing*, December 1987, p. 30. Reprinted with permission from *Climbing*. Quotation of Luisa Jovane:

Beth Wald, "Profile" [of Luisa Jovane], *Climbing,* August 1987, pp. 87–88. Reprinted with permission from *Climbing.*

Grateful appreciation is also extended to the following individuals for contributing photographs or other illustrations: Appalachian Mountain Club, Steve Arsenault, Henry Barber, The Black and White Image, Gerry Bloch, Bob Clark, Russ Clune, J. B. Gardner, Jim Goodwin, Tony Goodwin, Greg Gordon, Trudy Healy, Ken and Betty Henderson, Henry Kendall, Joe Lentini, Jim McCarthy, Don Mellor, Joe Muir, Ken Nichols, Percy T. Olton, Jr., Bonnie Prudden, Russ Raffa, Paul Ross, John Turner, Julian Whittlesey, Rick Wilcox, and Dick Williams. ∎

Introduction

"Each story-telling grandparent or great-uncle
had his own details and his own kind of moraliz-
ing to add. What I tell you is what is left in my
memory of what all these people told and of
what they all thought it meant . . . What else
does the 'study of history' give us, I wonder."

Dorothy Canfield Fisher
Something Old, Something New

"Foolish History (ever, more or less, the written epitomized synopsis of Rumor). . ."

Thomas Carlyle
History of the French Revolution

W HEN THE SUBTITLE identifies this book as a history of climbing in the
northeastern United States, that sounds like a clear-cut description.
But like most clear-cuts, a lot of confusing slash remains underfoot
to stumble over. May we clarify at least three words?

Northeastern? When we began work ten years ago, one friend of ours
said northeastern must include West Virginia and Ohio. He evidently envisioned the map of the United States quartered, and everything in the upper
right quadrant was "northeastern." Another friend (from Maine) allowed
as how "northeastern" would certainly not cover anything as far south as
Boston. Our definition lies between these views: New England plus eastern
New York (Adirondacks, Catskills, Shawangunks, Hudson Highlands).

History? Most short "histories" that accompany guidebooks tend, understandably, to focus on when the hardest climbs were first done. This is a proper preoccupation in its place. But for a great many climbers, what's going on at the leading edge of difficulty is not relevant to how they view the sport. For many, the most difficult climb *they're* interested in is the climb *they're* on at the moment. The breakthroughs at the leading edge are important, and we'll describe them. But it is a skewed perspective, to which we are all prone to one degree or another, to see this sector of climbing as more important than any of the other parts of this great game. We have tried to give the social history for the climbing population as a whole, as well as for those few who are pushing the standards of difficulty to new extremes.

Another point about the word history. We have been intimidated by the prospect of trying to gain a valid historical perspective on very recent climbing trends. Time and distance are needed to understand what's happening under our noses. So we have not attempted to carry this history into the 1990s. We wind down somewhere in the late 1980s, leaving to later historians to coolly judge—or current climbers to hotly debate—the exciting things that have been going on in the sport during the past couple of years. It's still a dynamic, fast-paced story, but not yet history.

Climbing? In general, we mean roped rock and ice climbing. People will say, "I climbed Mount Washington last weekend," and that's a perfectly valid use of the word "climbed," but that kind of climbing (or hiking) is not part of this book. We'd refer to our subject as technical climbing, except that's a bit stuffy and suggests too precise a meaning. For the most part we're describing climbing where the difficulty and/or danger are such that the climbers use a rope and other specialized gear. But even this rule is not always accurate, as we'll include steep scrambling where the rope wasn't used and solo climbing with or without rope.

Perhaps the real distinction is not so mechanical as whether a rope is used or not but has more to do with the spirit of the undertaking. Defining this spirit is exceptionally hazardous.

Climbing is often called a sport, but it may also be a ballet, or a gymnastic exercise, or a way to wilderness, or an exploration of the inner self, or a romp of the spirit, or a way of life that beats working. The striving, the obstacles, the achievements we all experience in climbing are surely a metaphor for something much more important than the vertical rock or ice, which is all the nonclimber sees. It is that metaphor which gives standing to what Lionel Terray called conquering the useless and Warren Harding called a fine kind of madness.

We won't attempt to go further but will fall back on Louis Armstrong's well-known comment, when asked to define jazz: if you have to ask what it is, you'll never know. ■

1: The Prehistory of Northeastern Climbing: Before 1916

W
HEN DID PEOPLE first climb in the northeastern United States? One answer would depend on when you first want to call the evolving species "people"—i.e., some individuals among the ancient aboriginal inhabitants of this part of the continent must have been a bit more adventurous than others in scaling difficult rocky ledges, in pursuit of food or escape from beasts or maybe at some point for the sheer pleasure of physical challenge and display. Among the native Americans who inhabited this region before the coming of Europeans and their better-documented history, there must have been individuals who climbed rock faces or enlarged boulder problems with flair. However, history has no record of any of these escapades.

When European immigrants first settled these shores, they had little interest in mountains. Their first priority was to tame some corner of the wilderness in which to survive. Mountains were hostile, cliffs dangerous. Interest in recreational mountain climbing of a nontechnical nature—hiking or tramping to summits—began in the first half of the nineteenth century. Until about 1900 remote and less accessible corners of the northeastern ranges—the White Mountains of New Hampshire, Green Mountains of Vermont, Adirondacks and Catskills in New York, and the scattered mountains of Maine—provided sufficient challenge to the adventurous in the form of exploration. Thus, during the 1880s, George Witherle of Castine, Maine, found excitement in pushing into remote peaks and passes north and northwest of Katahdin. Had he lived fifty or one hundred years later, a man like Witherle might perhaps have pushed into 5.8 (1930s) or 5.13 (1980s). But before 1900 there was plenty of adventure in exploration of previously unknown terrain. It was only after northeastern mountains were fully explored that those seeking further challenge turned to the vertical world of rock and ice climbing. That was in the beginning of the twentieth century.

Still, the occasional scramble of early years had the spice of adventure not unlike what modern climbers seek. Only a few early instances were recorded in print. Hundreds of others must have gone undocumented;

Moses' cliff. Nearly 200 years ago this modest slab in Shelburne, New Hampshire, was the locale for one of the earliest rock climbs on record. Moses Ingalls scaled it "as easily as a cat," thereby winning local acclaim and title to a piece of land.

nameless in dark oblivion let them dwell. Here are but twenty that we know about.

One. In the 1770s Ethan and Ira Allen were swashbuckling soldiers of fortune along the northwoods frontier of northern Vermont. The former has become the state legend, but his younger brother seems to have had a true climber's spirit. Once when running a survey over mountainous terrain, Ira Allen scaled a tall spruce at the edge of a cliff which he estimated was at least 300 feet perpendicular. He chopped off the top of this tree to get a better view.

> While thus amusing myself, the day being some windy, a sudden gust of wind caused the top of the tree to wave over the ledge aforesaid. At this unlucky moment for the first time, I chanced to cast my eyes down the tree, waved by the wind over, it had the appearance that I was going to the bottom. This gave me sensations not easily expressed.

Another time, Ira Allen found himself at the top of a rock face that angled steeply down for 60 feet, then dropped vertically for 100. A large boulder lay partway down the sloping section. Motivated by the dark passion for boulder-trundling not unknown to later climbers, Allen took off his shoes and climbed down to the boulder, using narrow cracks for foot and handholds. When he was dislodging the boulder, a projecting corner of it brushed him and nearly knocked him off the cliff, after which, he says, "I moved carefully to the top of the hill." This may qualify as the first recorded instance of genuine rock climbing in the northeastern United States.

Two. Back around 1800, one Moses Ingalls won renown and title to a desirable piece of land in the town of Shelburne, New Hampshire, as reward for scaling a 150-foot slab on what is now known as Mount Winthrop. It was said "he ran up in his stocking feet as easily as a cat and thus, by a single exhibition of skill and daring, gained a remembrance and a monument that martyrs and heroes might envy." Looking at that rock slab today, one may speculate that by the time Ingalls had walked up the first low-angle 50 feet, he had made a few moves that he preferred not to reverse, so he kept going up the moderate but pure friction until within a few yards of the top. There the angle definitely turns up. History does not disclose how Ingalls exited, but subsequent climbers have been glad for the protection of a rope.

Three. In the realm of pure legend, be it noted that while the great New Hampshire cliff on Cannon Mountain (largest in the east) had no confirmed ascent until 1928 (chapter 3), one Penacook brave had been up much earlier. This fellow found a large hollow branch shaped by nature into an oversized peace pipe. Seizing this rare opportunity to strike a blow for international relations, the Indian lopped off the branch and ascended the Cannon cliff with it so as to thrust it into the jaws of the Old Man of the Mountain, that great stone profile of Franconia Notch. This would be about the second-to-last pitch of Fritz Wiessner's 1933 route (chapter 7). The story goes that great puffs of smoke instantly enveloped Old Man and Indian, and when the cloud lifted, the latter was gone. This report of the first pipe pitch on Cannon, however, remains unconfirmed.

Four. A colorful Adirondack innkeeper of the late nineteenth century, Henry Van Hoevenberg, was given to imaginative flights of fireside fancy for the diversion of his paying guests. One of Mr. Van's epic assays told of an early ascent of the 1,000-foot cliff of Wallface. The motive for this early big-wall climb consisted of secret Indian treasure buried in a cave hundreds of feet up the side of the cliff. A solitary woodsman made the ascent, barefoot, by moonlight, using extensive vegetable holds and one death-defying lunge move across a blank slab, thus displaying poor form by the present century's standards. The quality of his climbing, and of Mr. Van's poetic talents, may be evaluated from the following excerpt:

Upward—still upward; advantage I took
Of every crevice and angular nook.
I crawl'd, climb'd, and squirm'd around the rough rocks;
Sometimes I lovingly hugged the huge blocks.

Upon reaching the cave our hero found the treasure but was driven out by the ghost of the first ascent party, and in the ensuing thousand-foot fall, he survived only by wiping out a branchy hemlock tree that had represented an indispensable hold for the ascent, thereby rendering a third ascent of the mythical route unjustifiable.

Five. Another less fanciful cliffside cave is "Devil's Den," a prominent dark hole high on the side of Mount Willard. This evil, rotten orifice is visible to motorists driving north on Route 302 through New Hampshire's Crawford Notch today, almost at the top of the great south face of Willard. Early Crawford family legends tell of Old Abel Crawford visiting this cave around 1800; if he did, he must have been exceptionally daring indeed, as access to it without a rope can be had only by technically advanced and wildly exposed moves over some of the most undependable loose and crumbling rock in New England. Early White Mountain historian Benjamin Willey recounts a "venturous young gentleman, some years since" (placing the

Wallface. A nineteenth century mock-epic tells of a treasure-seeking ascent— and rapid descent—on this 1,000-foot Adirondack wilderness cliff.

DON MELLOR

date before 1850) who persuaded his friends to lower him from the top so he could look into the Devil's Den. On seeing "bones and skulls" therein, he had himself hauled up in a hurry. Samuel Eastman's White Mountain guidebook of 1858 relates that the eccentric physician Dr. Benjamin Ball had himself lowered by ropes to this cave, carrying candles and a knife to defend himself from the bears that he thought guarded the entrance; he found only "two hawk's feathers." Franklin Leavitt's early maps showed the cave's location and carried a marginal sketch with the caption, "They are lowering Leavitt down the side of Mt. Willard to go into the Devil's Den." In 1927 some mischievous railroad workers in the notch let themselves down by rope and set an American flag, supported on a framework of poles, across the entrance of the cave, visible from the highway and train track far below. In the 1980s the authors found that one of the poles from that framework was still in the cave, along with the remains of the wire with which the flag had been attached. Skull and bones do not survive.

Six. Another instance of being lowered on a rope involves the ingenious Catskill lad who was sent down to rescue a hunter's prized hound that had slipped into a cavern initially estimated to be 40 feet deep. As told by the artist Charles Lanman, the hunter's son was lowered 40 feet, then sat there out of sight and pulled down another 200 feet of rope before tying the

*Francis Parkman.
America's celebrated
historian of the frontier,
Parkman made an
adventurous ascent of a
slide in New Hampshire's
Crawford Notch in 1841.*

FROM *A LIFE OF FRANCIS PARKMAN*

hound on, thereby deluding the villagers into thinking he had coolly descended more than 200 feet. When he clambered out on his own, his reputation as a climber of a 240-foot solo earned wide local repute. This boy
takes his place with many subsequent climbers—to identify recent examples
would be hazardous—as among the great con artists of northeastern climbing history.

  Seven. The Catskills were also the scene of an early exercise of that dis-
reputable if tradition-hallowed branch of the art of rock climbing: boulder-
trundling. In 1820 a party of young men from Cairo and Catskill, New York,
decided on a new way to celebrate the Fourth of July. They ascended to the
top of Kaaterskill Falls where a boulder measuring 175 feet across rested in-
securely poised at the top. They succeeded in undermining its precarious
supports, whereupon the boulder started down. The concept of grandeur
and the sublime, so central to that romantic era's perceptions of mountain
scenery, took on enriched meaning in the next few seconds:

> The effect was awful and sublime, the crash tremendous,
> exceeding the loudest thunder—the tremulous motion of
> the earth and the long murmuring echo rolling from point
> to point through the ravine gave to the scene an indescrib-
> able degree of grandeur. The rock was shattered in a thou-
> sand pieces. Toasts were then drunk and vollies of mus-
> ketry fired.

Other nineteenth-century illustrations of the dark science of trundling can be found on Maine's Katahdin as early as 1855 and such White Mountain bowling alleys as Huntington Ravine, the Great Gulf, the Webster cliffs, and Cannon cliff.

Eight. Back in the realm of more serious climbing, one noteworthy incident involved no less a figure than Francis Parkman, later to become the brilliant historian of the American frontier. In 1841, a young man on the eve of his western travels, Parkman took a brief sojourn in the White Mountains to expose himself to some sample "wilderness" in preparation for the great West. During this trip, while staying at the Crawford House, Parkman wandered off by himself one day to have a close look at the scene of the infamous slide on Mount Willey that had engulfed a whole family, tragically shaking the notch just fifteen years earlier. This slide had exposed a long, bare scar of rock, an "inaccessible precipice" as a previous traveler had described it. Parkman elected to scramble up. After surmounting not one but two precipices "with considerable difficulty and danger," he had one final move over a decaying wall of loose stones. After nearly coming off once, he resorted to a jackknife both to dig footholds and to sink into the rotten cliff as a handhold. He said he climbed 50 feet in this manner before reaching safe ground, calling it "the most serious adventure it was ever my lot to encounter." A fellow traveler at the Crawford House relates that on Parkman's return:

> The condition which he presented betokened the perilous
> adventure of the day. His clothing was badly torn, his
> fingers were lacerated, and his legs showed injuries which
> had been caused in almost super-human exertions in the
> preservation of his life.

Nine. The Colden Trap Dike was the scene of early American rock scrambles. In 1837, on an expedition of exploration during which the Adirondacks' highest peaks were first climbed, geologist Ebenezer Emmons made

DON MELLOR

The Colden Trap Dike. This dramatic cleft in the Adirondacks' Avalanche Pass was first climbed partially in 1837 and completely in 1850, two of the earliest documented rock climbs of note.

a partial ascent involving some 5.0 to 5.1 moves. Around midcentury, the local Iron Works employed two of the owners' nephews, Robert Clarke and Alexander "Sandy" Ralph, in the management of the works. In the summer of 1850, Clarke had been living in Cincinnati but came up for a holiday jaunt. In July the two men decided to go up the dike and climb Mount Colden. They set out at 5:00 A.M. with bread, pork, and tea, together with tea pot and cups, a blanket, compass and spyglass, ax, rifle, and a brandy bottle affectionately known as the "Admiral." By 10:00 they had walked up the forest path along Calamity Brook, around the shores of Lake Colden, and reached the base of the dike. Here they left most of the baggage, probably took an affectionate leave of the Admiral, and began the climb. In the lower part of the gully they soon came to the steepest climbing they would face, a series of jumbled rock steps. The angle was sufficiently steep to make a slip inadvisable, and the towering rock walls on either side afforded an intimidating psychological setting. After about 300 feet, according to their estimate, they scrambled out of the dike onto the smooth slabs on its right. These they followed cautiously to the top, keeping to the edge of vegetation where they could and pausing to sit down and rest every few rods. The slabs are not steep by modern rock climbing standards, but their exposure is impressive and the cousins must have been truly exhilarated. The route carried them right to the very top, great sweeps of clean rock dropping beneath them to the lakes 2,000 feet below. Their time from bottom to top was one and a half hours. They spent another hour and a half up there, delighted with the view, fascinated with the vegetation at 4,700 feet, and marveling at an eagle that soared up from the peak as they approached. The account is not clear whether they descended the slabs or came around through the woods; most likely they went down a less exposed route, but they evidently circled back to the base of the dike. Here they reclaimed all their gear, doubtless toasted their achievement with the aid of the Admiral, went down and shot a deer on the shores of Lake Colden, enjoyed a comfortable night by a huge fire, caught fresh trout for breakfast, and poked on down the stream, fishing, as they returned to the Iron Works. The whole enterprise seems to have been pulled off in what a modern climber would describe as "good style"—i.e., with competence, confidence, and a certain flair (for example, bagging that deer on the very afternoon of their climb). This was the first recorded ascent of Mount Colden, at 4,713 feet ranked eleventh highest in the Adirondacks.

Ten. A primitive roped climbing took place on the Adirondacks' Gore Mountain on August 25, 1877. Verplanck Colvin was engaged at the time in a comprehensive topographical survey of the region. Colvin was a hardy and bold spirit. He and his guides went up the steep northwest side of the mountain, encountering vertical ledges en route. Colvin's account testifies:

> Exploring among these ledges, we experienced some difficult climbing, having in one place to aid the ascent of some of the men (who were unpracticed as climbers) with the rope which we fortunately had with us. The slippery rock and deep abyss below were sufficient to try the nerves of a novice.

Eleven. In the Hudson Highlands in the 1870s and 1880s occurred a few incidents that showed that rock scramblers were adventurous there too. W. Whitman Bailey wrote of climbing the "Tors" of traprock overlooking the Hudson's Haverstraw Bay during the 1870s. Sometime in the next decade a character named Old Hager and his youthful admirer, W. T. Howell, used a rope to climb "a steep crevice" on the side of Crow's Nest. Howell was a fearless spirit ahead of his time. He later did some unroped climbing on the Timp face long before the later generation of orthodox New York rock climbers (chapter 2). Wrote Howell in his journal for June 14, 1908:

> As a diversion, [I] attempted a climb as nearly as possible up the face of the Timp face. It was exciting work and, it must be confessed, a little dangerous.

Twelve. College traditions of building-climbing can be found as early as the 1860s. At Wesleyan, one student, returning from vacation, climbed to his room over lattice and vines, "to the consternation and alarm of his landlady." At Harvard, scaling the Mount Auburn cemetery fence is reported as early as 1866. Doubtless many other examples were unnoticed by contemporary college officials or, alas, history.

Thirteen. One of the Adirondacks' pioneer rock scramblers was Newell Martin, who had honed his climbing skills as a Yale undergraduate on that university's hallowed ivy-covered steeples and towers. A summer resident at Saint Hubert's in the Adirondacks, the youthful Martin frequently clambered around the cliffs and ledges of the lower parts of Sawteeth above Lower Ausable Lake. In 1875, the year of his graduation from Yale, he ascended all the way up Sawteeth, and despite his own modest protests that others must have done so before, the Keene Valley guides knew of no prior ascent. Martin of course couldn't pass up the Colden Dike. With the guide Charlie Beede, he also was the first to climb Gothics from the Ausable side, descending the great Rainbow slide, an open rock slab of exciting angle. To silence skeptics, the pair left a large white handkerchief spread on the slab, plainly visible from the valley.

Fourteen. Not to be outdone, guide Mel Hathaway and another summer guest went up that slide twenty years later and fastened a huge white undershirt on its face. According to report:

> Bleached by snow and rain, [it] held its place for two seasons. In the morning, it would catch the sun, and be visible, as a speck of twinkling white, to tourists on the Upper Lake and they would ask "What is that shining jewel on the dark breast of the mountain?"

Fifteen. Over in the White Mountains, Appalachian Mountain Club scramblers of the same vintage mention occasional rock climbing feats. A deaf-mute named William B. Swett, employed as carpenter by the Profile House in 1865, crawled around the cliffs of Cannon and Eagle crags in Franconia Notch, reaching places described as "extremely hazardous" and "where no man had ever been known to go there before," including one spot "directly under the chin [of the Old Man's profile], about twenty feet below it," which might be the exposed ledge currently used as the second-to-last belay by climbers doing today's Lakeview route.

Sixteen. During the 1890s several instances involving climbing are reported. A. L. Goodrich mentions a place near Greeley Ponds as "the most troublesome cliff I ever scaled." An 1896 chronicler tells of descending the Webster cliffs by a direct line. An 1899 ascent of Raymond's Cataract on Mount Washington involved the use of a rope for difficult sections. When Frank Carpenter crossed the seldom-visited Benton Range, he learned that a local man had ascended the steep west side of Sugar Loaf, driving "iron pins sunk in the rock" for direct aid.

Seventeen. The 1907 guidebook of the Appalachian Mountain Club recommended "interesting bits of climbing even to veteran rock climbers" in Huntington Ravine. At least one instance is documented, and several others rumored, of a party ascending the great "Pinnacle" in Huntington Ravine via its steep rock face: in 1910 four men led by George Flagg traced a route not far to the left of the current rock climbers' route, negotiating some moves of impressive difficulty and exposure, as testified by a series of drawings made by the talented Mr. Flagg.

Eighteen. Some early White Mountain slide climbing technique employed style that never caught on. J. Rayner Edmands, on the Flume slide in 1885, described the use of interchanging-heel technique:

> It was necessary to lie on the back and dig one heel into the
> gravel, to keep one's position while digging a similar socket
> for the other heel. Interchanging heels then freed the foot
> on the advancing side to make another socket. Thus, crab-
> fashion, the edge of the bank was reached and the ascent
> resumed.

A similar form is described by Hudson Highlands tramper Albert Stürcke, who dealt with the Timp face by lying on his back and using hands and heels "in a sort of crawling, pushing, paddling fashion, not omitting at the same time to cling to the precipitous rock for dear life." The Reverend Doctor J. M. Buckley, ascending the fresh-fallen North Tripyramid slide, also encountered loose ledges and employed the little-known abdominal press:

> There was but one thing to do. . . . It was to clutch my fingers and toes into the slide mass, and to bear heavily with my abdomen upon what was beneath, in the hope of accumulating weight enough with my body . . . to stop the mass long enough to get what mechanics call a purchase for a hurried scramble to the top. I had barely strength enough to do it. In three minutes I was out of danger.

An 1892 adventurer scaling the then new rock slide on the steep side of East Osceola overcame difficulty by alternating the abdominal press with the dynamic onslaught:

> Now and then I came to a pitch so sharp and smooth that I could not cling, even though I lay flat and pressed hard with both feet and hands. The only possibility of advance was by dropping back a few yards upon the less steep portions and getting momentum sufficient to carry me to another foothold.

Nineteen. Oliver Perry-Smith, Philadelphia-born in 1884, was one of America's most remarkable rock climbers, and it is our history's loss that he almost never applied his extraordinary talents to native rock. Taken to Dresden, Germany, to live in 1901, Perry-Smith walked into the most progressive and technically advanced pure rock climbing center in Europe. A gifted natural athlete, a huge man with bearlike strength and prodigious appetite for competitive feats of speed and daring, Perry-Smith soon excelled in Dresden's atmosphere of friendly competition. Routes that he and the top German climbers of that day did between 1901 and the First World War were more difficult than anything done in this country till about fifty years later. Yet when Perry-Smith returned to this country he had lost interest in climbing. As a result, his sole climbing exploit in the northeastern U.S. was on the sea cliffs of Maine when he was but a boy, when he and a visiting South American friend descended the cliff face of Champlain Mountain. "It was not difficult," wrote Perry-Smith with uncharacteristic laconic understatement, "but we had no rope."

Twenty. The first ascent of Joe English Hill in southern New Hampshire is perhaps the first time in the Northeast that a party set out directly to climb a cliff of several pitches for its own sake, treating it in the spirit of a real rock climb, with rope (fifty feet of one-inch hemp) and appropriate shoes ("our feet were shod with rubber soles"). This was in 1916. The tactics of the two first ascensionists, H. L. Emerson and a friend referred to simply as H. B., were anything but conventional by modern rock climbing standards. But it was a pioneering ascent of the first order. The two scrambled up over the fan of broken rock at the base until they came out at the bottom of the middle of the cliff. What developed from then on was a recurring pattern of the daring (or foolhardy) Emerson taking the boldest lines, which frequently left him hung up unable to go up or down unaided, while the prudent H. B. picked his way up easier gullies and cracks to places where he could rescue Emerson from his various cul-de-sacs. Much of the time this climbing was simultaneous and unroped, though there seems to have been much tying and untying. There was no belaying until the end when H. B. had reached the top, and of course no pitons, carabiners, or slings. Emerson, who wrote up the climb, was scaring himself silly but enjoying every minute of it (at least in retrospect), though he wrote of his relief at receiving the top-rope that was to help him out of his final predicament: "I am free to confess that a check in hand for a cool thousand could never have given the thrill of satisfaction I felt as I grasped that rope." What followed summed up the slapstick routine of this glorious ascent:

> With the rope around one hand and gripping the rock with the other, I gained a position where my knees partly held me. At this moment disaster threatened again, in the guise of a small dead tree that came slipping down, branches first. It knocked my cap off, entangled itself in the rope, slipping under my arms and behaved disgracefully in general. I called to H. B. to work himself down and disengage it. This did not work out, so after a time I managed to free myself from the octopus and consign it to perdition, down below.

The climb was accomplished safely at last, causing Emerson to comment gratefully that "I . . . was not so much elated over the ascent as thankful for the finish." So ended the first continuous roped climbing on New Hampshire rock, beginning a grand dynasty of "epics" of larger or smaller proportions that continue even to this day to contribute to history and legend. ▪

Reference Note

Because the sources for this chapter are so numerous and diverse, we'll mention only a few particularly interesting accounts of early climbs. The complete list of sources is on file at Dartmouth. An early report of Moses Ingalls' daring dash is in J. H. Spaulding, *Historical Relics of the White Mountains* (Boston: Nathaniel Noyes, 1855), p. 64. The Clarke-Ralph ascent of the Colden Dike is described in detail in a letter from Clarke to his mother dated August 17, 1850, which was reproduced with informative commentary by Warder H. Cadbury in "The First Ascent of Mt. Colden," *Adirondac*, January-February 1957, pp. 4–7, 20–21. George Flagg's 1910 ascent of the Pinnacle is drawn in detail in his "Sketchbook" for 1910, now in the possession of Shirley A. Hargraves, his granddaughter, who generously allowed us to see and copy these marvelous drawings. A short sketch of Oliver Perry-Smith is J. Monroe Thorington, "Oliver Perry-Smith: Profile of a Mountaineer," *American Alpine Journal,* 1964, pp. 99–120. For the 1916 escapade on Joe English, see H. L. Emerson, "A Rock Climb in Southern New Hampshire," *Appalachia,* June 1917, pp. 154–157. We are indebted to Bonnie Christie, Mark Dindorf, and John Dunn for helping us recreate and evaluate the Ingalls climb; to Kendall Query, Louis Cornell, Mary Jane Cross, and Robert Hall for helping to trace the 1910 Pinnacle ascent route; and to Peter Crane for a friendly belay while we descended to the Devil's Den.

2: A New Form of Exploration: 1916–1927

NTIL 1916 THE only serious roped climbing by northeastern Americans was on vacations in the Alps under the tutelage of European guides. Charles Evans Hughes, Governor of New York and later presidential candidate and Supreme Court Chief Justice, for example, "goes to Switzerland every year and climbs mountains for six weeks," according to a 1906 news clipping; "he has done that every year for thirteen years" (to which the gleeful Hudson Highland rock scrambler W. T. Howell commented: "He is indeed one of us!"). This practice was not unusual among

John Case. The first classically trained alpinist to attempt significant roped climbs in the United States, Case made first ascents on the Adirondacks' Indian Head and Wallface, the former as early as 1916.

the gentry of Boston, New York, and Philadelphia. Some also undertook mountaineering in the American West and the Canadian Rockies. But the Northeast's own abundant cliffs were ignored.

1916 merits immortality as the year when true rock climbing began in the Northeast. That is the date for two entirely separate events, each of which traces a direct descent to modern rock climbing in the Adirondacks and New England respectively.

In the Adirondacks the key figure was John Case, a summer vacationer at the Ausable Club who, since boyhood, had gazed at the same rugged lakeside terrain that had stirred Newell Martin to adventure on Sawteeth and Gothics. Case, however, had experienced real mountaineering in the Alps. As a young Technical Institute student in Zurich, Case had been exposed to some of the good European climbers and had joined George Finch (of early Everest fame) on an ascent of the east face of Monte Rosa in 1911. In 1916, back in the Adirondacks, Case took his rope out on the cliffs of Indian Head. Over the waters of the Lower Ausable Lake, he explored route possibilities with anyone he could find to tie into the other end of the rope, including his apprehensive fiancée. Though he never systematically exploited the rock climbing potential of the Adirondacks, Case continued to climb off and on there for the next sixty years. More importantly, he was a highly competent and classically trained climber and, as we shall see, extended his influence by teaching several younger climbers during the 1920s and 1930s, who carried on the tradition he started on the Indian Head cliffs in 1916.

Meanwhile, back in Boston, an active hiker in the Appalachian Mountain Club named Frank Mason had been avidly reading the *Badminton Library of Sports and Pastimes,* a quaint turn-of-the-century British series, in which a treatise on rock climbing by C. T. Dent especially attracted his attention. To give the exotic sport (pastime?) a try, Mason procured rope and went looking for something to climb in the suburbs of Boston. Rock outcrops in West Roxbury and a few outsized boulders in South Peabody caught his eye, areas perhaps less romantic than the storied heights of Chamonix or the east face of Monte Rosa, but good enough for a start. By 1916, according to early AMC sources, Mason had established a small group of friends who joined him regularly on Boston's suburban rock piles. Included were two of Mason's daughters, Margaret and Dorothy. Both married rock climbers of later consequence, and Margaret especially became a talented climber in her own right.

The next figure to contribute to the development of the sport was a big, self-confident young businessman named Willard Helburn. Robert Underhill, dean of American climbers in the 1920s, credited Helburn as "the man who got things started here." A veteran of guided mountain holidays in the Alps, Helburn became a regular in the Mason circle and married Margaret. Together the young couple became enthusiastic climbers and special devotees of Katahdin. In 1919 the Helburns climbed Katahdin's Chimney, Willard leading and using the rope to protect the party on the bottom chockstone. This was not the first ascent of the route, but no sure record of prior ascents survives, and Helburn's lead may have been the first competent use of the rope on a northern New England climb. Earlier ascents of the Chimney are implied in a Boston newspaper account of 1916 written by the hiker/journalist Allen Chamberlain:

> And as for stunts to satisfy the nerviest of cliff climbers there are enough and to spare on the walls of the Chimney Pond basin itself, including the ascent of the Pamola chimney, in the climbing of which one may readily imperil his neck and all his limbs at one and the same time.

Since an AMC party visited Chimney Pond in 1916, and Chamberlain was active in the AMC, he may have been referring to an ascent of that year or to legends of earlier ones. In any event, the Helburns' route was a respectable rock climb in 1919. Colonel T. W. Higginson, sitting atop the rim of the Great Basin in 1855, had declared the Chimney "absolutely impossible." It is a long gully of slabs and loose rock that rises for 1,000 feet from the floor of the south basin to a dramatic cleft between Pamola and Chimney Peak. For most of the way it is merely a steep scramble, though the exposure and loose rock call for care. But the first of three giant chockstones wedged in the gully requires about twenty feet of climbing at a moderate standard of difficulty, with the ground sloping so steeply below that a fall would have serious consequences. This one sequence of moves, plus the overall length of steep scrambling and the remote and harsh setting, make the Chimney a significant climb for such an early year as 1919.

Until the mid-1920s, Case, the Masons, the Helburns, and their friends only occasionally brought out the rope on this side of the Atlantic. After 1920 a growing circle of Bostonians took summer vacations in the Alps and enjoyed the excitement of exposure and tricky climbing. One family that regularly summered in Europe was the O'Briens, one of those exceptionally talented, strong-willed, tough-driving, close-knit Boston Irish clans of which the Kennedys are but a recent and unexceptional example. The O'Briens included Miriam, who became one of the greatest woman alpinists of her day; her mother, who also climbed a good deal in the Alps; and her younger brother Lincoln, of whom more will be heard in these pages. Others, mostly Bostonians, who sometimes encountered and climbed with the O'Briens in the Alps were the Helburns; Dean and Florence Peabody; "Trot" Chandler; Elizabeth Knowlton; Jessie Whitehead, flamboyant daughter of the great mathematician-philosopher Alfred North Whitehead; a rangy young investment banker named Kenneth Henderson; and a somewhat aloof, slightly older, urbane Harvard philosophy professor named Robert L. M. Underhill. Still, for a surprisingly long time, of this group of summer alpinists only the Helburns did anything on the rocks of New England during the rest of the year.

In 1925 a group of five young Boston "Appalachians"—Jack Hurd and his little sister Marjorie, Avis and Charles Newhall, and Emily W. Browne— planned a trip of their own to the Alps and sought out Frank Mason to initiate them in the mysteries of the rope. Their outstanding first season in the Alps showed that Mason had taught them well. That fall they began regularly frequenting the Boston rock outcrops. By the spring of 1926, these outings became official AMC trips, with one per month scheduled around Boston that spring and another series in the fall, plus a trip to Mount Washington's Huntington Ravine over the Memorial Day weekend.

The overture was over. The curtain now rose on the history of northeastern rock climbing.

Considering that roped climbing of steep terrain had already accumulated a long and exciting history in the Alps by 1925, it is hard to explain why this country should have been so slow in taking on the cliffs and crags that abound throughout New England and New York state. The main reason doubtless was the lack of really large, spectacular snow-capped and glaciated ranges and consequent lack of interest in formal mountaineering as long practiced in the Alps. Yet the lag behind Europe—where both rock and ice climbing were quite advanced by the turn of the century—seems surprising even granting the lack of "alps" nearby.

At any rate, in the late 1920s, four distinct centers of early rock climbing developed in the Northeast: Boston, the Hudson Highlands, the Adirondacks, and Connecticut.

Boston. By 1927 rock climbing was a full-fledged activity of the Boston AMC. Weekend trips were made to cliffs on Crow Hill, northwest of Boston, and across the New Hampshire line to Joe English Hill and the Pawtuckaways. A rare three-day weekend might take them as far as Huntington Ravine. But

Boston crags. Before 1920, Appalachian Mountain Club climbers found numerous short climbs on boulders and quarries around Boston, including this route which is still popular today.

WALTER HOWE COLLECTION

the characteristic Boston rock climbing activity—then as sixty years later—took place on Saturday afternoons or Sundays, when there was no scheduled weekend trip, when the many Boston area outcrops swarmed with the sport's new devotees. Popular places, then as now in most cases, were the Peabody boulders, the man-made "cliffs" of quarries in Quincy and Waltham, woodsy outcrops in both the Blue Hills and Middlesex Fells reservations, and the very popular "Black and White" rocks of Melrose. In the

KENNETH A. HENDERSON COLLECTION

Robert Underhill and friends. A pioneering AMC party after a Katahdin climb. The leading climber of his day, Underhill is fourth from left. Fifth from left is the colorful Jessie Whitehead, daughter of philosopher Alfred North Whitehead.

summer of 1927 the AMC climbers felt confident enough in their climbing competence to schedule a jointly sponsored "meet" in the Alps with the Climbers' Club of London. Robert Underhill was chosen to lead the AMC contingent—a recognition of his established role as America's leading climber.

The original nucleus owed much to the organizing spirit of Jack and Marjorie Hurd, especially the latter. Less than five feet tall, sharp-witted and sharper-tongued—a lawyer by profession—Marjorie Hurd became from the beginning and remained throughout the next fifteen years the most consistently active in promoting climbing excursions. "A spitfire" or "a little outboard motor" her fellow climbers called her, a nonstop talker all the way up the cliff. Though she herself rarely led, she'd try anything on a top-rope.

Indeed, women played a conspicuous part in these early climbing days. In the summer of 1926 Miriam O'Brien began to emerge as a top-flight alpinist and was soon exercising her talents on Boston area crags, though she reserved her best work for the Alps and other larger mountain ranges.

Appies at Joe English. Jacket, tie, and fedora were the regular climbing outfit of early AMC leader, Ken Henderson, shown here leading a party up the popular cliff on Joe English hill.

Margaret Helburn was still on the scene. Elizabeth Knowlton was a regular Boston (later New York) climber of those years and would later go to the Himalayas for one of the early attempts on Nanga Parbat. Jessie Whitehead was a colorful figure, with wit and temper to enliven any rope she was on; Ken Henderson recalled vividly that she "could push the leader up with a good string of profanity." Florence Peabody was the first of many New England women said to excel her husband on difficult rock. Of these women, however, only Miriam O'Brien consistently led on harder climbs.

Among the men, Helburn did not pursue rock climbing much after 1925. Robert Underhill began to step forward as the top climber and mountaineer in the United States, a status he enjoyed until the mid-1930s. Some more youthful strong men than Underhill led the first ascents of more difficult pitches, but he seemed always to be present as their second on their more celebrated achievements, and they universally acknowledged his superiority as an all-round alpinist. John Case and Hassler Whitney (we shall meet the latter shortly) are remembered by old-timers today as nearly in a class with Underhill for ability and overall mountaineering skill, but neither of these chose to play a major role in the mainstream of American climbing. Besides his position as principal leader among the early Boston climbers, Underhill made significant ascents in the West and played a key part in bringing technical climbing expertise to the earliest Sierra climbers. He also became editor of *Appalachia* in 1926 and gave rock climbing developments major attention in the next decade in that then-prestigious eastern journal. He is remembered by climbers of the 1920s as calm, unhurried, and graceful on rock, one who consistently substituted finesse for strength—"the cat is a better climbing model for humans than the goat," he counseled—an intelligent climber, capable of calling upon great reserves of experience and mountaineering judgment. "He knew the most," recalled Elizabeth Knowlton sixty years later, "and was the easiest and most graceful." An urbane, witty, erudite man, Underhill combined old-world manners and courtliness with a zest for fun and games and an iconoclastic appreciation of the absurdities that sometimes befall climbers. When in 1932 he married Miriam O'Brien, then regarded as incomparably the best American woman climber, the prestige of the couple can well be imagined. In the eyes of the 1930s climbers, as one of them put it, "Robert and Miriam Underhill were the parents of rock climbing in the Northeast."

The other Boston AMC leaders of that period included some mentioned before as active in the Alps: Lincoln O'Brien, Miriam's competitive kid brother, "a fascinating guy with a lot of Irish in him"; the well-dressed financier Ken Henderson, who always wore a jacket and tie on the hardest of rock climbs; prominent leaders of the Boston AMC aristocracy, like Dean Peabody and Trot Chandler; Carlton Fuller, the genial patrician who married the other Mason daughter, Dorothy; big, rugged John Holden; Leland Pollock and Will Allis, two younger men who rapidly emerged as bold new leaders under Underhill's tutelage; and a teenage prodigy of brassy energy, diverse talents, and unlimited self-confidence named Bradford Washburn, who unlike many teenage comets did not burn out but went on to sustain a long career of continuing contributions to American climbing.

Meanwhile other islands of interest in rock climbing had surfaced in the Northeast. In each case the local group was spearheaded either directly or indirectly by leaders who had learned roped climbing from vacations in the Alps.

The Hudson Highlands. From the New York area, a young man named Percy Olton graduated from college in 1926 and decided to blow all his savings on one summer in the Alps. There he met the O'Brien family in

Chamonix, as well as Ken Henderson. By September, Olton was feeling in great shape physically, with many successful alpine ascents, but in deteriorating condition financially—i.e., running low on cash, the necessary medium for hiring guides. To save money, he persuaded Henderson to join him in a guideless ascent of the prized Matterhorn. Since that dramatic spire was seldom done without a guide in those days, the two Americans moved cautiously, belaying in many places where the guides romped up, and ended up taking a long, long time, returning to Zermatt about 10:00 that evening, exhausted but exhilarated, with their prize safely and successfully earned.

The O'Briens and Henderson convinced Olton that rock climbing could be continued when he got back to the United States and persuaded him to start a New York AMC Chapter rock climbing group. Olton began weekend excursions via train up the Hudson River, where he and his friends discovered the riches of the Hudson Highlands crags. For their first venture, Olton selected a 100-foot cliff at Arden, an easy train ride from the city and almost within sight of the Arden station. This cliff proved to have several challenging routes on it and became a regular climbing destination for New York climbers for the next fifteen years. Smaller cliffs were found nearby, such as the Timp face, which Howell had scaled unroped in 1908, and the Ramapo Torne. Along the Hudson River itself, the larger cliffs of Storm King, Crow's Nest, and Breakneck Ridge soon attracted their attention.

The prime movers in New York climbing of the late 1920s besides Olton included the irrepressible and adventurous Nicholas Spadevecchia, Daniel Underhill (only distantly related to Robert), Lawrence Grinell, Ed Wolf, and Winthrop Means—mainly people who had learned roped climbing from guides either in the Alps or in the Canadian Rockies. For what they didn't already know, they leaned heavily on the few books available, always starting with Geoffrey Winthrop Young's *Mountaincraft*, and on their own cautious self-teaching experiments at Arden and elsewhere.

The Adirondacks. In 1927, as Boston climbers were exploring Joe English Hill and the Quincy Quarries and New Yorkers were at Arden and Storm King, John Case introduced the climbing rope to a young Adirondack mountain tramper named Jim Goodwin. The pupil became the most active and enterprising rock climber of the Adirondacks for the next generation, and in turn a teacher of many to come. Among others for whom Case was an early mentor in the 1920s, Bob Notman and Lewis Thorne also became proficient rock leaders and dependable all-round Adirondack mountaineers.

Case and these younger men began exploring more rock faces around

Women and men. Early rock climbing held no sex barriers: women were as active as men from the earliest days. Here Elizabeth Knowlton leads Dean Peabody on a route at Connecticut's Sleeping Giant.

the area and even made several bold attempts on the huge unclimbed cliff of Wallface in Indian Pass. Apart from the small lines at the Ausable Lakes cliffs, these excursions did not produce notable routes during the 1920s, but they were good training for more ambitious routes to come in the next decade. Beyond that, they showed that rock climbing was gaining competent practitioners around the entire region.

Connecticut. Down in the civilized corridors of Yale University, more rock climbers were surfacing in the mid-1920s. Hassler Whitney entered Yale in 1924 following secondary schooling in Switzerland, where he had been exposed to climbing with alpine guides. He was a brilliant student destined for a distinguished career as mathematician and educator at Harvard and the Institute for Advanced Study at Princeton. In personality Whitney was an introvert and loner, mildly eccentric, of strong convictions quietly and tenaciously held. He was a fluid and elegant climber, "an artist on rock" (according to a Yale contemporary), a true disciple of the Geoffrey Winthrop Young philosophy that judgment and skill were more important to a leader than muscle or bravado—or protection. Like the ideal Young leader, he possessed a cool and decisive nerve when the route demanded, as he was to show on Cannon cliff in 1929. Whitney took up an isolated niche in American climbing, aloof from the mainstream, tending (like Miriam O'Brien Underhill) to do his best climbing in the Alps yet occasionally showing up in the Northeast to produce excellent routes.

In his sophomore year, Whitney discovered the Sleeping Giant, that long, low hikers' haven just eight miles north of New Haven. Ambling along the hiking byways of the Giant, Whitney observed its many cliffs, ranging in height from 20 to 30 feet to the 100-plus-foot precipice of the Chin. He spent much time there during the next three years, sometimes with ropemates, sometimes alone. Whitney's solo climbs on the Giant illustrated a facet of the Young ideal that the later and more rigid devotees of Young tended to forget—that the seasoned leader's judgment could tell him what he could get up *and* down safely, so that solo climbing at a reasonably demanding standard was regarded as justifiable. (More on this point in chapter 4.) When later Yale climbers resumed exploration of the Sleeping Giant cliffs, they could never be sure when they were on new ground, so thoroughly had Whitney probed the possibilities.

Among his early partners at the Sleeping Giant were his brother, Roger Whitney, Tom Rawles, and Steve Hart. This nucleus formed the first incarnation of the many-lived Yale Mountaineering Club, which lapsed into inactivity after Whitney went to Harvard but was soon reborn with a more active group of Yale climbers in the early 1930s, disappearing again by World War II, only to be born again in 1947. In 1928 historian William Willcox, with a background of alpine climbing, came to Yale Graduate School. When Hassler left in 1929, it fell to his brother Roger, along with Rawles and Willcox, to continue the saga of Yale climbing. They even worked on a guidebook to the Sleeping Giant climbs, though this project never reached fruition.

Thus from Yale to the Ausable Club, from Storm King to the Quincy Quarries, northeastern rock climbing was warming up by 1927. Beginning in the following year, this solid base of technical competence throughout the region became the springboard for the first classic routes on northeastern rock. ∎

Reference Note

Primary written sources for the earliest efforts at northeastern rock climbing are rare. For Boston origins, see Marjorie Hurd et al., "The Development of A.M.C. Rock-Climbing," *Appalachia*, May 1951, pp. 345–347. Much more than from written sources, the authors benefited from conversations with original participants or their friends and relations, notably Frank Mason's daughters, Margaret Helburn and Dorothy Fuller, John C. Hurd, Robert L. M. Underhill, Kenneth A. Henderson, and Elizabeth Knowlton. In the Adirondacks the font of all knowledge was John C. Case. Pre-1928 climbing in Boston, the Hudson Highlands, the Adirondacks, and Connecticut must be drawn almost exclusively from the memories of surviving participants, among whom the authors were especially fortunate in conversations with Hurd, Underhill, Henderson, and Knowlton; Percy T. Olton, Jr.; Case and James A. Goodwin; Hassler Whitney and William Willcox. For acquainting us firsthand with the many crags of the Boston area, thanks are due to Deborah and David Duncanson and Glenn Allen.

3: The Classic Routes: 1928–1933

IN VIEW OF the novelty and primitive level of rock climbing for New Englanders up through 1927, the burst of activity and progress in climbing standards over the next six years is remarkable. In the history of this region's roped climbing since that time, we shall note definite moments when climbing took great leaps forward: 1928–1933, 1958–1960, 1967–1968, 1972–1974, and 1983–1986. But this first period, beginning with a bang in 1928, may well rank second only to the ice climbing revolution (after 1969—chapter 21) for its sudden rise in the standards of the climbing.

The single year 1928 saw great changes. By 1927 little had been done save the easiest and most obvious routes in the smaller areas. Then in 1928 four of the five big cliffs of the White Mountains were climbed for the first time, including the largest cliff in the East; several routes were worked out on far-away Katahdin and on the pink granite of Mount Desert in Maine; and harder ways were found up cliffs along the Hudson Valley in New York. All in one year!

It was a year, as historian Barbara Tuchman says of another era, in another sphere of activity, "of vigor, confidence, and forces converging to quicken the blood." It proved but prologue: the following year saw even more spectacular advances in difficulty, and major new climbs continued to be racked up throughout the early 1930s, especially in 1933.

The first ascent of Cannon cliff was the landmark climb of 1928. This huge rock face, the western wall of Franconia Notch, ranks with Katahdin and the Adirondacks' Wallface as the East's most intimidating climbing terrain. It stands so far away from and higher than the highway through the notch that the passing motorist fails to appreciate its size, unless it is pointed out that climbers on the cliff are so dwarfed by its scale as to be almost undiscernible to the naked eye from the road. On Memorial Day of 1928 a party of six Boston climbers, with Underhill in charge, drove into Franconia Notch, gazed at this mile-long expanse of vertical rock, boldly picked out a potential climbable line almost in the middle, then crossed the brook, plunged into the woods, and headed for the boulder field at its base. On that day Underhill sent Will Allis into the lead to negotiate the first two pitches of moderate difficulty. Above that, easier ground led through two grassy terraces, above which they were daunted by a steepening section of broken rock that led to a smooth slab broken only by two parallel vertical cracks some 20 feet high and four inches wide. The crack on the left appeared accessible from below but led nowhere; that on the right appeared to lead upward through apparently climbable rock but to be inaccessible from below. The Memorial Day party retreated. Later that summer, however, Underhill gathered up the agile Lincoln O'Brien and returned. The two scrambled up through the wooded slopes to the right of the cliff, circled around on top, and descended cautiously to a point directly over the route, a reconnaissance that convinced them that the route above the double cracks would "go." Thus encouraged, Underhill and O'Brien came back again on September 18 and quickly reclimbed Allis's bottom pitches, dragging along a thick birch log, tapered at one end. From the grassy ledge, O'Brien climbed up to reach the left-hand crack, where he jammed in the birch stake securely. Looping the rope over this projection, he backed down to a point opposite the base of the right-hand crack. With Underhill securing the bottom end of the rope, O'Brien moved out across the blank face, pulling on the rope with his left hand until his right hand and foot could barely reach the right-hand crack. With a strenuous pull, he swung around and lodged himself in the farther crack. Climbing up the crack proved strenuous too, but where it narrowed near the top, O'Brien found good handholds further out on the right and swung out onto the rock above. This indeed proved climbable, as they had surmised. In following this pitch, Underhill (with the security of a top-rope) attempted to cross to the right-hand crack without the tension of the rope but found the holds too small. When he slipped off, O'Brien easily held him, and his fall gently pendulumed him over to the crack. From this point on, they encountered more problems than anticipated but managed to get over them all and emerge in the bushes at the top.

The highest cliff in the East had been climbed. In the very first year of paying serious attention to the Northeast's prime rock faces, Underhill and O'Brien had seemingly made almost any other achievement an anticlimax. The remaining cliffs were all smaller, and both felt that theirs was the only possible route up Cannon. By modern rating methods, their route is 5.6 in difficulty. For 1928 at least, Underhill and O'Brien—with Allis's assist on the bottom pitches—had pulled off the premier climbing feat in the Northeast.

Meanwhile, however, during that summer other New Hampshire cliffs had felt their first imprint of human feet. Over in Crawford Notch, the big

Ken Henderson

The Whitney-Gilman

THE TWENTIES AT A GLANCE

Principal climbing event: first ascents of the north country's
biggest cliffs
Climbs of the Decade—rock: Whitney-Gilman
                     —ice: Odell Gully
Hardest single climb: Pinnacle (the rock climb, not the ice gully)
Emblematic item of gear: rope-soled shoes
Most important climber: Robert Underhill
Most underrated: Will Allis
Most colorful: Jessie Whitehead
Most prominent woman: Miriam O'Brien (later Underhill)
Child prodigy: Bradford Washburn
Still-active father figure to climbers of this decade: Willard Helburn
Best-looking (or at least best-dressed): Ken Henderson
Brainiest: Hassler Whitney
Patrician: Carlton Fuller
Vanishing act (Climber who was prominent in this decade but
who disappeared off the face of the climbing map in the
next decade): Lincoln O'Brien
Couple of the Decade: Robert and Miriam Underhill
Person you'd most like to have climbed with: John Case

KENNETH A. HENDERSON COLLECTION   KENNETH A. HENDERSON COLLECTION

south face of Willard which overlooks that scenic notch was attacked by
Underhill and O'Brien. They found a good route for the lower half, attaining
an ample tree-covered ledge halfway up. Seeking a direct line from there to the
top, Underhill led up into a rotten chimney. A few feet below its top, where
he thought he could see the cliff ease off to a lower angle, he encountered
one move that required the use of a distinctly shaky hold. Unwilling to trust
that hold, Underhill took the chance of untying, throwing down the rope,
and instructing O'Brien to traverse off the tree-covered ledge into the
wooded slopes on the side, climb up to the top, circle around over the cliff,
and throw down the rope. Long after O'Brien started off, it occurred to
Underhill that perhaps he had grossly underestimated the time it would take
O'Brien to accomplish these maneuvers, so he eventually steeled himself to
make the move over the suspect hold. The loose rock held, and Underhill
emerged over the top of the chimney, only to discover with horror that
above his new stance stretched far more than one rope length of difficult
climbing over some of the rottenest crumbling rock in the state of New

Classic routes of 1928. Left to right: Jack Hurd on Old Cannon; Ken Henderson (hat) and friends on Willard; Dana Durand leading an ascent of the Pinnacle.

KENNETH A. HENDERSON COLLECTION

Hampshire, the stretch of rock immediately below the black hole known as Devil's Den (chapter 1). The psychology of Underhill's reactions as he moved up over this pitch is an interesting illumination of the mind of a rock climber and is therefore worth quoting at length:

> The next half-dozen or more steps are unique in my climbing experience, and I hope without counterpart in that of most others. The only possible course was slightly upward and to the right, and even that wasn't properly "possible." In soberness I estimated my chances of sticking on, at any of these steps, as decidedly less than fifty-fifty. At any moment I quite expected to be on my way down the cliff. I still remember vividly how, after accomplishing a certain one of these steps, the absurd idea shot through my mind: "Well, that's interesting! We're still here! Let's try another." One thing only, in the whole performance of that day, still

gives me real satisfaction, and that is that, although on the one hand an insane temptation to rush the passage, to get it over with as quickly as possible, and on the other a tendency to slump, to think fatalistically, "What's the use? I'm bound to go off, if not on this step, then on the next, or the one after"— although both these made their appearance, I managed to reject them and to climb at each moment just as carefully and skillfully as I knew how. Indeed, I have always felt that under the great stress of the occasion I gained for the time being a quite abnormal ability to perceive quickly what holds there were and make the very best use of them.

After the half-dozen steps the climbing began to improve, becoming, though still very difficult, what we call "legitimate." And now note the curious psychology of the rock climber. Only a few seconds previous nothing had interested me less than the sport of rock climbing. The only thing that mattered had been getting across that cliff face alive; my entire consciousness had been flattened down to a single idea, namely, to Hamlet's good old question of "To be or not to be," with no extras whatever. But I had taken only a few steps on really climbable rock when my whole attitude underwent a quick spontaneous change, reverting with a bang to normalcy. Suddenly I found myself thinking: "Look here, this isn't so bad at all. If only we could get some pitons in for protection on these places, it might be a grand route!"

Eventually, after further difficulties, Underhill grasped the rope lowered by O'Brien and reached the top in safety, thoroughly chastened. A more justifiable route up Willard remained to be worked out by O'Brien and another partner the following May, after a long traverse to the left. Willard became a favorite cliff for 1930s climbers, though it fell into a long period of obscurity during the 1960s and 1970s, only to be reopened in the 1980s.

Later in 1928, Underhill spearheaded an attack on Huntington Ravine's great Pinnacle. This magnificent alpine megalith had seen unknown numbers of scramblers along its left (southern) edge, where bits of steep rock alternate with patches of bushy terraces and grassy gullies and yield to amateur heroics with comparative ease. In 1910 a Randolph, New Hampshire, summer resident, George Flagg, led a group of friends up a somewhat bolder line, starting on the steeper right-hand (northern) edge but drifting slightly

Allis's chimney. The crux move on the 1928 Pinnacle route, rarely done today, was getting started on this chimney. Note short pitch, copious coiled rope, hatted climber waiting his turn.

Atop the Pinnacle. The ever-well-dressed Ken Henderson, a member of 1928's first ascent party, shown at the airy top of Mount Washington's celebrated Pinnacle.

WALTER HOWE COLLECTION

The Brown Spot. This crux move on the first route on Whitehorse Ledge defeated early attempts of the cliff. Here a 1930s climber surmounts the notorious "Brown Spot."

leftward to avoid some of the difficulties higher up. In 1927 a party led by Lincoln O'Brien and animated by the fiery kibitzing of Marjorie Hurd had attempted a direct line up the right-hand edge, gaining about half the height before being stopped by steepening rock, the only breach in which seemed to be a steep chimney, the base of which lay around an awkward out-sloping corner. On October 14, 1928, Underhill showed up with Allis, Ken Henderson, Jessie Whitehead, and one other climber. To get into the chimney, Allis was given a shoulder to stand on from a ledge directly beneath. Once lodged in the cleft, Allis found that there were no good holds and realized that he had never climbed a pure chimney before:

> But as a boy I knew how to get up between trees not too far
> apart & I tried the same thing & it worked. Underhill told
> me to alternate feet & it worked even better. He was rather
> solicitous & asked if it felt safe, but I was quite comfortable.

The pitch completed, Allis held a tight rope for the others to pendulum around the awkward corner into the base of the chimney. The rest of the climb proved less taxing, and the route became a standard one for climbers of the 1930s. The Pinnacle is such a broad and complex feature that postwar parties have found endless variations to weave, and few modern climbers repeat the 1928 route. The original Allis chimney pitch, solid 5.7 in difficulty, is almost never climbed today.

Elsewhere around New England, further routes opened up during that momentous summer of 1928. A partial ascent of the graceful arches of Whitehorse Ledge was made, John Holden leading, seconded by Underhill. Willard Helburn returned to the fray to lead a gully climb on the Webster cliffs, across the notch from Willard, which he called *Willey House Gully* and compared in difficulty with Katahdin's Chimney. (Today's climbers know this route primarily as an ice climb and call it *Shoestring Gully*.) Other White Mountain cliffs that saw action ranged from the Mahoosucs and Devil's Slide in the north to Green's cliff and Mount Hedgehog in the area off today's Kancamagus Highway (not then cut through) and such remote cliffs as Mount Lowell and Bondcliff in between. Underhill led a group to Katahdin in late September 1928 that included Lincoln O'Brien, Marjorie Hurd, and the Helburns. There O'Brien led two new routes, one on either side of Helburn's original Chimney. Underhill praised these new routes as comparable in difficulty to anything he had encountered in the Alps. On Mount Desert an Appalachian Mountain Club party made a roped ascent on Dog Mountain, leaving untapped some cliffs in that island paradise that have subsequently proved more popular. In late 1927 Percy Olton invited Underhill and the Boston climbers to sample the Hudson Highlands rock, and in 1928 Underhill and O'Brien returned to pick off several prize routes on Storm King, ably supported by Olton, Spadevecchia, and other locals.

In 1928 Underhill had pronounced the original route up Cannon "the only possible route up the cliff." In less than a year Hassler Whitney proved the hazards of such predictions.

Whitney and his cousin Bradley Gilman, with whom he had just enjoyed a successful season in the Alps, selected one of the most striking and unusual lines in the East. About one-third of the way from the southern end of Cannon cliff, the huge face is broken from bottom to top by a deep, dank cleft of rotten, dripping rock known ominously as the Black Dike. The left edge of this discontinuity is an exceedingly sharp and vertical 600-foot arête of very fine, hard granite. In the ancient glaciated hills of the Northeast, a true knife-edge arête is most rare. The 1928 parties had looked at this arête, but, as Allis said, "We thought it obviously couldn't be done." Actually the upstart cousins had come to Cannon in 1929 intending to do the second ascent of the 1928 route, but finding it wet from recent rains turned to the

The infamous "Pipe Pitch." In 1929, Hassler Whitney and Bradley Gilman first ascended this dramatic section of Cannon's cliff. Note gaping exposure below the climbers. This has been called the most impressive climb in the United States at the time it was done.

arête over the Black Dike instead. Standing free and tall, this feature sheds water sooner than any other part of Cannon.

Up this arête Whitney and Gilman worked their way on the morning of August 3, 1929. They kept at first to the left side of the knife edge, finding a reasonable route on the clean, sunny granite. About 200 feet up they found this way blocked by an overhanging section. With cool nerve, they swung around the corner of the knife edge for one particularly exposed and delicate pitch, poised airily over the evil void of the Black Dike. Above, the route unrelentingly clove to the crest of the arête, with the steep face of Cannon's sunny granite on the left, the dark emptiness of the Black Dike on the right. An admiring Underhill later described the climb as "a long series of passages of great technical difficulty, high exposure, and dubious outlet." Suddenly one final move brought them out on relatively level ground sloping up into dense trees, and the jubilant cousins descended by a long, arduous traverse over the top of the cliff to the north.

The *Whitney-Gilman* route greatly impressed the climbers of their day. Underhill and Henderson repeated the climb in 1930, and Henderson was so impressed with the exposure on that one pitch 200 feet up that he subsequently installed a section of iron pipe at its base, with the idea that the belayer could snake the rope over the pipe to provide protection for the leader. Henderson's contribution forever gave the notorious sequence of moves the name of "the pipe pitch." Underhill bestowed his prestigious blessing on the route as "the best White Mountain climb to date." For all the postwar advances in difficulty, the *Whitney-Gilman* has remained perhaps the single most respected of the prewar climbs in the eyes of modern climbers, one of whom has said: "I'm impressed every time I go up there."

What adds to its luster is the fact that, ever the purists, Whitney and Gilman used no pitons, neither for protection nor anchors. Whitney on more than one occasion later descended the route as well, deftly flipping the rope over projections to safeguard the last man down (himself).

Just how difficult was the original *Whitney-Gilman?* Whitney himself

Classic route, classic climbers. This party celebrating at the scenic finish of Mount Willard's big cliff includes two key figures of the 1928–1929 pioneering climbs. At left is Bradley Gilman, of the Whitney-Gilman route; at right is Lincoln O'Brien, pioneer on Old Cannon and other early routes.
KENNETH A. HENDERSON COLLECTION

compared it in difficulty to the Grépon, an Alps route regarded as roughly 5.6 in today's ratings. Subsequent rockfall has raised the level of difficulty of both the second and third (or pipe) pitches, numbering them as done today; to the earliest parties, with their short ropes and lack of protection, the corresponding moves were met on the fifth and tenth out of seventeen pitches. With these changes, the *Whitney-Gilman* is now rated a solid 5.7. Although easier when first climbed, it has enjoyed a reputation as probably the hardest climb done in the United States until well into the 1930s. Actually, the technical difficulty of the Allis chimney on the Pinnacle was probably greater, but the overall sustained and exposed nature of the *Whitney-Gilman* makes it more impressive then and now.

In the next five years further exploration continued on northeastern rock. In the early 1930s Underhill discovered a new bold leader in Leland W. Pollock, whom he later described as "my favorite partner" and "a natural born rock climber." In June 1931, with Underhill seconding, Pollock created a splendid line up a prominent crack system in the center of one of the steepest cliffs in New Hampshire, Cathedral Ledge. The effort was flawed slightly by bypassing the obvious direct start at the bottom and by some acrobatic rope work involving nearby trees to protect the first moves. Subsequently Will Allis, with strenuous effort, muscled his way up this direct start, rated today at 5.7. (With both this and his work on the Pinnacle, Allis was clearly outstanding among the early leaders—a man who has never been given as much credit as he deserves.) Pollock's original route has become the popular *Standard* route on Cathedral and deserves a respectable 5.6 rating.

In 1929, after a reconnaissance from above, Underhill and Henderson completed Holden's route on the beautiful arching slabs of Whitehorse Ledge, Cathedral's southern neighbor. However, they still felt that they had avoided the best line. In July 1932 Pollock led another Underhill party that finally pieced together what has become the Whitehorse *Standard* route, which a leading modern climber calls "the single most popular rock climb in New Hampshire." Pollock solved the key problem, an awkward move near the top, later known as the notorious "Brown Spot." The move is rated 5.5 today.

In 1929 a Harvard Mountaineering Club party of six climbers, again under the leadership of Underhill (this time in his mantle of Harvard philosophy professor rather than AMC leader), went to Katahdin and established no fewer than eight new routes. Aside from Underhill himself, leaders in these efforts were Henry D. and G. L. Stebbins. The crusty old Katahdin guide Leroy Dudley, watching askance from his cabin at Chimney Pond, could only shake his head in disapproval: "What we need around here is a fool-killer," Dudley warned. "Untrained people mustn't come in here expecting to follow those trails [sic]. They'll get killed if they do." Thus was born a spirit of disapproval on the part of Katahdin's locals that has been directed against adventurous activities on Maine's greatest mountain to the present day.

In 1931 and 1932 AMC rock climbers led by Pollock brought their gear and their spirit of adventure to the fabulous wealth of clean pink granite cliffs on the seashore idyll of Mount Desert. They "explored a different mountain every day . . . and only once during the six days of climbing did two ropes go up the same course." Among many areas explored were the cliffs of Champlain Mountain, destined to become one of the more popular rock climbing areas on the isle.

Over in New York state, John Case continued to develop Adirondacks rock climbing on its separate but parallel course. In the early 1930s, Case and Jim Goodwin made several attempts to climb a direct route up the "grim titanic guardian" of Indian Pass, Wallface. Their best efforts were insufficient to find a feasible way through the final steep sections. At length, in 1933, Case returned with his son and Betty Woolsey, a talented and versatile athlete, Olympic skier, and one of the strongest woman rock leaders outside the Boston circle in the 1930s. This time, nearing the top, Case opted to diagonal away from the steeper rock, zigzagging up and right over moderate but wildly exposed moves to complete the first ascent of the Adirondacks' tallest cliff. About the same time Case and Bob Notman climbed another large Adirondack face, the big slab at the south end of Chapel Pond, prominently visible from the highway. They called this route *Bob's Knob*. Case's routes were somewhat easier than the counterpart achievements in the White Mountains—in today's ratings, more 5.3 than 5.6—but the lack of other climbers and the remote setting of Wallface added spice often lacking in New Hampshire's busier and more organized scene. ∎

Reference Note

Primary sources for the path-breaking climbs are contemporary write-ups in *Appalachia*, usually in a section called "Rock Climbing," throughout the period 1928–1933. Especially helpful to the authors were the personal recollections of participants, notably Underhill, O'Brien, Allis, Henderson, Holden, Whitney, Gilman,

Hurd, Case, Goodwin, and Woolsey. Of special interest is a landmark article by Kenneth A. Henderson, "Some Rock Climbs in the White Mountains," *Appalachia,* December 1929, pp. 343–350. Secondary sources of merit include Chris Jones, *Climbing in North America* (Berkeley: University of California Press, 1976); Robert Kruszyna, "Climbing Nature's Walls," *New England Outdoors,* May 1978, pp. 40–45 and June 1978, pp. 44–47; Al Rubin, "New Hampshire Climbing: A Historical Essay," *Mountain,* July-August 1978, pp. 18–26; Michael Macklin, "Fifty Years of Granite State Climbing," *Climbing,* March-April, pp. 22–28, May-June, pp. 15–19, and July-August 1980, pp. 19–29; and historical essays in local guidebooks, notably Al Rubin's in Paul Ross and Chris Ellms, *Cannon, Cathedral, Humphrey's and Whitehorse: A Rock Climber's Guide* (North Conway, NH: International Mountain Climbing School, Inc., 1978; revised edition, 1982), and Don Mellor's in his *Climbing in the Adirondacks* (Lake Placid, NY: Lake Placid Climbing School, Inc., and Sundog Ski and Sports, 1983). Among those who traced original routes of classic climbs with us, thanks are especially due to Bob Hall and Mary Jane Cross (*Old Cannon*) and Jack Taylor (Willard and the Pinnacle). Bob Kruszyna (Gilman's son-in-law) was most helpful in analyzing changes in the *Whitney-Gilman* route due to rockfall.

It's a Grand Old Flagg

IT IS THE authors' stern intention to leave ourselves—our own experiences, modest climbs, and personal opinions—entirely out of the chapters of this history. In one respect that will be easy: we have done nothing to merit the attentions of posterity, nothing like those gods and goddesses of whom we write.

However . . . sometimes the very process of our collecting the historical record generated incidents that we thought unusual, bizarre, or just plain funny. So we shall interrupt our regular chapters now and then with interludes of a more personal nature. Occasionally these experiences shed unexpected light on the original events, possibly enriching a view into a time long past. We hope readers may pardon this intrusion, or may enjoy sharing some of our experiences in gathering history and the insights they helped us toward. Herewith the first of these interludes.

The distinguished European historian, H. R. Trevor-Roper, once mused:

> One of the most delightful experiences, for a scholar, occurs
> when, after long search, or perhaps by chance, he discovers
> a small key which is found to open a long-locked door and
> reveal, beyond it, a totally unexpected vista.

A series of happenstances and doors almost left unopened led us to that small key which did indeed open a long-locked door to reveal a small but gleaming jewel of an early rock climbing adventure. The story concerns the Pinnacle of Huntington Ravine, a ninety-year-old woman, and some faded sketchbooks gathering dust in a suburb of Washington, D.C.

The Pinnacle of Huntington Ravine is a massive bulk of dark rock looming out from the jagged gullies of the cirque, an obvious attraction to the earliest rock climbers. In 1928 the Underhill-Allis party proudly recorded the first ascent, duly memorialized in an *Appalachia* account by Ken Henderson, a member of the party, and also duly reported in chapter 3 herein.

More than half a century later, when researching this history, the authors stumbled by pure luck onto an account of a prior climb of the Pinnacle—a bold scramble eighteen years *before* the Underhill-Allis "first ascent."

Like many another gem of purest ray serene, this feat might have remained in dark obscurity, unfathomed by posterity, condemned to blush unseen in the oblivion of unrecorded history, had it not been for a tenuous chain of events.

A casual friend who works for the Appalachian Mountain Club at Pinkham Notch Camp in the White Mountains makes his home in the nearby small mountain town of Randolph, New Hampshire. Knowing of our history project, Walter urged us to go see a summertime neighbor of his, one Marion Flagg Foynes. Said Walter, this lady has been coming to Randolph since the turn of the century and she's nearly ninety years old and she's a real character. (This was in 1983.)

Well, lots of people have been spending lots of summers in the White Mountains during this century. Lots of our friends were urging us to go talk to lots of their friends who had been around lots of years. Having spent lots of time already researching the early Randolph scene, what could we learn from yet one more elderly reminiscer? So we almost didn't go to see Mrs. Foynes.

To humor Walter, who's a nice fellow, we agreed to write to the old girl and make a date to go see her if she still managed the trip in 1984's summer. We anticipated listening to the bemused, barely audible ramblings of an armchair-ridden nonagenarian.

What we found instead, on arriving at the modest summer home in Randolph, was a vigorous, blustery, open, candid, can-do dynamo of an eighty-nine-year-old woman who talked our ears off, dashed up a steep flight of stairs repeatedly to find old photos or other memorabilia, and provided fresh insights enlivened by visual evidence of what mountain holidays were like for not one but three generations back.

Visual evidence? Mrs. Foynes' father, George Flagg, had been a newspaper cartoonist, had summered in Randolph from before 1900, and had

The Pinnacle in 1910. Eighteen years before the recognized "first ascent" by Underhill, Henderson, Allis, Whitehead, and Durand, this group of four adventurers made their own way up the celebrated Pinnacle on Mount Washington. Sketches show clearly the approximate line, the unorthodox techniques, and the clearly recognizable finish (from the sketchbooks of George A. Flagg, courtesy Marion Flagg Foynes and Shirley Foynes Hargraves).

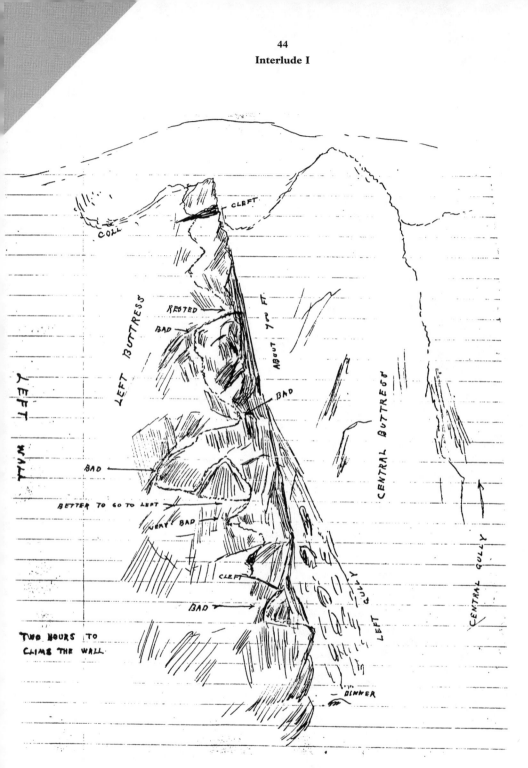

Interlude I

MR. DENNIS COMES OVER

THE FIRST BAD PLACE

ONE WAY TO GET OVER A LEDGE

Interlude I

OVER WITH THE ROCKS

set down his impressions of mountain life in innumerable drawings, carica-
tures, and parodies. His art was a gold mine for researchers seeking to see
back into not just the dusty facts but the vivid spirit of a lost era.

Among George Flagg's works was a series of "sketchbooks," one for
each summer in Randolph. Most of these, however, were unavailable to us
on that first visit, because they were not in Randolph then. Mrs. Foynes had
removed them to her winter home near Washington, D.C. and consigned
them to the care of her daughter there.

Washington, D.C. seemed far away, and anyway, we rationalized, we've
probably assembled all we need on early Randolph, so maybe we'll forget
about those other sketchbooks.

That winter, however, other research sources required us to go to Washington. We decided that if (and only if) our schedule had any free time, we
might call on Mrs. Foynes (now turned ninety) at her winter home and have
a look at those other sketchbooks. During our trip, it first appeared we'd be
too busy, but at the last minute an uncommitted afternoon opened up, so
we did drive over to see the wonderful woman. Before we could see the
sketchbooks, we first had to pass inspection by a slightly suspicious daughter. Reassured of our legitimate historical purpose, the daughter warmed
up and produced a series of thoroughly delightful, warmly evocative, and
very funny sketchbooks by her talented grandfather.

Leafing through the 1910 edition, our eyes were suddenly arrested by
a page headed "Huntington Ravine, Aug. 20 1910, Party: Geo. Flagg—Mr.
Dennis—Mayo Tollman—Paul Bradley." Beneath these words was a sketch
of three men perched on a boulder directly beneath the unmistakable out-
lines of the Pinnacle buttress. There followed, to our wonder and joy, a
series of eight drawings depicting an ascent of the Pinnacle—eighteen years
before the Underhill-Allis climb.

As always, Flagg's drawings were clever. The climbing technique was
more Charlie Chaplin than Robert Underhill. In place of the sophisticated
British classification of "Difficult," "Severe," and "Extreme" or the modern
U.S. numerical gradings (5.0 to 5.10 and beyond), the 1910 cartoonist
marked crux moves as "bad"—and one as "very bad." Mr. Dennis seemed to
have been particularly inept and in need of unorthodox assists from his
more agile companions.

But the revelation was that route details were explicitly delineated. We
quickly realized that here was all the evidence required to trace this 1910
ascent with far better assurance than most purely written accounts of early
climbs.

TRAMPERS BELOW OBJECT TO OUR ROCKS

ON TOP

PAUL BRADLEY
IN A BAD PLACE

END OF TRIP.

We secured permission from Mrs. Foynes and her daughter, Shirley Foynes Hargraves, to copy this series of sketches—they are reproduced herein on adjacent pages with the generous acquiescence of the family—and speedily made plans to climb the Pinnacle during the following summer, with George Flagg's drawings as our route description.

On September 1, 1984, a few days more than seventy-four years after Flagg, Dennis, and associates had passed that way, we and four friends perched on that boulder and gazed at the unchanged rock monolith. On the early pitches we had little difficulty following where Flagg and company had gone. Then matching the drawings to the terrain became more problematic. We began to hypothesize that this early party had drifted well to the left of the 1928 line and onto far more climbable rock. Will Allis's difficult chimney, for example, seems to have been avoided in 1910. But much of the lower route was identical, and the earlier climbers certainly climbed the entire Pinnacle, as the triumphant view "on top" shows.

In one sense, our conclusions were very satisfying. Proper credit remained due to the Underhill-Allis party for their uncompromising straight-up line—yet a generous share of honor remained for those untrained, unequipped pioneers of 1910 and their magnificent spirit of adventure and joy.

Our own 1984 researches were unceremoniously halted by the onset of a violent thunderstorm. It came upon us from over the mountain when we were about two-thirds up the big wall. An exposed buttress on Mount Washington is no place to be during an electrical display, sheets of cold driving rain, boisterous wind, and rapidly falling temperatures. Some of us were close to hypothermic before we completed our hasty series of rappels and tenuous downward climbing through loose, rain-washed gullies. It was as if the mountain gods wished to preserve the glory for those resourceful pioneers of 1910 and 1928 and to condemn these 1984 upstarts, with their fancy new climbing aids, to ignominious retreat.

Retreat we did: on that day at least, we were honored to leave that hallowed ground of the Pinnacle to the undisturbed spirits of George Flagg and his merry companions, who stole the first-ascent tiara from the noble brow of Underhill himself. Seventy-four years is a long time to wait for glory.

Ah, but in what other attic, in what other faraway city, lurks yet another sketchbook or journal entry by what other adventurous cartoonist or diarist, showing abundant evidence of an 1890 ascent of the Whitney-Gilman ridge? ■

4: Mountaincraft: Ethics and Style in Prewar Climbing

NORTHEASTERN ROCK CLIMBING during the creative years of 1928 to 1933 had certain qualities that differ sharply from the climbing of today or even of the later 1930s.

A spirit of jointly shared exploration characterized the attitudes of the leading climbers, in contrast to the more competitive spirit of the postwar (and especially post-1969) era. Under Underhill's benign hegemony in New England and Case's in the Adirondacks, a cooperative approach toward solving the difficulties of the big cliffs was nurtured. The purposeful pursuit of first ascents to mark a leader's reputation had not begun. Write-ups of new routes often omitted specifying who led, a procedure that would mystify most modern climbers. Percy Olton, writing up New York rock climbs for *Appalachia* in 1938, explained that many routes had been left "uncatalogued so that future climbers may share to some extent the pleasures of climbing an uncharted route." This quality is singled out not necessarily to praise the older as against the newer spirit. Many climbers enjoy the spark of friendly competition, and it is often argued that the most impressive advances in technical difficulty have resulted from periods of intense rivalry between ambitious leaders. Nonetheless, the cooperative spirit of the early years is not altogether unattractive.

In the 1928–1933 period, each cliff was regarded as a single problem, and once one route had been found, that cliff was regarded as climbed. This view contrasts sharply with the modern search for as many different routes as possible on each cliff. In the 1930s you climbed Cathedral or Whitehorse or the Pinnacle or Willard, and it was unnecessary to specify what route because in most cases there was but one. Cannon and Katahdin were prominent exceptions, but on Cannon there were only two routes, referred to as *Old Cannon* and *New Cannon* (today's *Whitney-Gilman*).

One minor corollary of this principle was that early routes had the dullest of names (the *Standard, Old Cannon, New Cannon*). Imaginative, humorous, and evocative names—*The Prow, Repentance, Sliding Board, Bloody Mary, Inferno, Wonder Wall,* the *Ghost, Screaming Yellow Zonkers*—lay far in the future.

Equipment was minimal, largely limited to the rope. An AMC climber of the 1930s, Ron Gower, proclaimed this Spartanism as one of the virtues of the sport:

> It is so perfectly natural, there being no artificial aids ex-
> cept the rope. . . . In this respect rock-climbing runs close
> to tramping and swimming in its essential simplicity.

The extensive shopping list that outfits the modern climber was unknown to this first generation of their tribe. Racks of protection were limited to a few carabiners and, for some leaders but not others, a handful of pitons and a hammer. Today there exists an imposing array of various types of nuts and even more exotic forms of protection, gaily colored sling material for various functions, seat-harnesses, belaying devices, rappelling devices, hard hats, chalk bags, not to mention carefully studied fashions in climbing clothes. For boots, highly specialized (and expensive) today, the 1930s climber wore sneakers, or perhaps rope-soled shoes or some other favorite footgear, such as the stylish Ken Henderson's golf shoes.

Leads were done with short ropes and little or no protection, so one striking difference in early climbing was the much shorter pitches. The tendency was to climb a short distance, surmount one series of difficulties, then stop and bring up the rest of the party. The *Whitney-Gilman* route, done in five pitches normally today, was done in seventeen pitches in 1930. Olton, describing one New York route, warned: "This pitch is quite long and requires a full 60 feet of rope." Today's ropes are 150 feet or longer.

In the 1920s the use of pitons was controversial. The feeling among climbers was that rock climbing should test the climber's ability to climb a route on his own. Almost universally, direct aid was condemned as unsporting. Beyond that, in the 1920s at least, many leaders disdained the use of pitons for intermediate protection on leads. In event of a long fall, piton protection would have been dubious anyway because prewar ropes would break. The well-known maxim "the leader does not fall" was oft quoted from the "bible" of early American climbers, *Mountaincraft,* by the great British alpinist Geoffrey Winthrop Young. But even had the ropes been strong, many leaders felt that it was part of the challenge of their role to climb without meaningful protection—to have such judgment, skill, strength, and cool nerve that "the leader does not fall." Many of the outstanding early northeastern leaders (e.g., John Case) never or rarely drove a piton throughout long (and quite safe) climbing careers. Miriam O'Brien Underhill said: "When I began climbing we knew about pitons but we didn't think nice people used them."

The corollary of not using pitons, of course, was that most of these leaders never—literally never—took a fall on the lead. Note that Young's maxim was not "should not fall," nor even "must not fall"; it was flatly the leader "does not fall." John Case once said, "If I ever take a fall, then I'll quit." What he meant was not simply that he would be embarrassed or disgraced by a fall, but that to fall would display such inexcusably poor judgment as to disqualify him from leading.

Two consequences flowed from this philosophy. One was that prior to the advent of strong rope and acceptance of pitons, few climbers were willing to lead. Most settled for the far less demanding role of following.

The other consequence was that the standards of difficulty of prewar climbing were much lower than postwar. When trustworthy climbing rope became available, along with better pitons and other means of protection, leaders could try much harder routes, secure in the knowledge that a fall would not be fatal. When postwar leaders realized the implications of this higher safety margin, they began to climb at levels of difficulty that would have been unthinkable to their predecessors. Many leaders of this later era fell a lot too, but with safety; and they certainly got up harder lines. Routes done since the late 1950s, and especially since 1970, scale rock that Case and the Underhills never considered remotely possible.

It's worth dwelling some more on the implications of the prewar Youngian maxim that became the cliché "the leader does not fall." With it grew a demanding and subtle philosophy on the role of the leader quite different from anything in modern climbing.

For Young and the prewar climbers weaned on his precepts, the role of the leader was a far broader one than it is today. It meant more than merely going first or being the best climber, and much more than skill or muscle alone. The critical points were intangibles—judgment, cool presence of mind in tight situations, vast reserves of experience and technique, and psychological elements of leadership vis-à-vis the other(s) in the climbing party. Young defined mountaincraft as:

> . . . an education alike in self-development and in self subordination; a discipline of character . . . a test of personality for which no preparation may be considered excessive, and a science for whose mastery the study of all our active years is barely sufficient.

Remember that the English tend toward understatement. One Adirondack disciple, Jim Goodwin, stated his understanding of the terms of leadership more bluntly: "The main idea was the leader never made a mistake. Period." Some of the ramifications of this philosophy should be noted.

First, to be *sure* never to fall, a leader had to be able to back down anything he went up (in case he should meet an insurmountable obstacle higher up). Therefore you could never do a move that you could not also down-climb. One interesting manifestation of this principle was the rule observed in bouldering in the Dartmouth Mountaineering Club in the 1930s:

> If any climber, even on a six-foot boulder, tried a route, he
> had either to complete it or to *climb* down; if he *fell*, the for-
> feit was to bend over and be paddled by the other climbers.

This approach to bouldering problems would be viewed by many postwar climbers as defeating the purpose of bouldering. In the modern view, bouldering should be used to find just where your limits are: pushing yourself until you fall off is precisely the point. A widely respected current how-to book says:

> Bouldering has played a major role in the advance of
> climbing standards. Often the boulderer operates only a
> few feet or even a few inches above gentle ground, and if a
> fall is inconsequential, he may push himself to the limit of
> his ability and make repeated efforts until he finally masters
> an extremely difficult and complex problem.

A second ramification of the no-fall imperative involved a different attitude toward loose rock. It was part of the responsibility of leading not to be thrown off by a breaking hold. The modern leader certainly does not want a hold to break, but if one does, he is inclined to regard it as bad luck, a sort of *deus ex machina;* if it causes a fall, it is not his fault in the same way as failing to complete a hard move would be. Not so for the prewar leader: he regarded it as his full and unshirkable responsibility to *know* whether that rock would break off. Admonished Young:

> Stones loosened by the party upon itself . . . are matters for
> the correction of climbing technique, and cannot be rated,

either mentally or vocally and emphatically, as risks from external causes.

In a prewar treatise on climbing technique, Underhill devoted many pages to describing how to deal with loose rock, "the unremitting testing of all holds," how to apply weight gradually to a suspect hold while retaining the ability to sink back on lower holds if the new one broke. Modern how-to texts virtually ignore the subject of loose rock. Consider the implications in the plain fact that most of the great prewar leaders—John Case, for example—literally *never* fell, though they climbed for more than half a century; also the fact that *none* of the 1920s leaders died in climbing accidents (indeed, many lived vigorously into their late eighties or nineties—a fortunate fact for the writers of this history). These remarkable facts mean that in all their exploratory first ascents up rock of dubious or downright rotten quality, in all their years and years of leads, they never once erred in placing undue reliance on a hold that gave way.

Thirdly, early leaders made much of the concept of always having a *reserve* on which to call in emergency. Quoth Young: "While exerting himself to the utmost, the leader has always to keep some strength, nervous and physical, in reserve, to meet a sudden emergency." One reason why postwar climbing has progressed to such extraordinary levels of difficulty is that the postwar leader expects to climb right up to the very limit of what he can physically stay on. In fact, he is often prepared to determine that limit by pushing himself until he falls off—safely caught by nylon rope and sophisticated protection apparatus. This approach was of course completely foreign to the prewar leader, schooled in the idea of always maintaining a comfortable margin between what he could barely hang on to and what he would actually lead. Miriam Underhill, writing in 1957 after the adoption of nylon rope and improved pitons, recognized what a change this meant, in that the modern climber "can afford to climb right up to his limit," whereas the old leader on difficult rock without protection needed "reserves of strength, skill and control."

And fourthly, underlying everything was a much broader concept of leading on rock. Among the requirements of leadership, Young's book delved into such topics as "the collective confidence" ("Their [the party's] confidence in his [the leader's] confidence is a more important asset than their confidence in his skill"), "keeping touch," "preventable humours," and "will and nerves." Will was crucial:

Ethics and style in prewar climbing (left to right): Pitoncraft: Irvin Davis drives a steel piton. Follow-the-leader: unroped practice, with Davis again at the front. Shoulder stand: Hudson Highlands climbers show that "two men are one attacking unit." Geoffrey Winthrop Young: this British alpinist-writer wrote the "Bible" for prewar climbers, Mountaincraft.

KENNETH A. HENDERSON COLLECTION

WALTER HOWE COLLECTION

M. GIRARD BLOCH

FROM *MOUNTAINCRAFT*

> Far more than any muscular strength or even physical fit-
> ness, will-power is the dominant force in maintaining nor-
> mal energy. . . . The leader is most efficient who can protect
> his party against influences that irritate the nerves and so
> interfere with the power or desire to bring the will into
> play.

If this sounds mystical today, perhaps it was so even then. Miriam Underhill
similarly stressed moral qualities:

> Where there is a genuine penalty for failure, you have to be
> a real man [*sic*] to play at all. You must have experience,
> skill, strength, courage and, above all, those moral quali-
> ties of self-knowledge and self-control.

All these constraints on early leaders are useful to keep in mind when
comparing the difficulty of routes done prewar and postwar. With the exception of a few short routes led by Fritz Wiessner, no prewar route is known
to have exceeded 5.7 in difficulty. For a full decade after the war and the introduction of nylon rope, that remained true in the Northeast. The advancing standards of difficulty thereafter are chronicled in later chapters: the
breakthroughs to 5.9 and 5.10 around 1960, to 5.11 in the late 1960s, and on
to 5.12 and 5.13 in the 1970s and 1980s. The difference lay not so much in
improved technique, skill, or strength as in a radical change in the conditions
under which climbers climbed—and a consequent transformation of their
perceptions of the possible.

Ethical questions involving climbing technique and tactics divide the
climbing community of the postwar world. These were not unknown to the
1928–1933 explorers. It may not have escaped the reader's attention in
the last chapter that these high-principled disciples of Geoffrey Winthrop
Young's purity were not above employing a pendulum on *Old Cannon*, a
shoulder stance on the Pinnacle, elaborate "rope tactics" on Cathedral, and
prior inspection from above on Whitehorse. Opinion was divided on some
points: Case and Whitney disdained pitons, but Underhill would use them
to protect a lead otherwise unjustifiable, and Henderson put in his famous
pipe (and on Whitney's route!). In general the entire generation was in
agreement that the actual climbing must be without benefit of pitons or
other artificial aids. In this respect all shades of northeastern ethics, from
the purist Whitney to the pragmatist Underhill, followed the British

precept. (Young had scoffed: "Artificial aids have never been popular with us. . . . The only two pegs I can recall having seen in our hills were left by two foreigners, and were not needed.") However, the shoulder stance was not regarded as an artificial aid, since only human limbs were involved. "Two men are one attacking unit," Fritz Wiessner reasoned. Even Young had sanctioned this tactic, recalling:

> I have had a guide of some weight, but of delicately managed feet, walking from my shoulder to my head and back again for twenty minutes, while he was trying to noose the lower pinnacle of the Charmoz, without feeling any great discomfort.

As these words suggest, "rope tactics" occupied an uncertain middle-ground ethically. Underhill and his generation regarded them as a compromise, possibly acceptable for a first ascent but to be subsequently eliminated as soon as possible. Thus the tight-rope-from-above with which Allis pulled his followers into the chimney on the Pinnacle was soon eliminated when a way was found to get around the corner by fair means. The same for the pendulum on *Old Cannon* and the tree-rigged protection of the bottom move on Cathedral. Underhill argued that the ethical line should be drawn according to whether climbing skill was used: to pull up on a piton or top-rope involved no skill, but to lasso a rock projection from below to protect a lead was quite an art!

An interesting twist on the ethical arguments may be observed in an article written by Miriam Underhill in 1957, representing the older generation's comments on the growing acceptance of pitons. The modern ethic nearly universally condemns the use of pitons (or rather their counterparts in modern hardware—nuts, Friends, etc.) for direct aid but completely and totally accepts their validity for protecting a lead. To Miriam, weaned on 1920s climbing ethics, the precise reverse was true. "I have no quarrel whatever with direct-aid pitons" (to overcome rock otherwise unclimbable), she conceded, "but the piton for security is something else." She rejected the claims of younger climbers that pitons merely make the climb safe, that they don't use them for ascent, and . . .

> that it is exactly the same climb it was before, only safer. *It most definitely is not the same climb.* These modern climbers are getting from their pitons enormous help, without ad-

Hassler Whitney. Pioneer at the Sleeping Giant in the mid-1920s and on Cannon's classic Whitney-Gilman route, the great mathematician-climber is shown here during a return to the scene of his Sleeping Giant climbs almost sixty years later. In a 1951 essay, Whitney lectured postwar climbers on techniques then falling out of fashion.

mitting it or, perhaps, even realizing its extent. . . . It is not the same climb, because the piton removes or greatly mitigates the penalty for failure. . . . For even if the modern climber never needs to use these pitons, they are there, removing from his mind a great weight of responsibility. [Italics in original.]

In these early years, when the Youngian maxim "the leader does not fall" reigned supreme, leaders took a relaxed view of soloing on rock—i.e., climbing without rope or any protection whatever. After all, to lead on the old ropes was virtually tantamount to soloing anyway. When two Penn State climbers joined John Case to do his old route on Indian Head, Case was seventy-two years old. The youngsters roped up, but Case at first prepared to solo alongside them, reluctantly agreeing to tie in, though regarding the precaution as unnecessary. When the authors (and Connecticut climber Ken Nichols) joined Hassler Whitney to explore one of his old routes on the Sleeping Giant, they encountered a similar reluctance. In fact, Whitney soloed all but the crux section, where he accepted a rope. He was seventy-six at the time. In both cases (Indian Head and Sleeping Giant) the routes involved 5.3 moves. Into his eighties, when climbing at the Shawangunks, Fritz Wiessner made a regular practice of avoiding the standard descent route after climbs (the Uberfall) in favor of soloing down one of the easier climbs. In this one respect, the earliest climbers were more in tune with recent trends, where solo climbing has regained respectability in some circles (not in all!). To build confidence for aspiring leaders, Underhill and his contemporaries would sometimes play a form of "follow-the-leader" on Boston's practice crags, in which an experienced leader would work out a long series of moves, traversing up and down and around the crag, while everyone else followed behind, all unroped. By the late 1930s, concern about safety and the retirement of most of the original leaders had begun to make this sort of thing unacceptable. When Henderson darted, unroped, around the lower slabs of Willard to take pictures of the other climbers, he was viewed with skepticism despite his prestige as an old-time leader. In another ten years the strictures against solo climbing had hardened into absolute dogma, not to be relaxed until relatively recent times.

Rock climbing in 1928–1933, for all the shining achievements of those years, was still seen by its practitioners primarily as training for the big mountains. That was how it started in Boston, with Mason's pupils in 1925, and that was largely the spirit of such alpine veterans as Underhill, Henderson, Case, Olton, and Whitney. Henderson recalls:

> In the eyes of most climbers of that period these [the routes on Pinnacle, Whitehorse, Cathedral] were merely practice climbs on which to gain experience for bigger things or on which to keep in practice. They were not regarded as major accomplishments in themselves as many later climbers regarded the new routes that they set up.

Still, it was undeniable that the splendor of those classic first ascents on Cannon and Cathedral and Wallface constituted a triumph in themselves. To the younger leaders like Allis and Pollock, New Hampshire was world enough to conquer. A visiting British climber in 1936 was invited along on a New Hampshire weekend jaunt and later wrote to the AMC weekend leader:

> White Horse Ledge is a perfect climb of its kind and it both delighted and impressed me. . . . Mr. Pollock's lead over the difficult section was a fine bit of work and it is my considered opinion that anyone who has led this climb as surely and safely as he led it, is fit to lead the Grépon.

Northeastern rock climbing had come of age. ∎

Reference Note

For an understanding of early climbing philosophy and the role of the leader, an indispensable primary source is Geoffrey Winthrop Young, *Mountaincraft* (London: Metheun & Co. Ltd, 1920). Also of great value are the writings in *Appalachia* by Robert L. M. Underhill, notably his general treatises on "The Technique of Rock Climbing," in December 1933, pp. 565–590, and December 1939, pp. 486–496, but also his shorter essays on special problems—e.g., in June 1928, pp. 53–64; June 1929, pp. 298–301; June 1930, pp. 79–81; December 1930, pp. 181–183; December 1932, pp. 288–293. See also Hassler Whitney, "Practical Belaying," *American Alpine Journal,* 1951, pp. 90–97; and Dean Peabody, "On Belaying," *Appalachia,* June 1930, pp. 105–107. For the authors, conversations and correspondence with the leaders of that period were of inestimable value, among whom especially helpful were Underhill and Whitney, as well as John C. Case, James A. Goodwin, Kenneth A. Henderson, Percy Olton, and Fritz Wiessner.

5: The First Ice Age: Before 1927

ROPED OR TECHNICAL climbing in the Northeast has two parallel but separate traditions: rock and ice.

In high mountains these two media are less precisely differentiated. It is not uncommon in climbing large mountains to start out scrambling on rock, walk up a glacier for awhile, encounter a difficult ice climbing problem crossing the bergschrund, then return to a steep rock ridge, perhaps ducking in and out of ice gullies or steep snow fields. The climber must deal with both rock and ice on the same day, or perhaps even with mixed terrain: one foot on ice, the other on rock, one hand clutching a rock hold, the other planting an ice ax.

In the Northeast, although some winter routes are mixed, the great majority of climbing is distinctly one or the other: either summertime rock climbing, usually on warm dry rock under sunny friendly skies, or ice climbing in the dead of winter, often under those horrendous conditions of cold, wind, and driving snow that give Mount Washington's winter weather such an infamous reputation. This sharp differentiation between three-season rock climbing on the one hand and what Geoffrey Winthrop Young called "the sterner and more primitive discipline of ice" on the other gave the two sports different but at first parallel histories. In the late 1920s, when Underhill and his circle were creating the first classic rock climbs of the Northeast, they also made a start on ice routes that remained the popular test pieces for forty years. Yet despite this similar starting time and cast, the twin sports progressed from there at vastly disparate paces.

Instances of ice climbing can be found back around the turn of the century in the great glacial cirques of Mount Washington and a bit later on Cannon and Katahdin. Though moderate in difficulty by the standards of today or even of the late 1920s, they must have had the spice of high adventure in their time.

Tuckerman Ravine. The first person who made a regular practice of snow and ice climbing was Herschel C. Parker, who later rose to mountaineering fame on Mount McKinley. Parker used the Presidential Range in winter as his principal training ground, as so many alpinists have since. Parker made eleven winter ascents of Washington, mostly during the last decade of the nineteenth century, by such various routes as the carriage (now auto) road, the cog railway tracks, Tuckerman Ravine, the northern peaks, and the Crawford Path.

Like many subsequent climbers who spend a lot of time in the Presidentials, Parker had his share of adventures, some of epic proportions. One ticklish moment occurred when he was alone, having undertaken, on December 31, 1890, to climb Mount Washington from Gorham via the carriage road. He broke trail through extremely soft snow, a very fatiguing effort, getting only as far as the Halfway House, where he passed a solitary night. On New Year's Day in threatening and heavy clouds, he continued on. "It may interest friends who have accompanied me on some of my later climbs," he wrote, "to know that I had no ice-creepers or alpenstock of any description, that I wore moccasins of the softest and lightest kind, and was further handicapped by wearing an overcoat." While crossing one of the huge drifts that covered the carriage road, Parker slipped, dropping one of the snowshoes that he had been carrying under his arm, and slid out of its reach. "Here was a very unpleasant situation," he wrote.

> I could not keep my footing on the icy snow in order to climb up and reach the shoe, neither could I return through the deep soft snow on the lower portion of the carriage road without it. Luckily I remembered that I had a large pocket knife with me, and by means of this I was able to cut steps in the hardened snow, and so regain the shoe.

Despite low visibility and high winds, Parker succeeded on this solo ascent.

Parker saw Tuckerman Ravine in winter as a splendid gymnasium for practicing "real alpine work." On December 26, 1894, he and his friend Dr. Ralph Larrabee, with a college buddy named Andrews, set off for Tuckerman Ravine. Anticipating a straightforward snow climb, they took no ice axes, only "long poles furnished with a spike" typically used in alpine climbs of that era. Young Andrews was also armed with a hatchet which was to be pressed into unwonted service that day. To their chagrin, they found the headwall gleaming with vast stretches of hard water ice, and even much of the snow was too hard to permit the usual step-kicking. Bearing further right than planned and using the hatchet to hack small nicks for steps, they reached a point two-thirds of the way up before finding further progress barred by sheer ice ledges. Here they spent "a bad quarter of an hour" fearing that "to return seemed only less dangerous than to proceed." Retreat they did, however.

Parker returned in February 1895, alone but equipped with ice ax, and found the entire slope well draped in its more customary mantle of snow, so ascent was comparatively easy. Still, the long headwall climb was exciting and Parker did not reach the summit until 4:50 P.M. He descended the cog railway in gathering darkness and had "a long dark walk" out to his inn at midnight. The following two winters, he and Larrabee returned in December, again finding ice but having no difficulty in climbing it with ice axes. Thus ice climbing is known to have taken place in Tuckerman Ravine as early as the 1890s.

Parker's impressive record of diverse winter ascents in the Presidentials notably omits two approaches soon climbed by others—Huntington Ravine and the Great Gulf.

Huntington Ravine. In February 1902, on one of the Appalachian Mountain Club's mass vacations (114 people at the Iron Mountain House in Jackson), a group of ten snowshoed into neighboring Huntington Ravine, where two of them ascended the headwall of that far more formidable cirque. Records fail to disclose either their identities or the exact route of ascent. In view of the later importance of Huntington Ravine in northeastern ice climbing, one can only lament the anonymity of this pioneering duo. The route is most likely to have been on or near today's summertime trail or the adjacent gully known as the *Diagonal,* the least imposing of the direct lines up the headwall. This ascent was repeated the following winter by a party of six, including a man named George Whipple, of whom more will be heard presently.

The ascents of Huntington Ravine at these early dates command respect. There is a world of difference between Tuckerman, grand and immense as it may be, and Huntington, which an early botanist called the "dark ravine," with its bristling crags, narrow ice-choked gullies, and much steeper precipices. Tuckerman is beautiful and benign—most of the time. Huntington is stark and menacing, but also beautiful beyond compare on the right day and in the right frame of mind. A later (1924) visitor to Huntington in winter notes this contrast and the angst inspired by the latter:

> As we stood gazing up at the majestic headwall [of Huntington], instead of beckoning to us as did the Tuckerman

Headwall, it seemed to tell us to go back. One or two venturesome spirits did climb up the fan a little way, but they were only too glad to come down.

In later years, Tuckerman won renown as a downhill skier's test piece and paradise (for those proficient enough to handle its celebrated upper headwall). Huntington remained obscure to the general public and became the mountaineer's tough training ground for those with ambitions of Alaskan or Peruvian 20,000-footers.

Great Gulf Headwall. Even bigger than either Tuckerman or Huntington,

and far more difficult of access—seven rugged miles from the nearest road—is the Great Gulf. In 1905 the road was unplowed and there was no trail from it into the Gulf's interior. From Gorham to the base of the Great Gulf headwall was twelve miles, less than half of it by road.

On January 27, 1905, three doughty winter warriors sallied forth from an Appalachian Mountain Club gathering at Gorham. George N. Whipple had been Parker's companion on winter climbs. Warren W. Hart was the builder of spectacular hiking trails in the Great Gulf. Harland Perkins was another leading AMC official and trail-builder. For five miles on the unplowed road and seven over the frozen streambed the trio snowshoed toward the base of the headwall. That is to say, the streambed was mostly

The Great Gulf. This formidable cirque of snow and ice, remote from roads and topping out almost at the very summit of windswept Mount Washington, was first climbed in midwinter in a 1905 epic. Probable route ascended the middle of the section facing the camera.

PETER CRANE

frozen: trail-breaker Hart was subject to "occasional partial disappear-ances," as Whipple's account relates:

> Without the slightest warning he would suddenly subside,
> sometimes as far as his waist, sometimes as far as his shoul-
> ders, carrying down with him a large segment of the roof
> of the stream. The first time this happened Perkins and I
> rushed to his assistance in considerable alarm, as it is no
> joke to get one's feet wet under such circumstances, but
> were met with such imperturbability and *sang froid* that the
> subsequent proceedings interested us no more. His feet
> entirely fast in the mass of debris rapidly being converted
> into slush, he would survey the landscape in a meditative
> manner, hazard the prediction that the water must be at
> least four inches deep, extricate his snowshoes by the aid of
> a remarkable mountaineering implement in the shape of
> a long-handled boat-hook which he affected, and clamber
> out to repeat the process further on.

Well after noon they reached the base of the Great Gulf cirque. Above them loomed the 1,800-foot headwall, draped in snow and ice, and above that the exposed alpine ridge leading to the summit. The pleasant weather of the morning had gone the way of so much Mount Washington weather: as they cowered under a ledge for a bite to eat, "a fierce squall swooped down, blotting out all but our immediate surroundings." The temperature was 14 degrees Fahrenheit.

At 1:30 P.M., having exchanged snowshoes for ice-creepers, they started up. Not far up the slope it became necessary to chop steps for every upward move. Sometimes one of the party attempted to go ahead without steps, but a couple of slips and falls, in which disastrous descent was prevented by a 1905 version of self-arrest with the ice ax, persuaded them to settle into a tiring and tiresome routine of chopping out each step, eight to twenty strokes per step.

> Chop, chop, chop, chop, chop, chop. The bits of ice and
> crust went hissing down the slope; the snow squalls de-
> scended and enveloped us; the dark rim of the wall above
> us certainly seemed no nearer than an hour ago. How
> slowly we moved! How slowly time went by!

As the hours dragged along, darkness crept into the Great Gulf. Before they reached the top, they could no longer see the steps they cut. In the dark the ice particles seemed to hiss the louder in their rapid descent down the growing distance below. Snow and wind swirled around them. The three men became increasingly conscious of what alpinist-philosopher Leslie Stephens had described in a similar situation on the Eiger, words that Whipple recalled:

> The result of a slip would in all probability have been that
> the rest of our lives would have been spent in sliding down
> a snow slope, and that the employment would not have
> lasted long enough to become at all monotonous.

The marvel is that their spirits seem not to have been dampened. They were, according to Whipple, "thoroughly delighted with what we were doing." What little conversation passed in the roar of the storm and the hard breathing forced by their labors tended to jokes and self-congratulation. Whatever the quality of the humor, Whipple remembers the jokes as being "received with appreciation."

It was 9:00 P.M. when they pulled themselves over the rim of the headwall. They had been seven and a half hours on the wall, following seven of uphill trail-breaking on snowshoes. The storm was in full progress, the temperature at 10 degrees. In the dark they groped to the cog railway tracks and up them to one of the summit buildings. Dinner consisted of the remaining handfuls of lunch. They found a straw mattress and for bedcovers employed the carpet. Undressing "was brief, and stopped with the removal of our creepers." Huddled under the rug, they indulged in about five hours' sleep. After a breakfast even slimmer than dinner—"the commissary department had gone to pieces"—they started back out into the cold, dark storm at 4:45 A.M. and managed to find and descend the carriage road. By 8:15 they were down to the valley and headed back for Gorham.

Cannon. The main cliff of Cannon is a most hostile environment in winter, and it was not until the 1960s that climbers would consider approaching it directly. In the Dartmouth Outing Club's flaming youth, however, the wiry little Sherman Adams, later Governor of New Hampshire and presidential adviser, was one to dare challenges that most of his contemporaries soberly acknowledged as imprudent. On March 3, 1919—a half century before the first official winter ascent of Cannon cliff—Adams led his DOC mates, Ellis

RICK WILCOX

Above: Katahdin. Maine's lonely mountain mass, further north than Montreal, was the scene of early winter adventures.

Top of the Chimney. Three climbers from Willard Helburn's 1926 party surmount the final moves of the 1,000-foot snow-and-ice gully, one of Katahdin's most striking features. It remains a popular winter climb today.

ARTHUR COMEY

Griggs and D. W. Trainer, in the words of the DOC Annual Report of that year: "up the face of the cliff just under the profile." Adams later recalled that they were not really committed out on the cliff itself but skirted snow and ice chutes to the right of the northernmost slabs, flirting with the exposure while trying to avoid real trouble. "We had a lot of fun," he explained laconically.

Katahdin. The redoubtable Willard Helburn contributed a chapter to the prehistory of northeastern ice climbing by leading an ascent of the awe-inspiring Chimney on Katahdin in 1923. Helburn himself made no boasts, claiming the route was "easier than in summer," and his wife agreed. Having been with him on both winter and summer ascents, Margaret shrugged: "There is more soot than fire in Ktaadn's Chimney." Nevertheless, they did rope up for part of it, and were "glad to have our axes." The party of seven included three women—Margaret Helburn, Jessie Doe, and Margaret Whipple—along with Helburn, his friend Henry Chamberlain, Roger Holden, and Owen Kennedy.

Helburn also led this party up the south slide on Turner in 1923. In the winter of 1926 he repeated the Chimney and led the Elbow Gully in North Basin, followed by a large crowd that included Margaret, Robert Underhill, Miriam O'Brien, and Chamberlain.

The technical difficulty of these climbs of Helburn and his friends, while not great by modern standards, was as hard as anything done on Katahdin in winter until some forty years later.

Doubtless other isolated escapades on steep ice occurred with increasing frequency during the first quarter of the century and contrived to escape the notice of history. But as a true sport in its own right, ice climbing began at the start of the second quarter of the century, in the locale with which the sport was almost exclusively identified for forty years: Huntington Ravine. ■

Reference Note

Herschel C. Parker gives a full acount on his many winter climbs in "Winter Climbing on Mt. Washington and the Presidential Range," *Appalachia*, May 1902, pp. 19–28. Two marvelous write-ups of the Great Gulf climb are George N. Whipple, "A Winter Ascent through the Great Gulf (Mt. Washington)," *Appalachia*, June 1905, pp. 7–13; and Warren W. Hart, "Appalachian Club's Winter Excursion to White Mountains," *Boston Globe*, February 19, 1905, p. 4.

6: Huntington Ravine: 1928–1945

APPALACHIAN MOUNTAIN CLUB rock climbers had visited Huntington Ravine over the Memorial Day weekend of 1926. Perhaps inspired by the recognition then of its potential as a winter climbing area, a group returned in February 1927 to take on the first of its six major ice gullies. Well to the right of the looming Pinnacle buttress, a broad band of snow and ice descends in a remarkably straight gully of several hundred feet, prominent even from the highway far below. Because of its dominant location square in the middle of the cirque, it was first called Main Gully and since has come to be known as Central Gully. On February 23, 1927, long John Holden and Dartmouth's Nathaniel Goodrich led two rope teams up this route to inaugurate the first era of ice climbing in New England. Central Gully was not technically difficult—it is the easiest of Huntington's six—but this was the first venture on uncharted ground and, for one bulge, required chopping steps in steeper New England water ice than had previously been attempted.

(The six major ice gullies recognized today are, left to right as seen from below, Odell, Pinnacle, Central (formerly Main), Yale, Damnation (formerly Nelson Crag), and North. In addition, the summer trail and an adjacent snow gully ("Diagonal"), which lie between Central and Yale, are sometimes climbed, as well as an aesthetic gully route to the left of Odell ("South"), which is also usually all snow.)

The first real stimulant to New England ice climbing standards took the adventitious form of a visiting professorship. During the academic years of 1927 to 1930, Harvard University hosted the British geologist Noel E. Odell, a name that readers of the romantic epics of early attempts on Mount Everest will at once recognize. Odell occupied, for a brief span, a position in New England ice climbing somewhat analogous to that of Fritz Wiessner on rock (chapter 7) and the great skier Jackrabbit Johannsen on snow: a migrant from an area with more advanced standards who raised the sights of the New England locals. On February 12, 1928, Odell climbed Holden's Central Gully route leading a large party that included Jack Hurd, Nick

Spadevecchia, and half a dozen others. The next year, on March 16, Odell returned with a more uniformly strong party of Hurd, Underhill, and Lincoln O'Brien. This time they attacked the ice floes to the left side of the Pinnacle. Odell boldly chopped steps through and around bulges of ice, the steepness of which was an entirely new world for the New Englanders. Though Odell himself felt that "the standard of difficulty . . . was less than that of many ice-climbs in the British Isles, Norway and the Alps," it was a revelation and an incentive to the locals. Adding to the zest of the climb was a bad turn in the weather, seemingly obligatory on Mount Washington winter climbs: a hailstorm sent a continuous stream of "tapioca snow" rustling down the chute, which has ever since been denominated Odell Gully.

Odell's route showed the formidable team of Underhill and O'Brien what Huntington ice had to offer. Besides enjoying their ascent of Odell's, these two men had also looked into the near-hidden gully that lies just to the right of the Pinnacle. This is the narrow, steep, dark, evil band of ice that snakes up behind the rock buttress. Known to early Appalachians as "Huntington's Cascade" or "Fall of the Maiden's Tears" but for the last sixty years as *Pinnacle Gully*, it is the classic route of Huntington Ravine.

In 1929, three weeks after the first ascent of Odell's, Underhill and O'Brien were back kicking steps up the steepening snow toward the right side of the Pinnacle. As they rounded the base of the rock, they found the snow steepening dramatically and ending in a near-vertical wall of ice that swooped up right against the imposing precipice of the north wall of the Pinnacle. Finishing the last of the snow with great caution, they stepped left into a little alcove against the rock wall, where they could stamp out a reasonably level little platform in the otherwise unrelenting steepness around them. Here they roped up and moved out to chop steps on that wall of ice. Never having coped with verticality so unforgiving, the two climbers (taking turns at the lead) found each stance more precarious for the next step to be chopped. After two hours they reached the top of that initial steepness. Here the gully moderated temporarily as it arched inward to the left under a huge, dark overhang of rock, then steepened again into ice bulges above. Calculating the time and energy required for the pitch below against the unknown difficulties above, Underhill and O'Brien gave up the ascent and down-climbed to the snow below.

What they did next, we may judge in retrospect, is no less a tour de force than the ascent of the first pitch of Pinnacle Gully and indicates what an appetite for climbing these two men had. They rapidly traversed the upper snow slopes of the floor of the ravine, heading for a long, narrow trace of ice that seemed to offer a continuous if tenuous line up the highest part of the right (north) end of the ravine where it culminates in Nelson Crag, a prominent 5,620-foot eminence high on the northeast shoulder of Washington. Entering the base of this couloir, they met more moderate ice climbing for one pitch and then some good going over snow to a short vertical ice wall that blocked further progress. Having their fill of steep ice for one day, and being resourceful mountaineers by training, they sought and found a way around by climbing the snow-covered rock to the right side of this ice step. Above, they worked back into the gully and on up, pitch by pitch, to the lip of the ravine. Then they still had time and energy left to "stroll" (Underhill's word) to the summit and descend via the Tuckerman headwall, "terminating in a splendid glissade . . . over steep snow as one could desire."

This second route is the longest gully in Huntington and ranks second only to Pinnacle Gully in elegance and prestige. This was one of at least two occasions on which Underhill went up it, the other recorded time being with Arthur Comey, unroped, during a year when it was more snow than ice and therefore easier. The crux, that little vertical wall which Underhill circumvented on rock, is often judged the hardest 15 feet in any of Huntington's six gullies. It was not climbed directly for sure until 1943. At that time the couloir as a whole was given its present name, Damnation Gully.

Thus in one eventful day, April 6, 1929, Underhill and O'Brien had climbed what was to prove the hardest pitch on Pinnacle Gully and all but the hardest pitch on Damnation. Considering that they came away without credit for an official first ascent of either, and considering that they started from the road, went to the summit and descended the headwall of Tuckerman, it was quite a day.

Undaunted by these exertions, they went back the very next day and did the second ascent of Odell's while a rope of Harvard students, led by Alden Magrew, climbed Central. That may have been the first but was far from the last time that two gullies in Huntington were climbed on the same day.

Word spread fast about Huntington Ravine and Pinnacle Gully. Climbers with alpine experience, from Harvard and Yale as well as the AMC's Boston and New York contingents, began to consider their prospects for a successful ascent. In those days of long workweeks, slow roads, and spotty snowplowing, trips to Huntington Ravine in winter with time for a big climb were few and far between. But everyone knew that Pinnacle Gully was the big prize, "incomparably the most difficult and dangerous winter or

Fritz Wiessner

THE THIRTIES AT A GLANCE

Principal climbing event: "discovery" of the Shawangunks
Climbs of the Decade:—rock: *The Armadillo* (Katahdin)
　　　　　　　　　　　—ice:　*Pinnacle Gully*
Hardest single climb: *Vector*
Boldest lead: *Vector*
Most improbable coup by a nobody: *Pinnacle Gully*
Emblematic item of gear: hemp rope
Most important climber: Fritz Wiessner
Most underrated: Hec Towle
Most colorful: Red MacDonald
Most colorful group of climbers: the Boston Appies
Most prominent woman: Betty Woolsey
Still-active parental figures to climbers of this decade: Robert and
　　　Miriam Underhill
Best-looking: David Millar
Patrician: H. Adams Carter
Nice Guy Award: Walter Howe
**Norman Clyde Award (way out in the back somewhere, doing
good climbs with impeccable style, but hardly anyone knows
about it):** Jim Goodwin
Couple of the Decade: Lawrence Coveney and Marguerite
　　　Schnellbacher
Person you'd most like to have climbed with: Thelma Bonney
　　　(later Towle)

spring climb in the White Mountains," as Underhill phrased it—and still unclimbed!

Yale men William and Alan Willcox were early on the scene. Sometime in late winter 1929—whether before or after the Underhill-O'Brien attempt is not known—the brothers made an attempt, accompanied by Sylvia Knox and a beginner to the sport named Julian Whittlesey. Bill Willcox led that steep first pitch, "a long grind of step-cutting," then stood for hours belaying the others up ("damned cold"). At that point the brothers conferred and decided that it would be "crazy" to continue, partly because their two partners had little experience and partly because of time. "I knew then that we were too slow to make the top, whatever lay ahead," recalled Bill.

In January 1930 Bill Willcox returned, bringing the inexperienced Whittlesey again plus another Eli novice, Sam Scoville. Again they got up that first pitch, but again time (the short January days) and weather ("the bottom dropped out of the thermometer") worked against them. They traversed off over frozen rocks on the right, executed a perilous descent, and spoke confidently of coming back. However, in the extreme cold, Willcox had developed frostbite along the lines of his crampon straps and was bundled off to a local hospital, to be confined for several weeks.

By this time half a dozen Harvard climbers with snow and ice experience had designs on the coveted prize: Bradford Washburn, H. Adams Carter, Robert Bates, Charles Houston, Alden Magrew, and Francis Adams Truslow. One circumstance or another delayed their attempts. Nor did Underhill or his AMC friends mount another try during midwinter, regarding ice climbing as properly a March-April sport to take advantage of longer daylight hours and névé snow conditions of the sort they had experienced in the Alps.

With New England's most experienced ice climbers holding back and Yale's one solid leader stuck in the hospital, those two grass-green sons of Eli, Whittlesey and Scoville, looked at each other and at the job to be done, shrugged, and said some 1930 version of "What the hell!" On February 8, 1930, with still-short daylight hours, below-zero temperatures, little experience ("we were both novices") but copious aplomb, these fools rushed in where angels had been trying to work up nerve to tread.

It should not be implied that totally inexperienced climbers can ordinarily expect to pull off major breakthroughs in this difficult and dangerous sport. Whittlesey and Scoville had learned quickly from their few previous outings, and they approached the job with reason and care. Still, their accomplishment caught the contemporary ice climbing community by surprise.

It has continued to perplex posterity. Recent historical essays on New England ice climbing have praised the "proficiency and skill" and the "skill and tenacity" of Whittlesey and Scoville—understandably, since neither had contact with the ice climbing community for the next fifty years and all that was known was that they succeeded on Pinnacle Gully where no one had before. Posterity inevitably assumed that they must have been among the top technical ice masters of the day. But the fact was that Whittlesey and Scoville were newcomers to ice climbing. Willcox said of them, wholly without malice:

> Whittlesey and Scoville, to the best of my knowledge, were not regarded as climbers at all. They were the rankest of amateurs, and I'd whole-heartedly agree with Julian that they had beginners' luck.

Houston compared their coup to that of the Sourdoughs' zany 1910 first ascent of Mount McKinley—an absurdly inexperienced party stealing a major mountaineering achievement from under the noses of supposedly more qualified aspirants. Whittlesey himself, when questioned more than fifty years later, cheerfully confessed that he had no rock climbing experience at all, and when asked if the Pinnacle Gully was the hardest route he ever did, responded simply: "It was the only one." When asked when he stopped climbing, he commented: "Can't say I really got started!"

Whether with beginners' luck or skill and tenacity, or perhaps both, Whittlesey and Scoville climbed rapidly up that now-familiar first pitch and a second, working their way back under the overhanging rock. "Wildly blowing snow" obscured vision and the extreme cold hampered the simplest operations, but they continued alternating leads up a series of steep bulges, sometimes traversing around them, sometimes hugging the rock wall on their left. After five and a half hours of climbing they emerged on the more gradual snow leading to the top of the Pinnacle, traversed west and glissaded back to the bottom (apparently down South Gully), and headed back for Yale (the college, not the climb). Dismissing the magnitude of their accomplishment, Whittlesey later commented:

> The trip back at 20 below in an open top-down car overnight to New Haven on roads that others could not deal with—hence no traffic—was perhaps more notable.

Modesty and beginners' luck notwithstanding, the Whittlesey-Scoville

FRANCIS FARQUHAR, *CLIMBING IN NORTH AMERICA* BY CHRIS JONES

Pioneers on Huntington Ravine ice. This quartet played key roles in opening up the central locale of ice climbing in the Northeast for forty years. Top to bottom: Prestigious visiting Britisher, Noel Odell, pioneer of 1928's Odell Gully; dean of American climbing, Robert Underhill, shown starting a route in King Ravine; Julian Whittlesey (left), one of the two Yale students who first ascended the classic Pinnacle Gully; and Bill House (right), a later Yale climber who did the second ascent of Pinnacle Gully.

FRANCIS FARQUHAR

COURTESY JULIAN WHITTLESEY

FRANCIS FARQUHAR

first ascent of Pinnacle Gully in 1930 is *the* landmark climb of prewar northeastern ice. For almost forty years it remained the most difficult winter route regularly climbed in the Northeast. Adding to its objective problems was the dark, ominous look of the place, concealed back there behind the gigantic greenish black rock wall of the Pinnacle, the middle pitches actually overhung by the gloomy rock. It is a fearsome place. While the revolution in ice climbing standards after 1969 reduced its reputation for technical difficulty, it will always be one of the true classics of northeastern ice—and a tribute to two green Yale underclassmen who gritted it out on a cold day in 1930.

Actually what this climb demonstrated is an interesting phenomenon about breakthroughs in climbing standards that we shall see more of in later chapters: the importance of vision and mental attitude—just as important as strength, skill, or experience. Royal Robbins, a top climber of the 1960s, in commenting on a breakthrough climb by a young climber in 1973, called it an act of creative imagination. What he meant was that the new man had a vision that he could accomplish something that more experienced climbers had not believed could be done. In 1930 Whittlesey and Scoville did not have the experience to perceive Pinnacle Gully as "incomparably the most difficult and dangerous," as Underhill did. They didn't know it was hard. (When asked in 1980 if their 1930 climb created a stir among ice climbers, Whittlesey replied: "I have no idea.") So when Willcox was hospitalized, they failed to perceive this as the loss of the experienced leader they needed and instead saw only that, with just two of them, maybe it wouldn't take so long to get up the first pitch. To be sure, a heavy dose of "skill and tenacity"—or at least tenacity—and a lot of concentrated effort and will went into the climb. But the main thing was the vision that they could do it.

Within a year of the Whittlesey-Scoville triumph, a Harvard party made another partial ascent and yet another the following winter, but the second full ascent is traditionally awarded to another Yale party, this time Bill House leading Alan Willcox on March 30, 1934. How many other ascents were made in the 1930s is not properly recorded, and claims that two 1948 ascents were only the fifth and sixth must be viewed with caution. Washburn, Bates, and Carter all recall climbing Pinnacle Gully in the 1930s, and a film made by Ken Henderson in 1940 or 1941 shows an ascent by William Lowell Putnam, Andrew Kauffman, and Maynard Miller, the latter nattily attired in green shirt and red-checked necktie. By then it was still no routine stroll, but it clearly had become the great standard lead that it remained.

Thus by the 1930s ice climbing was well established, albeit for a tiny community of climbers. The 1934 AMC *White Mountain Guide,* intended

The step-cutting era. Left: Maynard Millar cutting steps up North Gully in Hunt-ington Ravine, Andrew Kauffman belaying. Right: Florence Peabody on an early ascent of Pinnacle Gully. Prior to the 1960s the only known method of getting up steep ice was to cut every step and handhold all the way up, a time-consuming art requiring skill and stamina.

mainly for hikers, carried descriptions for five standard routes in Hunting-ton Ravine: the summer trail ("the easiest way"); Main Gully (now called Central); Odell Gully ("of considerable difficulty"); Pinnacle Gully ("ex-tremely difficult and dangerous"); and Nelson Crag Gully (today's Damna-tion). It is not clear whether Nelson Crag Gully included the crux move, as the route description calls it "a steep and narrow snow couloir, which may be barred at one point by an icy overhang." In 1929 Underhill and O'Brien circumvented that ice cliff by going around on rock to the right. However, Underhill and Arthur Comey later climbed the route in a year when it was mostly snow and may have gone right over the crux then (unroped!). How many other parties climbed Nelson Crag Gully in the 1930s is not known, and whether the "icy overhang" was done during that decade remains a mystery. By 1940 the AMC guidebook writers had decided that it begged trouble to print descriptions of ice climbing routes, so beginning in that year the AMC guide omitted them.

One of the most active contingents in the early 1930s was the Harvard group, many of whom went on to considerable success in Alaskan and Himalayan mountaineering—Houston, Bates, Carter, Arthur Emmons (primarily a snow-and-ice man), and Brad Washburn ("a prime spirit in the winter"). This group negotiated the right to build a small cabin in Tuckerman Ravine, primarily as a base for skiing. A prodigious effort of hauling lumber and supplies went into the construction of this little edifice. Later it was moved away from the overpopulated Tuckerman to a more obscure glade below Huntington. Here it has remained and become an institution to generations of climbers as the base used by almost everyone who climbs Huntington ice.

College outing clubs live in short spurts, due to the quadrennial turnover of guiding spirits. By the years 1939 to 1943 the Washburn-

House in North Gully. One of the outstanding prewar performers on both ice and rock, Bill House went on to a distinguished career on climbs all over the world, including first ascents of Devil's Tower and Canada's difficult Mount Waddington and the celebrated House's Chimney on K2, second highest mountain in the world.

KENNETH A. HENDERSON COLLECTION

Houston-Bates-Carter generation was long lost to adulthood, a brief span of inactivity had passed, and a new generation of snow-and-ice tigers arose, led by Maynard Miller, William Latady, Andrew Kauffman, and William Lowell Putnam. With Ken Henderson as instructor and adviser, this wave spent many weekends in Huntington Ravine. In December 1942 Miller and Latady climbed a short but fierce (for those days) couloir on the northern edge of the cirque, claiming a first ascent of what has become one of the standard Huntington routes under the name of North Gully. In January 1943 Kauffman and Putnam climbed the Nelson Crag Gully, tackling the ice crux head-on; so small and uncommunicative was the ice climbing community of that era that they were unaware of earlier ascents and christened their "new" route Damnation Gully, a deserving name which has stuck.

In view of the large number of northeastern ice climbing areas of the 1980s, it seems difficult to conceive how exclusively Huntington Ravine was "the" locale until well after World War II. Ice was chopped in Tuckerman and King Ravines, possibly even a repeat or two of the 1905 Great Gulf Headwall route, but no other area on Mount Washington compared with Huntington. The popular ice floes on Willey, Willard, and the Webster cliffs in Crawford Notch were apparently unvisited before World War II, perhaps because the road through Crawford Notch was not at first plowed in winter. Helburn's work on the Webster cliffs in 1923 is the only recorded instance of a technical climb in prewar Crawford Notch. There is no evidence that any Vermonter set cramponed foot on the steep ice of Smugglers Notch, nor that anyone on Katahdin climbed anything but the Chimney and other early Helburn routes. Some other areas that became popular later, like the Frankenstein cliffs of lower Crawford Notch and the big floes on Mount Pisgah near Lake Willoughby in northern Vermont, were shunned in the 1930s as far too steep for the state of the art.

In the Adirondacks, pioneering ice climbing was spearheaded by the versatile Jim Goodwin. In 1935 he chopped steps up the Colden Dike with a friend, Eddie Stanley. This was the hardest ice route done in the Adirondacks at the time; it had turned back a Yale party the previous winter. By today's standards it is an easy route, but its stunning locale made it a grand one. More imposing technically was the big slab of ice just south of Chapel Pond, near the summer rock route known as Bob's Knob. In 1936 Goodwin and Notman (the Bob of Bob's Knob, appropriately) chopped their way up the first ascent of this enormous face, completely without pitons or screws, belaying only from stances on chopped-out platforms—an impressive achievement in a locale that did not have the stimulus and sympathy of other climbers around. The next year the pair did the steepest slides on Giant-of-the-Valley, even longer and more taxing than the Chapel Pond slab, though technically easier. The pair made an unsuccessful attempt on nearby Roaring Brook Falls, a steep floe that awaited better tools and techniques. There is no record of others active on Adirondack ice before World War II.

There are several explanations for this general delay in the development of ice climbing and for its initial emphasis almost exclusively on Huntington Ravine.

First, despite its fast start in 1927–1930, ice climbing did not catch on as widely or as enthusiastically as rock climbing. Probably the happy crowds of summertime rock climbers were deterred by the uncomfortable conditions under which ice must be pursued, the expense of the equipment, and the greater objective danger.

Another obstacle, particularly in southern centers like Connecticut and New York where competent rock climbers were springing up rapidly, was the problem of getting to dependable ice. There are good ice routes in the Catskills and even as far south as the Hudson Highlands and the southwest corner of Massachusetts. But rare is the winter when these routes come into condition for more than a few weeks or maybe just days, and not necessarily on a convenient weekend.

Meanwhile, for the long journey north, the lack of full two-day weekends was a major deterrent. With Saturday morning work, shorter daylight hours, and the more primitive state of roads, cars (especially heaters in cars!), and the art of snowplowing, it is a wonder that any ice climbing got done at all. As noted, Whittlesey and Scoville rated the ice in Pinnacle Gully as scarcely less perilous than the long night drive back to New Haven.

Another factor that contributed to the slower advance of ice standards was the preference of one dynamic force on rock—Fritz Wiessner—for skiing. Wiessner could and did climb ice well; he instructed ice climbing in the Adirondacks in the early 1950s. But in the 1930s he ran a ski wax business and devoted most of his winter attention to the boards rather than crampons. Had some Scottish hard man emigrated to New England during the 1930s, ice climbing might have had quite a different history, but that didn't happen. After the brief visit of Noel Odell, no major outside stimulus showed the way to the locals.

A further factor that limited the pre-World War II ice climbing largely to Huntington Ravine was the alpine background of the leading Boston climbers like Underhill and Henderson. These men were primarily all-around mountaineers. They saw rock climbing as a means to an end, the end of getting up mixed terrain on big mountains, but a skill well worth polishing on smaller crags in the off-seasons. What they looked for in ice climbing was, similarly, practice for the mountains. The 1930s climber Bob Bates said of Huntington Ravine: "You did it for fun . . . to give you practice for expeditions." In the alpine setting the usual "ice" encountered is actually hard snow, or "névé," formed by repeated alternation of freezing and thawing. The hard water ice characteristic of the very cold New Hampshire winters was different, more difficult to climb, and to these men less attractive. One reason why so much of the ice climbing by Underhill and O'Brien was done in late March, or even April, was that they were hoping to find conditions more like alpine névé.

Whatever the causes, the record of ice climbing before 1945 is largely the record of the classic routes of Huntington Ravine. It is interesting to observe, half a century later and more than two decades after the revolution in ice standards of 1969 (chapter 21), that these fine early routes, in their splendid alpine setting and with all the risks of Mount Washington's uniquely cruel weather conditions, remain highly respected and popular routes. Not difficult by today's standards, they are still perceived by today's ice climbers, as they were by those of 1928, 1930, and 1943, as magnificent climbs in a magnificent place. ∎

Reference Note

Ice climbs of the late 1920s and 1930s were written up for *Appalachia* on a regular basis in much the same way that rock climbs were. Of special value are a full-length article by Noel E. Odell, "Comparisons Are Not Odious!" *Appalachia,* June 1929, pp. 205–207; and Julian H. Whittlesey's note on the first ascent of Pinnacle Gully, "Pinnacle Gully of Huntington Ravine," *Appalachia,* June 1930, p. 83. The authors also drew heavily on conversations and correspondence with Adams Carter, Bob Bates, James A. Goodwin, Kenneth Henderson, John Holden, William P. House, Charles Houston, Noel E. Odell, William Lowell Putnam, Robert Underhill, Bradford Washburn, Julian Whittlesey, and William B. Willcox.

Anniversary Waltz in Pinnacle Gully
Or, Four Climbing Generations on
Huntington Ravine's Classic Route

THE YEAR OF Pinnacle Gully's first ascent—1930—was a different America. Herbert Hoover and Prohibition ruled the land. In February 1930, as Whittlesey and Scoville chopped steps pitch after pitch amid "wildly blowing snow," the sheet music to "Stardust" had just been published. Big Bill Tilden dominated tennis, while Sonja Henie won her fourth consecutive world figure skating title. New York Yankee management received "with dignity, scorn, and a deal of silence" Babe Ruth's absurd demand for $85,000 a year, a salary higher than President Hoover's ("I had a better year than Hoover," explained the Babe). A Fifth Avenue shop sold men's suits for $26.50. On Broadway, Wanamaker's offered "Sprightly Spring Frocks" for $9.75, ladies' Oxfords, slippers, and high shoes at $2.95 a pair, and men's shirts at $1.95. Studebaker's latest "long and low-slung chassis," with seventy-horsepower engine and genuine mohair upholstery, commanded a price of $895. New York's Loew's offered an "All-Talking" film version of *The Virginian* starring Gary Cooper, and Charles Lindbergh suggested a radical innovation in aeroplanes: "a shield designed to make both cockpits windproof." A House Judiciary Committee formally sat to hear "The Star Spangled Banner," sung by Mrs. Elsie Jorss-Reilley of Washington and Mrs. Grace Evelyn Boudlair of Baltimore and played by the Navy Band, with a view to deciding whether to make the song the national anthem. The ladies wished "to refute the argument that it is pitched too high for popular singing." One witness expressed concern that "the tune is suspiciously like an Old English drinking song."

The world has changed much since Hoover and Lindbergh and Whittlesey and Scoville. Well, actually, the world of ice climbing changed little for the first forty of those sixty years. For four decades Pinnacle Gully remained as Robert Underhill had classified it: "incomparably the most difficult and dangerous" ice route in New England. It was the Grand Prix, the Wimbledon center court, the Super Bowl of winter climbing.

Beginning in 1969, a revolution in ice tools and techniques made much more difficult climbing possible. Ice axes with sharply drooped picks, serrated teeth, and much shorter handles, plus new kinds of crampons and ice screws, gave climbers security for hanging on ice of extreme verticality.

Suddenly new routes of undreamed-of difficulty absorbed the attention of a new generation of New Hampshire climbers. All gullies in Huntington Ravine now seemed easy, and Pinnacle Gully was routinely soloed by the young tigers.

But from a purely aesthetic standpoint, Huntington is still a significant setting, and Pinnacle Gully is still its hidden jewel. Among the truly classic lines of New England ice, most discerning climbers, of whatever generation, still rank that twisting band of blue-green ice overhung with green-black crags as one of the three or four finest natural lines in the east. At least half the time the whole is suffused with a noisy cacophony of raging wind, blowing ice particles, hissing sprindrift, ominous foreboding. On rare good days, though, the majestic setting is inspiring, a privileged place wherein to walk among the mountain gods. One of the best of the modern ice hard men has said:

> Although I have been up that gully over a hundred times my stomach always takes a flop when I see the cold green ice bulging out on the left side guarded by the overhanging rock that looms overhead. To be there in 1930 with alpenstocks, hemp rope, ten-point crampons and looking up at ice that is far steeper than anything the climber had previously contemplated is an awesome concept.

Whittlesey Revisited

Sixty years to the day after the first ascent, one of the authors enjoyed a different sort of climb in this singular place. It was one of those interesting outgrowths of our research for this book.

In the fall of 1989 Laura and I made a lunch-time pilgrimage to the Connecticut home of Julian Whittlesey. The sole surviving member of Pinnacle's first ascent party, this ex-Yale student had gone on to a brilliant and varied subsequent career as New Deal planner and designer of such cities as Virginia's Reston and British Columbia's Kitimat. He also designed slum clearance projects in Asia and Africa and pioneered innovative archeological techniques in the Mediterranean.

At age eighty-four Julian Whittlesey was still a dazzlingly innovative mind, and his wife, the beautiful and beloved Eunice, a former Broadway actress and colleague in archeological research, was equally remarkable.

In their hilltop backyard Whittlesey had recently built a slender tower of vertical pipes soaring 107 feet into the clear autumnal sky. A few short and narrow pipes were stuck in horizontally at intervals, and these, Whittlesey alleged, constituted a ladder. The purpose was to suspend a pendulum so that he could study something esoteric about the earth's movement. (Still many fascinating things to find out when you're only eighty-four.)

That day his pendulum had, in nonscientific terminology, got stuck. So he ordered his visiting climbers to scamper up and fix it. The tower of pipes looked frail, but he assured us that his friend Bucky (Fuller) had designed it to be perfectly stable.

Accordingly, with considerable apprehension, we dug out our climbing gear and Laura led all the way to the 107-foot top, placing protection around the pipes en route. An impressive lead, I thought, but the 1930 conqueror of Pinnacle Gully took it as a routine procedure for climbers or those interested in studying the movement of pendulums and planets.

After a few hours back on the ground, filled with absolutely scintillating discourse from the Whittleseys on a broad range of subjects, we reluctantly prepared to leave. Julian ducked into the house a moment and emerged with a capacious heavy canvas "Zenith" rucksack with leather straps and buckles still intact, proclaimed it the pack that had climbed Pinnacle Gully in 1930, and, disclaiming intention of further mountaineering ventures (being too busy exploring other frontiers), thrust it upon us to keep.

In the exhilaration of the moment, conscious that next winter would mark exactly sixty years since his historic first ascent, I promised Julian Whittlesey that his 1930 Zenith pack would go up Pinnacle Gully again on February 8, 1990.

A Partner for the Waltz

As winter approached, I eyed that canvas monstrosity and wondered if I could maintain the balance that modern ice climbing technique requires with that thing loaded and sagging far down my back. Laura, more sensibly, disclosed she had little zest for a full day's drive and plod up the ravine for such a duty. The project and promise teetered.

Then, at a gathering of climbing friends where I recounted the tale of visiting Whittlesey, Henry Barber demanded to know if I had a partner for the anniversary climb. Back in the 1970s the youthful "Hot Henry" had set the world afire with his brilliant climbing on both rock and ice. Unlike many modern stars, Henry always knew from whence he came and deeply respected the achievements of those pioneers in the realm of verticality on whose shoulders his generation stood to accomplish their great advances. He wished to join in honoring the anniversary of Pinnacle Gully's first ascent.

1930 pack in 1990. The first pitch of "the" classic prewar route, Pinnacle Gully, appears in the rear of this scene. During the 1930 first ascent, Julian Whittlesey carried a "Zenith" canvas rucksack. In 1990, to honor the sixtieth anniversary of the climb, author Guy Waterman (right) carried the same Zenith pack back up Pinnacle Gully, also wearing a 1930 style straw boater and other antique gear. Accompanying him was Henry Barber (left) clad in 1990's latest climbing fashion.

DON SCARF

At first we spoke bravely of doing it in the old style, with straight-angled ice axes and ten-point crampons, chopping steps all the way. Our courage failed us. We wanted the security of Chouinard-era drooped axes, front points, and ice screws that anchored securely. So we decided that the 1930 Zenith pack would constitute tribute enough.

To add a little flavor, I decided to don a 1930s-style straw hat for the occasion. Henry suggested the notorious Mount Washington wind would surely blow it far out across the state, but I pointed out that if I was wearing it, it would be affixed to a sharp¬pointed object and thus would be stable.

On the morning of the climb, Henry made sure the contrast in our two generations was as distinct as that between mine and Julian Whittlesey's. I wore my usual old-style, unfashionable wool Air Force pants, plain tubular gaiters, and L. L. Bean parka, all in drab blues and grays. Henry is a Patagonia sales rep. So he emerged for the day in flashy scarlet windpants, "neon green" sweater, and other brightly colored accoutrements of the latest climbing fashion. With my canvas Zenith pack and straw skimmer to suggest the 1930s generation, we had all bases well covered.

We made an odd couple. I'm of the second or post-Whittlesey generation of climbers, while Henry is of course in the vanguard of the next climbing generation, with John Bragg, John Bouchard, and Rick Wilcox. Physically he's big, I'm little. He had a mustache and no beard, I a beard and no mustache. Comparing our relative climbing abilities, grace, and professional reputations, Henry and I rank relatively as William Shakespeare to the writer who composed the obscure "Directions for Assembling Your Jiffy Lawn Chair" and other dramatic farces. During the salad days of his climbing youth, a globe-trotting Henry visited fifty-three countries and formed lasting friendships from East Germany to Australia. In almost six decades on the same planet, I've visited Canada twice briefly, but otherwise the only foreign countries I've been in are Florida and California (once each, more than a quarter century ago). An occasional expedition to the Adirondacks constitutes my western trip for the year. Like Thoreau, I travel far in East Corinth.

The Sixtieth Anniversary Climb

At the Harvard Mountaineering Club cabin in the floor of the ravine, we were joined by the two young caretakers who capably patrol Huntington and Tuckerman ravines in winter. They kindly broke trail through the new snow as the older and yet-older generations moved upslope toward our quest to honor the yet-oldest generation and its historic climb of sixty years before. It was splendid weather and, in midweek, we had the magnificent "dark ravine" all to ourselves—we thought.

We paused to put on crampons, sort gear, and take photographs at a rock outcrop about 200 feet below and a like distance to one side of the base of our route. From here the incomparable prospect of Pinnacle ice gleamed above us. We saw, far below, another party of two emerge from the woods and follow our footsteps up the fan. Soon it became clear that the leader was (a) moving rapidly and (b) heading not toward us for a friendly word but straight toward the base of Pinnacle Gully. Evidently this party wished to move ahead of us on the route.

To Henry's and my generation this was a lamentable breach of etiquette. With my straw skimmer for hard hat I had no wish to have another party showering ice from above. As for Henry, his old competitive instinct as the "fastest gun in the west," when he outperformed all other climbers wherever he went, took over: Hot Henry never turned down a challenge.

Having my crampons already on, I grabbed our rope and headed for the base of the ice. I got there first and began quickly throwing out rope at the most advantageous belay stance.

The young leader of the challenging party arrived next and took up his own stance at the other corner of the ice. My automatic instinct in the mountains, to a fault, is to engage others I meet in friendly greeting. Many a party or individual seeking quiet solitude in the peaceful hills has been driven batty by my insistence on animated conversation. But on this occasion all attempts at good cheer and repartee met heavy sailing: the other party was not in a friendly mood. Clearly they had sized up the age of the party next to them—especially the clown with the beard, straw hat, and absurd canvas pack—and figured that they would move fast enough to pass these dinosaurs with ease.

Henry responded in kind. And raised the ante. He was annoyed because he had planned to climb the steep first pitch with just one tool, a seventy-centimeter ice ax (i.e., relatively long by modern standards), using the elegant techniques required for such tactics. This was to be his way of honoring the even greater innate elegance of the Whittlesey-Scoville ascent of 1930. Now more speed would be required, and a second tool for some moves, if we were to remain the lead party. As he approached, Henry fixed their leader with the icy stare that competitors of the early 1970s had known too well.

When I handed Henry the sharp end of the rope, I included a muttered assurance that I was familiar enough with this pitch not to require a belay if that suited his plans. He responded that, yes, he would rather like to put some distance between us and the challengers.

I have never seen the first pitch climbed faster. Henry in good form has always been a joy and an education to watch: power, precision, fluidity, flair, ever in perfect control. As he disappeared over the top of the steep bulge, the rope regularly paid out. So when it came to the end, I began to climb too, moving with as much dispatch as could be marshaled with sagging canvas pack, sagging (has-been) muscles, and none-too-brilliant (never was) technique. It went well, though I noticed that the brim of my straw boater kept bumping against my tools when I looked down at my footing, a common problem for straw-hatted climbers, I suppose.

Somewhere along the way, the rope stopped moving briefly, so I assumed Henry had stopped to belay. Thus assured, I switched from front points to the more subtle—and precarious, for me—French technique of one-tool, ten-pointed sidewise walking up the ice. As I thus teetered over the top of the bulge, I glanced up and observed that, no, Henry was far up the second pitch and still climbing. Hastily I skittered back onto the security of front points and two tools.

Eventually Henry fixed two ice-screw anchors at the end of the second pitch and handed me two more as I went by. I clawed up the third pitch to anchor at the base of a steep flow of beautiful bulging ice that cascaded down from the sunlight above at the top of the right side of the gully.

When Henry joined me, now three long rope lengths above the base, we looked down. Far below, the ice curved out of sight beneath that bulge on the first pitch—and no climbers were yet in sight. The team of young hotshots had proved to be paper tigers. Faint sounds floated up of thrashing and bashing and desperate calls ("How much rope?" "Repeat?" "Ten feet." "What?" "Don't pull!" and the like).

Pinnacle Resplendent

Henry smiled, looking relaxed and happy. He eased up the steepest part of the ice floe on the right, climbing smoothly with just one seventy-centimeter ax, emerging from shadow into brilliant sun, his silhouette against the kind of deep blue sky you seem to see only in winter in the mountains, and maybe only looking up from the green-black depths of a dark, cold gully toward the safety and serenity and glory of the alpine gardens on Mount Washington.

When I began to climb, what a change in the spirit of the occasion! Gone was the petty competitiveness that had so rudely intruded on this day, meant only for warm nostalgia and the stark beauty of the gleaming ice. Now was only affirmation, celebration. O what a wondrous floe of ice had formed up there in the upper right-hand corner of the Pinnacle Gully!

As I topped out, we mused aloud on the pleasures of old climbs and old friendships, the happiness of moving up high ice in winter sunshine. But mostly our thoughts drifted back sixty years to the same lovely place, back in a different world of Sonja Henie and Hoagy Carmichael and Charles Lindbergh, when two brash Yalies and their Zenith pack and their long ice axes took on the world of cold and blowing snow and vertical ice and thrashed their way up Huntington's crown jewel, up into the company of the mountain gods, where they remain forever in our minds. ∎

7: Fritz Wiessner

TO HAVE COME this far in American rock climbing with scarcely a mention of the name of Fritz Wiessner is akin to staging *Hamlet* without the prince. It is no disservice to the fine climbing of Case's or Underhill's various protégés to concede that the yet more brilliant achievements of the little man from Dresden put them in the shade. Fritz Wiessner did not come to the United States until 1929 and did not discover our climbers and cliffs until 1931, so he was not present at the dawn of northeastern climbing. But during the 1930s his presence was soon felt as is the presence of the sun on a summer's day.

A less likely physical specimen for a man who may well have been the greatest climber of his generation can scarcely be imagined. If the reader pictures a tall, handsome, hawk-eyed Teuton, godlike, with a shock of wavy blond hair, broad bronzed shoulders, slender hips, and an air of imperious grandeur and mystery about him, the return to reality may be hard. Fritz Wiessner might more readily have been taken for a baker or bartender than a great alpinist. More gnome than god, he was well below average height, balding, slope-shouldered and stocky, almost without a waist, his features readily creased in a wide and friendly grin. The shape did not easily disclose the strength of arm or catlike agility, while that cheerful grin concealed drive and determination almost unparalleled even among the world-class climbers of his day.

Born in 1900, Wiessner was a German who started climbing in the Austrian Alps with his father before World War I. By the age of sixteen he was a regular climber at the fairyland world of sandstone towers near Dresden, where the pure art of free rock climbing was then more advanced than anywhere in the world. The brilliant Fehrmann, the great bearish American Oliver Perry-Smith and others were leading far ahead of English and American standards, and Fritz was soon aspiring to the front rank of Dresden freeclimbers. By the 1920s he was repeating the most difficult and infrequently climbed routes throughout the Alps and doing his own first ascents at a very demanding standard. His special strength lay in wide crack climbing, which requires both technical mastery and uncommon strength.

*"A wide and friendly grin."
America's greatest prewar
climber, Fritz Wiessner
pioneered on routes all over
the Northeast during the
1930s, as well as world-
wide in ranges from the
Alps to the Himalayas.*

HENRY BARBER

Alone of all the top Dresden climbers, Wiessner elected to come to the United States, emigrating in 1929 and becoming an American citizen in 1935. Had others of the Dresden men come over, the course of American climbing might have been very different and more rapidly approached European standards. But since he came alone, his name and climbing achievements during the 1930s stand in a class by themselves.

It was not until 1931 that Wiessner made contact with American climbers. Living in the New York area, he met American Alpine Club climbers, few of whom climbed much in the East but who put him in touch with Percy Olton. In 1931 Fritz joined Olton and his growing band of Hudson Highland explorers at the Crow's Nest. On the first day he served notice that a new standard of climbing was in store for the New World by attacking that most characteristic of Wiessner attractions: "a wide, slanting crack." Above the strenuous start, intricate route-finding led up through delicate face climbing, laybacks, and an overhang. The excited New York climbers dubbed this intimidating line *Fritz's Ritzy Route* and hastened to introduce the newcomer to all of the principal cliffs they knew. At each he established routes of a difficulty they had been unwilling to try. On Arden it was the *Piton Route*, "by far the most difficult" on the cliff (in Olton's words), surmounting steep bulges and a strenuous hand traverse. On Storm King, Fritz worked out *The Chimney*, more difficult than the earlier Underhill and Pollock routes, requiring "a greater variety of climbing than any other course in the Highlands . . . and there is no doubt about the exposure," according to a thoroughly impressed Olton. On Breakneck Ridge, *Fritz's Prize Route* took a magnificent line up the steep, dark rock, with "the smallest margin of climbability" of any of the Hudson Highland climbs.

In 1933 Wiessner contacted Underhill and arranged a visit to New Hampshire's cliffs. At Cathedral Ledge, Underhill showed him the 5.7 direct start that Will Allis had barely managed to struggle up. Ever at home in a wide crack, Wiessner was up it effortlessly. ("They did not know how to do these climbs," explained the patient veteran of the Dresden circle.) When Underhill called up that he would not attempt to follow that way, so that a complex rearrangement of ropes and belays would be necessary, Fritz called back to ask if the route went straight up the crack. Assured that it did, Wiessner simply untied, threw down the rope, and soloed up the remaining three pitches of the Cathedral Standard (5.6).

At Cannon Wiessner opened a third line north of the *Old Cannon* route. This was the first to involve the "Old Man" profile, as it finishes by climbing a splendid corner among the various vertical planes that, seen from the road, compose the famous profile. Although technically easier than either the original or *Whitney-Gilman* route, Wiessner's route has become a much-traveled line, despite the risk of much loose rock. In seconding the original ascent, Underhill was impressed less with the technical skill of the lead than with Wiessner's agility in threading through so much loose rock and gravel without dislodging anything on his follower. "Like a cat on the rock," he marveled.

On this New Hampshire trip, Wiessner also opened up a new cliff, Humphrey's Ledge, in the neighborhood of Cathedral and Whitehorse. The route that bears his name on Humphrey's was not climbed in its entirety in 1933. Fritz's party (including Underhill and Pollock) avoided the bottom pitch by a circuitous detour and employed a classic shoulder stance at a later point in the climb.

While these New Hampshire triumphs were highly admired at the time, Wiessner's technical prowess reached its greatest American pitch on the unlikely ground of Connecticut's little traprock cliffs. In three years, 1933 through 1935, Fritz made several visits to the New Haven area, climbing with Hassler Whitney and his brother Roger, Henry Beers and William Burling, and two young New Haven climbers of promise, Betty Woolsey and Bill House. At the Sleeping Giant he established a splendid line up the highest section of the Chin, which remained the standard of the area for years. At

PERCY T. OLTON, JR.   COURTESY KEN NICHOLS

Two Wiessner classics. Left: The Prize Route on Breakneck Ridge in the Hudson Highlands, showing an innovative photographic technique of the 1930s in which Wiessner is shown at various points on the climb from bottom to top. Right: Tower Crack on Connecticut's Ragged Mountain. Wiessner was far ahead of his time: twenty years later a Yale climber said of the Tower Crack: "Your author knows it exists, but doesn't even want to see it, let alone you-know-what it."

East Peak he swarmed up a classic Wiessner jam crack that widens into a chimney, then leads out over an overhang into a double crack system above—all unrelentingly vertical and wildly exposed, rated 5.7, though clearly harder than the *Whitney-Gilman,* and still a popular and demanding climb today under the name of *Rat Crack.*

It was at Ragged Mountain that Wiessner's most imposing lines were put in. In the center of the highest cliff is a low-angle slab that rises to a broad ledge 30 feet below the top. From either side of this ledge, large vertical cracks lead straight to the top. Few holds help the climber; they must be dealt with by good jamming technique or wide stemming. Fritz climbed both with virtually no protection and in a style that modern climbers rate 5.8. This was a level of difficulty new for the United States. Twenty years later a Yale climber said of one of these cracks: "Your author knows it exists but doesn't even want to see it, let alone you-know-what it."

Even more astonishing at the time was *Vector,* which Fritz put up with Roger Whitney in 1935. The current authority on Connecticut rock, Ken Nichols, describes *Vector* thus: "Starting as a small, relatively easy inside corner, this fine route finishes as a flared crack through a bulge. It was a bold lead in the mid-1930s, with only a single pin being placed for protection below the bulge before a 20-foot runout through the crux above." Fritz went up twice to try it but each time turned back, reluctant to commit himself to such a strenuous and unprotected sequence of moves. On the third occasion he made the commitment and completed what probably remained the hardest single lead in the country for almost twenty years. (A 1952 climb in California's Taquitz area is sometimes called America's first 5.9. A 1937 climb, *The Mechanics Route,* also at Taquitz, has been called "the country's first 5.8." Not so. While some may fault Wiessner's Connecticut climbs for being short, there is absolutely no question that they were technically at least 5.8. In 1987 two climbers with extensive eastern and western experience climbed both *The Mechanics Route* and *Vector* within a few days' time; their conclusion was emphatically that *Vector* was a far more serious lead.)

In the late 1930s, Wiessner got to the Adirondacks. He had made a brief and unsatisfactory reconnaissance before with Henry Beers, at which time a cursory look at Wallface left him with the impression that the main face was unclimbable. Nevertheless, he was back at Indian Pass in 1936 and again in 1937, only to be snowed off twice. Finally on Memorial Day weekend 1938, he returned with Beckett Howorth and Bob Notman and pushed a line up the center of the face that had repulsed Case and Goodwin years before. Wiessner used Case's 1933 line as a down-route, generously praising

Case's route as "possibly an even nicer climb than ours . . . cleaner . . . interesting crack and face work." By this time, Wiessner had fallen in love with Wallface and its setting, which he ever after regarded as the most beautiful climbing area in the Northeast, because of the "feeling of altitude" and the "charm of solitude" so uniquely combined there. During this three-day weekend in 1938, Fritz's party also polished off new routes on Indian Head and at Chapel Pond, advancing the standard of difficulty at each cliff.

Besides pioneering new routes in the Hudson Highlands, New Hampshire, Connecticut, and the Adirondacks, Fritz Wiessner also discovered the Shawangunks (chapter 9), opened up new cliffs on Mount Desert's pink granite, and eventually moved to Vermont where he explored Green Mountain cliffs. Thus he is remarkable for the regionwide breadth of his activity. Even Lake Willoughby's crumbling cliffs, the long-dormant ice climbing mecca that seemed to be discovered for the first time in the 1970s, had been explored by Fritz and his climbing partners thirty years before. One might expect that the interstate highways and improved communication among climbers might have produced many more regionwide itinerants, but the ranks remain thin of those who have made such significant contributions over the entire Northeast. It is not until Henry Barber in the early 1970s that comparable breadth of innovative climbing can be found.

While Fritz himself felt that his rock climbing peak was reached in Europe in the 1920s, he emerged as a major mountaineer on the world stage during the 1930s. The catalog of his accomplishments during that decade is without parallel among his contemporaries—a major attempt on Nanga Parbat in 1932; coming very, very close to climbing K2 in 1939, years before any of the big Himalayan 8,000-meter peaks had been climbed; British Columbia's Mount Waddington in 1936 with Bill House, one of the top ascents of the decade; a bold and virtually unprotected lead of Wyoming's Devil's Tower, its first free ascent, in 1937, in which Fritz felt he was in peak form; plus innumerable other mountaineering coups around the globe. It has been said that half the mountain ranges of the world have a "Wiessner Crack." He was called the greatest climber of his generation.

Even more astonishing perhaps was the incredible staying power of this Dresden youth who began climbing in 1911. When he was still getting up all his old routes at the age of sixty, younger men thought him remarkable. At sixty-four he spearheaded an attempt on the unclimbed Elephant's Head cliff in Smugglers' Notch; the first complete ascent fell to another, but not until Fritz had worked out the technical difficulties of the crucial first pitch—a steep crack, of course. In his seventies he was still going strong, befriending young climbers, never dwelling on the past, always looking for the next climb. When nearly eighty, he would apologize that he no longer cared to lead above 5.6 but would willingly follow 5.9. Once at the Shawangunks, when he was well over seventy, he joined a young partner to climb *Madame Grunnebaum's Wulst,* a dead-vertical 5.6 of fearsome exposure, especially on the airy second pitch. On their way to the climb, his young friend disclosed that he had recently soloed this route, at which Wiessner beamed and commented: "Ah, you must vee climbing pretty goot!" The younger man led the first pitch, then handed the rack to old Fritz, who proceeded to lead the entire second pitch, with its three wildly exposed 5.6 bulges, without placing a single piece of protection—virtually the equivalent of soloing the upper pitch. When his partner reached the top, Fritz grinned impishly and said: "I must vee climbing pretty goot!"

In his middle eighties, to observe his countenance, the spring in his step, the animation in his conversation—to say nothing of his grace on steep rock or his effervescent enthusiasm for climbing every month of the year—one might have easily mistaken him for one in his fifties, though in unusual physical shape and confident attitude toward life and climbing. Finally, in his upper eighties, a series of strokes brought this most remarkable climbing career to a close. He died in 1988.

In his prime, Wiessner's personal style was not universally admired. Perhaps as tacit acknowledgment of his superior skill, he insisted on leading almost every climb he did in this country during the 1930s. Underhill recalled that one of the conditions that Fritz laid down in arranging for their tour of New Hampshire cliffs in 1933 was that Fritz would do all the leading. Some other climbers found this attitude overbearing and preferred not to climb with him. It would be incorrect to exaggerate the extent of this feeling among climbers, however; many partners thoroughly enjoyed Wiessner's company, felt he was a patient teacher, and commented on his freedom from overbearing self-importance. Perhaps it was merely that Wiessner recognized that only the leader undertook the genuine risk in climbing under prewar conditions. When he was over eighty, he followed a younger partner, Jim McCarthy, up a 5.6 route famous for its intimidating qualities (*High Exposure* at the Shawangunks—chapter 9); when congratulated afterward, he demurred: "I didn't climb it. Jim climbed it. I just followed." Then, as fifty years earlier, the old Dresden warrior felt that if you weren't out there at the front end of the rope, you weren't really climbing.

Although an inspiration to modern climbers, his impact on the 1930s scene is harder to evaluate. In a sense, Fritz Wiessner was *not* an important influence on American climbing in the 1930s, because what he was doing was so far ahead of what others were willing to try that he did not significantly improve the general standard. His influence was felt in his dedication to Dresden ideals of free climbing, so that northeasterners were further indoctrinated with the idea that to use aid was to cheat. Furthermore, of course, he left a legacy of routes for all to enjoy. Perhaps his greatest gift to eastern climbing was his "discovery" of the Shawangunks. However his influence be evaluated, Fritz Wiessner became by 1933 and remained for fifty years a dynamic presence, well known to all the northeastern climbing community. ■

Reference Note

Ed Webster's profile of Wiessner in *Climbing*, "A Man for All Mountains," December 1988, pp. 102–108, is an important source, although its emphasis is on Wiessner's worldwide achievements rather than the northeastern United States. For his Hudson Highlands early climbs, see Percy T. Olton, Jr., "New York Rock Climbs," *Appalachia*, June 1938, pp. 12–26. Our prime source for his New Hampshire ascents was conversations with Robert L. M. Underhill. His Connecticut climbs are covered in Rubin's historical essay in Ken Nichols' *Traprock: Rock Climbing in Central Connecticut* (New York: American Alpine Club, 1982). Wiessner's Adirondacks trips were written up in (unsigned) "Rock Climbers Route: New Way Up Wallface," *Bulletin of the Adirondack Mountain Club,* June-July 1938, pp. 8 and 14; M. Beckett Howorth, "New Routes in the Adirondacks," *Appalachia*, December 1938, pp. 259–260; and Wiessner's own "Wallface: Up the Cliff," *High Spots*, January 1939, pp. 49–50. Wiessner gave a more general write-up of the region's climbs in "Rock Climbing in the Northeast," *Bulletin* of the Intercollegiate Outing Club Association, Winter 1948, pp. 42–48, 72. Wiessner was very helpful to the authors in compiling this chapter, both in conversations and correspondence; and climbers too numerous to mention contributed to our understanding of how Wiessner was perceived by the climbing community of the 1930s.

8: Rock Climbing for Fun: 1934–1945

B ACK IN THE mainstream of northeastern rock (if such a metaphor be allowed), a definite watershed was reached about 1933. In six years all the main cliffs of the region had been climbed. Gradually most of the first generation of ground-breaking leaders drifted from the scene.

Robert Underhill married Miriam O'Brien in 1932, and although both continued to grace the crags for many years, the hard-driving days of first ascents on north country rock were over. Lincoln O'Brien quit more abruptly and altogether in 1931. Injuries slowed the smoldering pace of Will Allis, Leland Pollock, and Jessie Whitehead. John Case kept on climbing, but with less pioneering spirit after Wallface and Bob's Knob. Hassler Whitney continued on his solitary way but did more real climbing on his western and European travels than in the Northeast. The *enfant terrible*, Brad Washburn, launched his great Alaskan climbing career and was rarely seen on New England rock. Among the top Boston leaders, only Ken Henderson remained an active force: never an innovator by instinct, he gradually grew into an elder statesman role in which he commanded immense respect and influence for many years, both with the Appalachian Mountain Club and the Harvard University climbers. Jack Hurd became almost exclusively a canoeist, but fiery little Marjorie continued primarily a climber for years, a last link to the earliest AMC rock climbers, though like Henderson she slipped comfortably into the role of elder stateswoman.

In the years from 1934 to 1940, rock climbing entered a new era. In place of these fabled pioneers there emerged a generation of a wholly different temperament. To these climbers (Wiessner always excepted), the routes and climbing areas of the Northeast were accepted as given, not new worlds to explore. They sought adventure of a sort, explored their personal climbing limits, and even went looking for new cliffs occasionally. But the challenge of pioneering unknown new worlds, such as Underhill, O'Brien, and their generation had probed, was largely replaced by a different, more relaxed view of rock climbing.

The sport entered a period in which its participants viewed it more as diversion and pleasure than challenge. To the new faces, climbing was just

Fun on Boston crags. The popular Thelma Q. Bonney struggles at the keel of The Ship (also known as The Boat or The Ship's Prow), a Boston test piece which still discomfits Boston top-ropers today.

WALTER HOWE COLLECTION

plain fun, a social activity for a close-knit bunch of good friends, bubbling with camaraderie, good cheer, and laughter. On today's climbing scene, the monthly magazine reports of new first ascents at the highest technical levels of difficulty may blind us to the fact that rock climbing has gone through long periods where competitive conquest and one-upmanship were distinctly subservient to a more relaxed, sociable spirit of lower-keyed enjoyment. The second half of the 1930s was such a time. The age belonged not so much to Fritz Wiessner as to Walter Howe and Thelma Bonney, to casual weekenders at Arden cliff, Ragged Mountain, and even Rhode Island.

For the Boston group, there were still the occasional pilgrimages to the great shrines of Cannon, Willard, the Pinnacle, Cathedral, and Whitehorse.

"*A heavy fellow who lost all his weight on the cliffs.*" *Two charismatic leaders of the 1930s hide from the camera, yet reveal their unmistakable signatures: Irvin Davis (left) with the well-rounded figure that never seemed to stop him from graceful climbing; and Ken Henderson (right) with his ever-present jacket, tie, and fedora. Scene is at the crest of the Pinnacle on Mount Washington.*

WALTER HOWE COLLECTION

Even Katahdin received a visit almost annually. But the chief focus was now largely on the top-roped escapades around the crags of suburban Boston. Here, on friendly Black and White rocks, the 25-foot *Boat* (or *Ship's Prow*) route at Rattlesnake, or the Quincy Quarries, the new generation of Boston Appies basked in serene sunshine.

Their image was wholly different from the slightly aristocratic hard men of 1928 to 1933. The leading figures epitomized the new breed of middle-class origins and middling climbing ambitions:

• Walter Howe, a portly, balding bachelor with gruff manner and heart of gold, the butt of many jokes but a solid friend to one and all—"Mr. Rock Climbing from prewar through the early fifties," as he is remembered;

• Irvin Davis, also on the portly side but with a nimbler spring to his step and light grace to his movement on rock ("a heavy fellow who lost all his

The new Boston leaders. Quartet of key figures in the Boston area and New Hampshire climbing of the 1930s. Clockwise from upper left: Irvin Davis; Walter Howe; Hec Towle; Thelma Q. Bonney.

weight on the cliffs," recalled Allis), a lawyer with a pixilated sense of humor and fun, "an irresistible scamp full of the joy of life—we always wondered how he could be serious long enough to be the fine lawyer he was," as one contemporary later mused;

- Thelma Bonney, the popular mill girl from the other side of the tracks who charmed (and climbed as well as) everyone;
- Ron Gower, the Katahdinophile and renowned bushwhacker, who declined to lead on rock but would follow anyone anywhere;
- Herbert (Hec) Towle, a rough-hewn personality who was probably the boldest leader of the generation;
- Edith (Red) MacDonald, "a spunky, tiny (well under five feet), agile redhead," a salty Scottish nanny, brought to America by her well-to-do employers, who burst on the rock climbing scene in 1938 and enlivened it for twenty years.

These and many, many more made up the Boston rock climbing scene of the second half of the 1930s.

In this egalitarian, noncompetitive world, it is noteworthy that everyone seemed to climb all the routes. On today's climbing scene, with its keen sense of ratings, each climber tends to categorize his ability: "a 5.8 leader," "a 5.10 leader," "I lead 5.7 and follow 5.9." In the late 1930s there were no ratings, and if you climbed at all, it was assumed you climbed any route. (Well, almost any route—a note from Walter Howe's journal for April 19, 1938, reads: "Tried Hurd's traverse. Too fat. Also new sneakers.") Ask the 1930s climber today which were the hardest routes on the north country cliffs and you may get conflicting answers, many of them vague. Ask a modern climber about those same 1930s routes, and you will receive a precise listing of which routes are 5.7, 5.6, or 5.5.

The one distinction of importance in those days was the matter of who led. Towle and Davis would lead anything, Howe most things, Bonney some things, Gower and MacDonald very few. The old unreliable rope and minimal protection separated leaders from followers with ruthless effect.

On one occasion Towle rose to heights worthy of the preceding pioneers. On a trip to Katahdin in 1935, Towle led an assault on the enormous buttress high on the wall above Chimney Pond, until then unclimbed and named the *Armadillo* by Towle's party. After a long approach brought the climbers to a high perch under an imposing triangular cliff 300 feet high, Towle launched into a vigorous struggle up a wide chimney. From the top of the chimney, he declined the challenge of a direct assault up the remaining face (rated 5.7 by postwar climbers) and worked out a slanting line to the right which went free at 5.5 but had intimidating exposure unlike anything

"Rock climbing for fun." A characteristic group of 1930s climbers cavort at the top of the Whitney-Gilman route, then called "New Cannon." Walter Howe is at left, Leland Pollock at right.

the Bostonians had learned at Black and White rocks. Characteristically, once Towle had led, everyone followed—Walter, Thelma, Marjorie, and eight others! Though not technically difficult, Towle's lead of the *Armadillo* was a bold venture for its day, in a league with the classic route explorations of Underhill's prime years.

This tour de force was not in the mold of the 1934–1940 era, however. Even the old explorers who turned out on the Boston crags from time to time caught the new spirit. One young man recalls, after having read and heard about the legendary Underhills for years, the first time he actually *saw* both god and goddess in person at the lowly Quincy Quarries, where he went as a novice. He remembers expecting that surely the great mountaineering pair's lunch would consist of gritty pemmican, munched hastily on a narrow ledge halfway up some wild slant of overhanging rock; and was quite dismayed to see a checkered tablecloth spread at the base of the cliffs and . . . creamed chicken, deviled eggs, wine, and all the trimmings.

Down in the New York area, a similar spirit glowed. A happy ambiance wafted over the New York metropolitan rock climbing scene. Like the New

Connecticut crag climbing. Betty Woolsey leads on the Sleeping Giant.

BILL HOUSE

York hikers of that era, the climbers often reached their cliffs by trains, picnicked on the clifftops that overlooked civilization, and evolved a rich mixture of midweek urban cosmopolitanism with weekend fresh air on steep crags. Though Percy Olton and Win Means were still part of the scene until the late 1930s, new faces began to emerge: Lawrence Coveney, Beckett Howorth, Walter Spofford, Howard Carlson. Toward the end of the 1930s, Roger Wolcott, Don Babenroth, and David Millar became regulars. Among the women, Marguerite Schnellbacher, Helen Fair, Helen Spaulding, Maria Leiper, and (later) Del Wilde were most active. The sociability of the circle is suggested by the observation that by the end of the decade Marguerite Schnellbacher became Marguerite Schnellbacher Coveney, Maria Leiper became Maria Leiper Millar, and shortly thereafter Del Wilde became Del Wilde Wolcott. The places they climbed were still primarily the old Olton haunts—Arden cliff, Storm King, Crow's Nest, and Breakneck Ridge—and little pioneering was done. As in Boston, it was enough to enjoy the sunny rocks and warm companionship of good friends on old familiar routes.

In 1930 a group of Appalachian Mountain Club members from the Connecticut Chapter visited the Boston rock climbing scene and brought back the word on safe top-roping practices and rudimentary climbing form. Soon Connecticut outcrops were studded with climbers too. At this time many moderate routes were developed on Ragged Mountain, where some of Wiessner's cracks were too hard for the average climber. Other cliffs were explored in nearby Plainville (Pinnacle Rock and Sunset Rock) and Farmington (Rattlesnake and Will Warren's Den). The Hanging Hills of Meriden were less often visited; again Fritz's standards were not for the typical 1930s climber. The Sleeping Giant was climbed, but most of the AMC climbers came from the central section of the state, so the cliff was out of the way for them. The short distances and good roads of central Connecticut lent themselves perfectly to the spirit of the late 1930s. On weekday evenings (traditionally Thursdays at first, Wednesdays later), climbers would go directly from their jobs in the cities of Hartford or Meriden or Waterbury to the favorite rock, climb until dusk, and then enjoy both picnic supper and animated post-mortems of the evening's climbs. On weekends the group might go farther afield, to the Sleeping Giant or to join the Boston climbers further north. Among club climbers, Bill Burling, Foster Sturdevant, and Mark Goedicke were principal leaders and organizers, but the top climber in the state in those years was Henry Beers, occasional partner of Wiessner's and later chairman of the Aetna Life & Casualty Insurance Company.

Even Rhode Island joined in this metropolitan mountaineering. Blessed with at least one first-class leader, Henry Childs, who had climbed with the Underhill entourage in the earlier period, the Narragansett Chapter of the AMC had an active program of Wednesday evening and Saturday afternoon climbs. In November 1935 this group proudly titled an *Appalachia* write-up "Rhode Island: the Rock Climbers' Paradise"—which might have been news to Dresden and the Dolomites—and described no fewer than nine different climbing areas, undaunted by the fact that the tallest was but 90 feet high, and some barely one-fourth of that. Only in Rhode Island, perhaps, could one of the choice locations (Lincoln Woods Reservation) include the recommendation: "A narrow crack about 20 feet high provides the best climb in this Reservation."

The relaxed spirit of all these Appie climbers of the 1930s was characterized not by good fellowship alone, but also by a growing concern for safety. After all, they were there to have fun, and it would be tragic to spoil it all by failing to allow for the inherently risky terrain and take appropriate precautions at all times. Gradually, safety procedures learned from the Underhill generation were more and more formalized, so as to guarantee no unhappy interruption of the good times. The old games of follow-the-leader (unroped) ceased after about 1936. Careful belaying habits, strictures against soloing, a preference for top-roping, a tradition that only the most experienced leaders should attempt to lead, and a spirit of not trying to do hard climbs till you were really ready for them—these and other safety precautions evolved unself-consciously, and without seeming to be a burden to that prewar group. It is only with hindsight that the observer of fifty years later can notice that those procedures contained the seeds of an over-formalization and system of rules that a later generation of climbers, who once again sought to push new standards of difficulty, would find confining. The climbers of the 1930s seemed universally content and indeed happy with an evolving system whose later stages would divide the climbing community in some cases into surprisingly hostile camps.

Of a wholly different nature was the development of Adirondacks rock climbing in the late 1930s. No one could run up to Wallface from the office on Wednesday evening. No large sociable groups could congregate on convenient top-roping areas. Rock climbing consequently developed far more slowly in that isolated wilderness. Far from the happy crowds, only a few Adirondack summer visitors showed any sustained interest in the cliffs in which the region abounds. Debonair John Case, now approaching fifty, continued the relaxed dabbling in rock climbs that he kept up most of his long life, but the most active and influential leadership for what little new climbing was done in the 1930s passed to his one-time student, Jim Goodwin.

A more different personality than the voluble, urbanized, sophisticated

Adirondack pioneer. Wilderness exploratory rock climbing was the special forte of the Adirondacks' Jim Goodwin.

Appies cannot be conjured. Though Goodwin was a history teacher in Connecticut during the winter months, to meet him in the Adirondack wilds, you would not have guessed it. Mild and soft-spoken with a deep love of woods and hills, he was happier tramping to distant trackless ridges than top-roping on sunny crags within sound of traffic. From boyhood he developed an affinity for wild places and remote forests and remained always a hiker and woodsman first, a technical climber only as a way to enrich his acquaintance with the more rugged places of the Adirondacks. His mastery of technical skills and formal safety procedures probably never came close to his contemporaries at Arden and Quincy, but his grit and resourcefulness on the vegetated cliffs that rise above the remote fastness of Panther Gorge or on the great open faces of Gothics might have quailed the more sociable spirits. Goodwin explored many of the Adirondacks' myriad of slabs and abutments, sometimes alone but sometimes leading parties. His routes never matched the technical difficulties being top-roped by the urban Appies, and he always stood somewhat in awe of Wiessner's occasional Adirondacks appearances, but Goodwin had the woodsman's natural love of adventure and the courage and shrewdness to pull off some bold routes, such as a poorly protected, grass-filled crack on the north side of Porter Mountain, climbed during a drizzle.

Besides the urban Appies and Goodwin of the Adirondack wilderness, only a very few other climbing circles existed in the 1930s. Most of these were the new college climbing clubs.

The Harvard Mountaineering Club, founded in 1924, originated primarily with summer vacation mountaineering with the Alps or the West in mind. Experienced leadership for the undergraduates was always available around Cambridge—from Underhill primarily in the 1920s, from visiting British Everest hero Noel Odell in the late 1920s, and from Ken Henderson in the 1930s and continuously thereafter. A contingent from this club, headed by Lincoln O'Brien (then an undergraduate) and the Stebbins brothers, had done some excellent rock climbing in the late 1920s, especially on Katahdin, Joe English Hill, and elsewhere. But the club's focus was mainly on the distant ranges. (O'Brien's best climbs were not really under the aegis of HMC.) In the early 1930s a corps of exceptionally talented and ambitious mountaineers came through this club—Bradford Washburn, H. Adams Carter, Charles Houston, Robert Bates, and Terris Moore (the latter a Williams graduate who went on to Harvard Business School). These men accomplished major climbs on big mountains in Alaska and the Canadian Rockies and later mounted a serious bid to climb K2, the Karakoram giant. In New England they logged many practice hours on Boston crags and in the White Mountains' alpine zone, but they were never terribly interested in high-angle rock climbing as such. "The only thing we were interested in was Alaska and the Yukon," recalled Bates. The same focus on the big mountains of the world was true for an early 1940s HMC crew of whom William Lowell Putnam, Maynard Miller, and Andrew Kauffman were leading lights.

More oriented to rock, the Yale Mountaineering Club suffered a checkered career. In the late 1920s it had been active under Hassler and Roger Whitney and Bill Willcox. After a brief period of inactivity, the club was reorganized and regenerated in 1933 with the coming of Bill House, Wilson Ware, Tom Rawles, and a British graduate student named Don Dudley. House blossomed into one of the country's best rock climbers, but his notable achievements lay, as with the Harvard group, in the big mountains. During the mid-1930s, though, House and his companions were active on the Sleeping Giant and throughout New England. A Yale party (R. S. G. Hall, Walter Spofford, and a third named Merrill) put up the second route on Cathedral Ledge, now known as *Refuse,* in 1935. Through the Oxford background of Dudley, they carried the fine art of building-climbing to its highest level in prewar New England, without benefit of permission from Yale authorities. This produced illicit roped ascents of Harkness Tower and attempted break-ins of Eli's secret societies, Skull and Bones (unsuccessful) and Book and Snake (successful). Curiously, one of the more capable and eager participants in these nighttime climbing capers was undergraduate Dick Bissell, who would black his face with shoeblack and don dark sneakers and gloves—foreshadowing his later prominence as a high-ranking CIA official.

Identified with the Yale contingent in Connecticut climbing circles is the isolated figure of Betty Woolsey, whom the reader has met with John Case on the first ascent of Wallface and as an occasional climbing partner of Fritz Wiessner. One of America's top woman athletes of the 1930s, Betty was one of five daughters in the household of Professor Woolsey of the Yale Forestry School. Best known for her Olympic skiing in 1936, she also did considerable climbing with House and his contemporaries at Yale and became a confident and proficient leader. When she moved west, the Northeast lost one of its very best woman climbers. Her memory lives on in this region through the popular beginners' route at the Shawangunks, the *Betty*.

Besides Harvard and Yale, Dartmouth was the only other northeastern college on record as having a rock climbing program before World War II. The key figure in Hanover was Jack Durrance, who had learned as a teenager in Austria. In the fall of 1936 Durrance organized the Dartmouth Mountaineering Club, patterning it after the HMC. The club was soon exploring nearby crags across the river in Vermont, many of which are still used today by DMC climbers (and virtually unknown to anyone else). In the fall of 1937 two ropes of DMC climbers—not including Durrance—pioneered a bold lead of a previously unexplored cliff on Owl's Head in New Hampshire's Oliverian Notch, comparable in size and difficulty with the other big cliffs opened up by the Underhill generation. This cliff has remained an almost exclusively Dartmouth preserve for half a century. Through Durrance's skillful diplomacy, mountaineering won an approved place in the eyes of Dartmouth authorities to a greater degree than at other eastern colleges, so that even building-climbing was permitted within reason. The celebrated Bartlett Tower (a demanding 5.7 at least) has been an on-campus training ground for DMC climbers ever since. Durrance himself went on to make significant climbs in the Tetons and elsewhere, but his chief contribution to northeastern climbing history was his formation of the DMC, which has been one of the more active college climbing clubs almost continuously since the 1930s.

Outside of the various AMC contingents, the three college clubs, and the remote Adirondacks climbers, almost literally no one else could be found on northeastern rock faces before World War II. One of the few exceptions was a group functioning wholly independently of the AMC climbers. The original leaders were Ray Garner, Bob Sanford, and Don Anderson; sometimes they called themselves The Mountaineers, sometimes Ka-Na-Da-Hi (allegedly Indian for "lovers of the outdoors"). Garner led a route on Breakneck Ridge in 1934 that was probably as serious a lead as any pre-1940 climbs other than Wiessner's. They and the New York Appies were the only climbers in the Hudson Valley then. "Believe it or not," recalled Garner fifty years later, "all [our] climbs were in perfect solitude. We never saw another group in action. We had no idea what was happening elsewhere." In the later 1930s, a youth named Gerry Bloch joined the Garner crowd and rapidly became a very good climber. Bloch did the first ascent of

M. GIRARD BLOCH

Man on the Rock. This slender spire was first climbed by Gerry Bloch, shown here (right) with friend and fellow independent climber, Ray Garner. Block and Garner and a small circle of friends climbed separately from the dominant New York AMC.

"The warm and flashing fire." Savouring the 1930s climbers' camaraderie, a Boston group ends their day, in Irvin Davis's words: "sweaty, dirty, tired but glowing with experiences of the day . . . this group of eager, living souls, feeling together all that life can mean. . . ."

a spectacular pinnacle on the New Jersey Palisades known as Man-in-the-Rock. It was not only spectacular and exposed, but also illegal and unfortunately exposed to view by the police: Bloch was very nearly jailed for his fine achievement. Once thought to be unclimbable by the New York Appies, the Man-in-the-Rock showed that the little Garner-Bloch contingent were first-rate climbers for their day. Although Garner left the area in 1935, Bloch continued to climb, largely in isolation from other climbing groups, for the next half century. At age sixty-nine, with the help of a Yosemite Valley guide, he became the oldest person ever to scale the vertical wall of 3,000-foot El Capitan.

Such was the rock climbing scene of the second half of the 1930s. Not an innovative period in the sport's history, it was one of great pleasure and good humor for its small bands of participants. The numbers were never large—typically ten or twenty on most outings. The cliffs were never crowded (though sometimes a single route might be, uproariously). Everyone knew each other, and everyone did all of the climbs. "We were all kids together," recalled New York's Maria Millar, "and we had a wonderful time." Boston's Irvin Davis (being a lawyer) prepared a mock "Last Will and Testament" for an incoming AMC Rock Climbing Committee Chairman (Oscar Dahlstrom), in which was bequeathed not only ropes, pitons, and carabiners, but also "Black and White . . . Castle Hill, Hammond Woods, Blueberry Ledge, the Chimney and the Boat"; and beyond that "the right to kibitz and advise, to make poor jokes—even puns—to encourage, to ridicule . . . and to rejoice in climbs well done"; and finally:

> To all the climbers, sweaty, dirty, tired but glowing with experiences of the day, to all this group of eager, living souls, feeling together all that life can mean, I give the warm and flashing fire, the songs, the jests, the chill of coming night, the stars' light—years away and yet so close—the late moon rising in the distant sky, the glowing embers of the dying fire, and then good nights and rustlings in the trees, until all drop asleep. ∎

Reference Note

The Boston rock climbing scene of the 1930s is thoroughly documented in notes, records, and photographs painstakingly kept by Walter Howe, long-time chairman of AMC's Rock Climbing Committee. This remarkable collection is now at Dartmouth College Library as part of the background papers for this book. Another invaluable source is the journals, photographs, and personal recollections of Thelma Bonney Towle. The Mountaineering Committee of AMC's New York Chapter has kept files similar to Howe's going back to this period. The authors are indebted to AMC's Boston and New York committees for the generous loan of all this material, and to Ms. Towle for sharing her collection and recollections. For lesser areas, see especially Foster E. Sturdevant, "Rock Climbing in Connecticut," *Appalachia*, December 1939, pp. 538–540; Richmond A. Day, "Rhode Island: the Rock Climbers' Paradise," *Appalachia*, November 1935, pp. 424–426; and James A. Goodwin, "Climbs in the Adirondacks," *Appalachia*, June 1938, pp. 27–32. Among the colleges, special note may be made of an unpublished "History of the Mountaineering Club" by Harvard's D. Stacey (1936) in the Pusey Library Archives; William P. House, "Mountaineering at Yale Twenty Years Ago," Yale Mountaineering Club *Journal*, 1955, pp. 23–25; and William B. Rotch, "Introducing the Dartmouth Mountaineering Club, Hanover, NH," *Appalachia*, December 1937, pp. 331–332. Many climbers shared personal memories of these years with the authors.

9: The Gunks Discovered: 1935–1945

A N OFT-TOLD LEGEND of American rock climbing concerns that brilliantly clear moment following an afternoon thundershower when Fritz Wiessner and his party topped out on Breakneck Ridge, gazed off to the northwest, and saw . . . the future of northeastern rock climbing. As a long, low line of sparkling white cliffs glittering on the horizon, the Shawangunks beckoned. Fritz was up there the following weekend and led the first routes on these cliffs, which became the principal arena for northeastern climbers throughout the 1940s, 1950s, and 1960s and remain among the most popular and important climbing scenes in the United States today.

The modern era of Shawangunk rock climbing certainly dates from Wiessner's arrival in 1935, but it is hard to believe that less skilled but equally enthusiastic sports were not tempted to try scrambling up those inviting cliffs in earlier years. Catskill historian Alf Evers went to high school in nearby New Paltz in the 1920s and recalled episodes on more than one of the Shawangunk cliffs, complete with rope and skills based solely on readings of such mountaineer-authors as Edward Whymper and Bolton Browne. Evers believes he heard of others before him. But serious modern climbing started with Wiessner's arrival.

It was not long before Fritz and his New York friends realized that the Smiley family's venerable Mohonk Mountain House, one of those grand nineteenth-century mountain resorts still operating, rich in antiquarian ambiance, was situated squarely amidst miles and miles of climbable Shawangunk conglomerate. An enchanted setting for their favorite pastime! Directly across Mohonk Lake from the resort, up a small wooded talus slope were beautiful, clean, solid cliffs known to climbers as the Skytop section of the Gunks. In an ensuing weekend in that same year (1935), Wiessner headed up that talus slope with John Navas and Percy Olton in tow. Today there are a dozen routes within a hundred yards of the prominent center of that cliff that go free at a grade of 5.4 or less. Nevertheless, with characteristic boldness and ambition, Wiessner picked a perfectly dead vertical line, up a broken crack (of course: always a crack for Fritz) squarely in the most ex-

Wiessner at the Gunks. In 1935 Fritz Wiessner "discovered" Shawangunks rock climbing, focusing especially on the Skytop cliffs where he is shown here.

posed and dramatic location. From the top of this route a rope can hang more than 100 vertical feet without touching the cliff at its base, so steep is the line. As Beckett Howorth put it demurely in the first write-up: "The exposure is unusual." It was an elegant line, a worthy inauguration for mainstream Gunks climbing. A projecting slug of rock near the top gave the route its name: *The Gargoyle.* It is rated 5.5 today.

What *The Gargoyle* proved—other than confirming the vision, technical skill, and physical strength of the leader—was that the steepest broken rock, indeed the most wildly improbable projections of horizontal flakes, which in almost any other range in the world would be avoided like death by a climber as most probably unsound, were, at the Shawangunks, almost always solid and unshakable. The implications for climbers were enormous. The solid, dependable quality of the rock, together with its extreme tendency to horizontal stratification, meant that climbs of an extraordinary steepness might prove to be surmountable at a reasonable standard of technical difficulty—as the incredibly steep *Gargoyle* route had demonstrated.

Wiessner was instantly aware that the Shawangunks were a superior arena for technical rock climbing. Not even Fritz could foresee, however, that this was to become the center of rock climbing in the East for years. When standards of climbing began their great advance in the late 1950s, and even more in the late 1960s, it was at the Gunks that the greatest accomplishments were first seen. Even when the big New Hampshire cliffs were, in effect, rediscovered in the 1970s, the Gunks remained the prime mecca for eastern climbers.

In the late 1930s, though, Wiessner was busy with many other climbing projects, including K2, not to mention the arduous demands of keeping a business solvent in the Depression. Other New York leaders were awed by the verticality of the Gunks. The first official New York Chapter AMC Gunks weekend was Memorial Day 1937, with twelve people registered. Until 1940, however, regularly scheduled weekends remained largely at Arden, Storm King, and Breakneck Ridge.

In 1940 a second European climber arrived on the Shawangunks scene. Born in Trieste, Hans Kraus had been tutored as a child by James Joyce, received a medical education in Vienna, and turned to sports medicine as his

Hans Kraus. Wiessner's close friend Hans Kraus became the dominant figure at the Shawangunks for many years. Note miniature piton on hat, given to him by fellow Gunks climber Dick Hirschland.

area of specialization, a field in which he rose to prominence as doctor, author, and proponent of physical fitness. He first visited the United States in 1934, then accepted a position on the staff of prestigious Columbia-Presbyterian Medical Center in 1938. During the 1950s his demonstrations of test results, showing that American youth of the automobile-television age was growing up in poor physical condition, led to formation of the President's Council on Physical Fitness. His fame as a physician was enhanced further when one of his back patients was President Kennedy.

But throughout this long career in medicine on two continents, the short, barrel-chested, athletic Dr. Kraus pursued an avocation with equal determination and flair: rock climbing. A friend and protégé of one of the greatest Italian climbers, Emilio Comici, Kraus perfected his climbing skills on the vertical towers of the Dolomites. For the first two years he was in the United States, professional responsibilities absorbed his attentions. Finally in 1940 he found out about the New York area rock climbing group. When Maria and David Millar picked him up in their car to go to the Shawangunks for his first American climbing, they recalled, his enthusiasm at the prospect of getting back on rock led him to more and more animated conversation and at length had him crouching excitedly on the floor of the back of the car, leaning over the front seat to chatter and gesticulate about climbing and to peer at the cliffs as they approached.

Kraus found his spiritual home in the Shawangunks. Climbers have long noted a resemblance in the type of climbing between the Dolomites and the Shawangunks—rock of excellent quality and extreme verticality seamed with a plenitude of holds. Both places are central playgrounds for the pure rock climber, rather than practice areas for the all-around mountaineer. In Hans Kraus the Northeast had its first major rock climber who was interested almost exclusively in pure rock climbing instead of seeing rock primarily as training ground for the mountains. Weaned on the Dolomites, he was instantly at home in the Gunks.

When Kraus arrived, the many long escarpments of Shawangunk cliffs had scarcely been touched by climbers. Wiessner had picked out a few choice lines on two or three of these cliffs but had avoided the single longest cliff in the area—known as the Trapps—because on a casual inspection it had seemed excessively vegetated and dirty. The Trapps run for about a mile in length and are about 150 to 200 feet in height for most of the way. Kraus was the first to put up a route on this cliff, a fine, easy line along the northern side of a 150-foot-high prominent extrusion bulging out from the upper part of the cliff. This *Northern Pillar* route, climbed in 1940, showed that the Trapps offered fine climbing—so fine that within a few years this cliff became and has ever since remained the most climbed high cliff in the Northeast.

During the war years, time and travel restrictions prevented full-scale exploitation of the new area. Nevertheless, Kraus and Wiessner—the "Hans and Fritz" of American climbing—managed to get to the Gunks on many a weekend with a handful of followers from the New York Chapter of AMC. Before 1950 a total of fifty-eight multipitch routes were put up whose identity survived to be listed in the 1980 guidebook. All but two of these routes had either Hans or Fritz on the first ascent party, and seven had them both. Of the fifty-eight, twenty-three are credited to Wiessner, twenty-six to Kraus, seven to both climbing together. (The remaining two are *RMC*, climbed in 1948 by Ralph Clapp and Grant Oakley, and *Alphonse*, climbed with aid in 1948 by Ken Prestrud and Lucien Warner.)

In those years Hans and Fritz picked out many of the true classic lines of the Gunks, climbs that still rate among the most beautiful and enjoyable in the Northeast. Most of their best climbs in those years fell in the 5.5 to 5.6 range: Fritz's *Baby* and *Layback,* both in 1941, and *Yellow Ridge* (1944); Hans's incredibly vertical and airy *Madame Grunnebaum's Wulst* (1943); and climbs on which they collaborated, including *The Horseman* (1941) and *Updraft* (1944).

The finest of these 1940–1946 climbs—indeed, some say the greatest route in the Shawangunks even today—was a line they did together in the fall of 1941, fittingly named the *High Exposure.* The climb began unexceptionally enough. Two routine pitches, perhaps 5.3 in difficulty, took them to a commodious if airy ledge underneath a large roof, still some 60 feet or so below the top. Hans climbed 20 feet up to the right edge of this roof, then placed a piton. When he swung out from under the roof, he found himself at the base of a 40-foot vertical wall, the first two-thirds of which were so steep as to be nearly overhanging. Below, the cliff curved underneath and out of sight, leaving nothing but oceans of empty space—high exposure indeed. Within reach were some excellent holds—but would there be good holds all the way? To commit himself to start up that steep face was an act of boldness almost unparalleled in northeastern climbing at that time. Yet that high, clean wall proved to be seamed with just enough cracks and holds to enable him to move steadily up and left, out over a 150-foot gulf of open air, placing one more piton along the way, until he could reach a passable stance two-thirds of the way up. Here he placed his third and last piton. Moving slightly further left, the exhilarated climber found himself on the nose of a prow leading to the very top of the cliff, high exposure on all sides, the clean white rock still yielding just enough holds for him to move on up.

The *High Exposure* later was rated 5.6, but the 1972 edition of the guide-

Wiessner on High Exposure. *Wiessner climbing Kraus's 1941 classic,* High Exposure. *Thirty years later a Shawangunks guidebook still called this route "perhaps THE Shawangunk climb to do."*

"Chust sheking." Kraus in a characteristic pose as he scouts one of his many new routes at the Gunks. The phrase, "chust sheking" was recalled by his frequent climbing partner, Bonnie Prudden, who seconded many of his pioneering climbs.

book noted it as "perhaps *THE* Shawangunk climb to do. . . . A tremendous line, not just for 1941, but for any time." When the California rating system was first applied, the route was called 5.7, but the word among climbers was that it was technically 5.5 and psychologically 5.9, so it averaged out to 5.7. For 1941 it was indeed a bold line, especially when it is understood that Kraus was leading on hemp rope, wearing sneakers, and of course had no reason to know for sure that good holds would be found all the way up. Indeed, considering the genuine commitment involved with hemp rope, as contrasted with the assumption of most modern leaders that they can safely

Kraus on Grey Face. *Kraus climbing a Wiessner 1940 classic,* Grey Face. *The route, rated 5.5, illustrates what breathtaking verticality could be surmounted at relatively modest levels of difficulty in the playground of the Gunks.*

fall, the 1941 lead of the *High Exposure* may well deserve rank as one of the greatest single achievements of northeastern climbing.

Besides their outstanding 5.5 to 5.6 routes, Kraus and Wiessner also put up some splendid easier lines, which have become popular beginner routes. No other climbing area abounds in so many multipitch climbs of high quality on which a beginner can feel comfortable. Among the best were Hans's *Northern Pillar* and *Southern Pillar, Easy Overhang,* and *Three Pines* (1940–1941), Fritz's *Minty* (1941), and their joint find, the *Easy Verschneidung* (1942). These climbs all rate about 5.2. The pure pleasure that hundreds, probably thousands of novice climbers have gained from those six routes alone defies measurement.

The relationship between these two expatriates was at first alternately competitive—Hans putting up a route one week, Fritz hearing about it and putting up another the next—and cooperative (many of the finest routes being done together), but it ultimately deepened into a friendship that lasted almost half a century. As late as the 1970s one of the privileges of climbing at the Gunks was the sight of the two small, gnomelike figures side by side on the carriage road below the cliffs, walking slowly, often with heads bowed and hands behind their backs, like two ancient dwarves from a Tolkien land, heading off for another classic Shawangunk climb, usually on a route that one or the other or both had put in three decades before.

But if Hans and Fritz found the new routes almost single-handedly, this does not mean that they were the only climbers at the cliffs. The New York climbers who had been content with the Hudson Highlands cliffs throughout the 1930s gradually switched their allegiance to the Gunks. During World War II military activities near Arden, Breakneck, and Storm King closed them to climbers. By 1945 the switch to the Gunks was complete. Every weekend found the Appie faithful headed for the gleaming white Shawangunk conglomerate. In those days a good turnout might mean a crowd of a dozen or a score at most, and almost no one showed up except AMC's New York Chapter. But the age of Shawangunk rock climbing had begun.

Back in June 1940, before Kraus arrived, Beckett Howorth followed Wiessner up an aesthetic line called *Grey Face,* then but the fifth route at the Gunks. Commented Howorth:

> Fritz and I both felt that this route was as difficult as anything we had done in the east. But there are other possibilities in the Shawangunks.

"Other possibilities?" Neither Howorth nor anyone else envisioned the explosion of rock climbing that was to come to the Gunks after the war, already in progress in Europe as he wrote those words. From the five routes that Howorth knew in 1940, at a time when Cannon cliff also had just five routes, Cathedral two, and Whitehorse two, the number of recorded Shawangunk rock climbs was destined to rise to 52 by 1947, 249 by 1964, 393 by 1972, 529 by 1980, 882 by 1986, and well more than 1,000 by 1992. Yes, there were other possibilities in the Shawangunks. ∎

Reference Note

The "discovery" of the Shawangunks is told by Fritz Wiessner in "Early Rock Climbing in the Shawangunks," *Appalachia,* June 1960, pp. 18–25. An early perspective is M. Beckett Howorth, "Rock Climbing in the Shawangunks," *Appalachia,* December 1940, pp. 245–258. Each generation of Shawangunk climbing guidebook has included a historical essay: see Arthur Gran, *A Climber's Guide to the Shawangunks* (New York: American Alpine Club with the Appalachian Mountain Club, New York Chapter, 1964), pp. 11–19; Richard C. Williams, *Shawangunk Rock Climbs* (New York: American Alpine Club, 1972), pp. 3–5 and (1980), pp. 33–38. The authors especially appreciate Williams' willingness to share his revised historical essay prior to publication of his most recent guide. A stunning collection of photographs of Gunks climbing, with brief historical text, is Richard Dumais, *Shawangunk Rock Climbing* (Denver: Chockstone Press, 1985). The authors are indebted to many conversations and much correspondence with the two leading climbers involved, Fritz Wiessner and Hans Kraus, as well as others present in the early days: Percy Olton, Maria and David Millar, Roger Wolcott, Lawrence Coveney, and M. Beckett Howorth. Records of the New York Chapter Mountaineering Committee (AMC) are also an invaluable source.

10: World War II as a Watershed in Northeastern Climbing History

D URING WORLD WAR II the Axis controlled the sources of both Italian and Manilla hemp, the traditional material for climbing rope. America's best climbers were commandeered in the war effort to seek and test alternative materials for mountain warfare. One warm afternoon in a Washington, D.C., office building, while evaluating an experimental synthetic rope made of nylon, Bob Bates decided impulsively to test it with realism. Bates anchored one end to a radiator, flung the rope out an upper-story window, and launched into a rappel past the incredulous eyes of office workers on the floors below.

It was a moment that changed climbing history. Bates and his associates decided that nylon made "almost as good" climbing rope as hemp, so full-scale production was ordered. In fact, nylon rope proved more durable, more flexible, less water absorbent, lighter in weight, and—more important—much stronger. By the time the war was over, the climbing world had a rope that would normally not break under the force of a leader fall. In addition, better pitons were developed during the war and again during the 1950s with the advent of a special chromium-molybdenum alloy, known affectionately to the climbers as cro-molly. The implications of these better tools of the trade, especially nylon rope, were enormous.

A rope that would not break provided a new level of security to postwar leaders. If you could survive a leader fall, then why not risk much harder moves than your prewar predecessors could ever consider? You could attempt much harder climbs, fall off on the first and second try, but perhaps get up on the third or fourth go. Armed with this new security, the postwar generation opened the gates toward much higher standards of difficulty.

For a few years, there was a pause before harder climbing was done. This was the age of the conservative tradition. But beginning in the late 1950s standards of difficulty began to move up. From then on, the horizons of climbers' perceptions of the possible continued to recede. 5.9 was reached in the Northeast in 1958, 5.10 tentatively in 1961 and more solidly in 1963, 5.11 in 1967, 5.12 in 1973, and 5.13 in 1983. Even more significant than this "leading edge," standards advanced throughout the climbing community. Proficient and relatively numerous leaders—say, the best club or college climbers—might be found leading 5.7s during the 1960s, 5.8s and 5.9s during the 1970s, and 5.10s and the odd 5.11 during the 1980s. Beginners were introduced on 5.2s during the 1960s, on 5.4s during the 1970s, and (if promising) 5.6s during the 1980s. Scarcely anyone in the Northeast climbed harder than 5.8 as late as 1960—yet by 1982 a guidebook referred to one 5.8 as "the best intermediate [*sic*] route on Cannon."

Perspective on this dramatic movement in climbing standards is essential if the reader is to properly evaluate the accomplishments of each wave of climbers. If on any given weekend in the 1990s, scores of climbers could be seen leading routes that Robert Underhill or Hans Kraus never could do, this assuredly does *not* mean that all these modern climbers are greater or "better" than Underhill or Kraus. The dynamic nature of the sport and the strong role of psychological factors must be understood.

Climbers exploring new levels of difficulty at each step of the way are coping with mental barriers that all subsequent climbers at that level will know nothing of. Once nylon rope was introduced, the attainment of higher levels of difficulty was a matter of psychological breakthroughs. In appraising Jim McCarthy's contributions to climbing in the 1960s (chapter 14) climber-historian Chris Jones puts it this way: "At each advance he carried the psychological load."

This principle requires slight modification to acknowledge the contributions to better climbing made by technology—the switch from pitons to nuts in the early 1970s, the still more sophisticated forms of protection introduced in the 1980s, the improvement of climbing shoes at several stages—and by more rigorous and better focused physical training. It also may be true that physical training and sheer strength in specifically trained muscles began to be decisive above the level of 5.12 or 5.13 during the 1980s. An even more significant modification of this historical principle was introduced in the late 1980s, with preplaced protection and extensive rehearsing of hard moves: then, many argued, advances became matters of physical training and perseverance rather than creative imagination.

Nevertheless, at least for the first forty years following World War II and the advent of nylon rope, harder climbing was the result neither of technology nor of training but of psychological factors. It was the *perception* by some leading climber that he (or she) *could* climb some stretch of rock that preceding climbers had *not* thought they could. One of the leading climbers in the breakthroughs of the 1980s, Lynn Hill, said: "The most important thing was the *idea* that you can do harder climbs."

This concept is essential to good historical perspective on postwar climbing. If Stannard climbed harder than McCarthy, and Hill harder than Stannard—to introduce names the reader will shortly know better—it was not that Hill was stronger than Stannard and Stannard stronger than Mc-Carthy; nor even, in the important sense, that Hill was "better" than Stannard and Stannard "better" than McCarthy, and all of them "better" than Wiessner. Each new wave of climbers must be judged by the climate of the time when they were climbing. Each new climbing generation stands, psychologically, on the shoulders of its predecessors and is thereby enabled to perceive new possibilities.

From a historical perspective, the respect due great achievements must be measured out at each stage when climbing standards advanced. Breaking through to 5.10 in 1961 was fully comparable to establishing a 5.13 in 1983— or to climbing 5.8 in 1935. Especially is this true when comparing prewar versus postwar climbing—the hemp rope unprotected leader versus the nylon and cro-molly (or chock or Friend) protected leader. Most climbers honor the first ascent of the *Whitney-Gilman* in 1929 or *High Exposure* in 1941 as much as they do the first ascents of pioneering 5.12s and 5.13s of the 1970s and 1980s. The principle applies in both directions though—that is, to honor the later accomplishments as well. The breakthroughs of recent climbers at the leading edge of the sport are every bit as impressive as those of earlier pioneers. Each generation must cope with new psychological barriers—and reap the rewards of overcoming such barriers.

When we consider ice climbing, the same principle holds, but with greater modification for the role of technology. Technological change looms very large at one critical turning point in ice climbing history. As the reader will see in chapter 21, the discovery that a drooped pick on an ice ax had vastly greater holding power than the traditional right-angle pick produced an immediate and radical change in standards of ice climbing. Thereafter further changes in technology—new tools and new techniques of hanging from them—played important roles in raising the standards. Nevertheless, the first leaders to exploit these changes battled psychological barriers similar to those overcome by the pioneering rock leaders. This is evidenced in part by the fact that breakthroughs were usually made by someone new, someone not trained in (and psychologically trapped by) the earlier technology.

The emphasis in this discussion on what was going on at the leading edge at each stage should not obscure the fact that similar psychological forces operated at all levels of climbing at any given time. As the leading edge raised standards from 5.7 to 5.9, or from 5.9 to 5.11, the message would slowly filter down to lower levels. Less proficient climbers would raise

Hans Kraus

THE FORTIES AT A GLANCE

Principal climbing event: World War II's equipment developments
Climbs of the Decade:— rock: *High Exposure*
                          — ice: *Damnation Gully* (direct)
Hardest single climb: *Minniebelle*
Boldest lead: *High Exposure*
Most improbable coup by a nobody: *Conncourse*
Emblematic item of gear: nylon rope
Most important climber: Hans Kraus
Most colorful: Bonnie Prudden
Most prominent women: First half: Maria Millar
                               Second half: Bonnie Prudden
Brainiest: William Shockley
Nice Guy Award: Roger Wolcott
Couple of the Decade: Herb and Jan Conn
Person you'd most like to have climbed with: Irvin Davis

their sights as well—say, from 5.5 to 5.7, or from 5.3 to 5.5, or from 5.7 to 5.9. Psychological barriers came down all along the scale of proficiency.

All of our discussion so far has focused on the simple matter of difficulty. Sheer difficulty is measured on a scale on which most climbers agree most of the time. But there had always been more to climbing than mere difficulty. Postwar climbers began to talk more and more about something called "style" and something else called "ethics." Here agreement was far less readily obtainable.

If Smith climbed a 5.9 on a top-rope or leading with a piton nearby at every hard move, the 5.9 was saluted as difficult. If Jones *led* a 5.9 in a situation where only an occasional piece of protection was available, not necessarily near the 5.9 moves—and if Jones remained calm and in control throughout the lead—then Jones was saluted much more for having climbed his 5.9 "in good style." If Johnson came along to try the same climb and decided he'd first drop a top-rope from above and practice the 5.9 moves before he led them, Johnson would be criticized for climbing in "poor style." If Johnson decided he needed more protection and placed a bolt to protect the hard move, he would be castigated for "very poor style" (perhaps with an adjective less printable). If Johnson should decide to bang on the rock so as to create a somewhat larger hold, the outcry would be more colorful. In the latter two cases, the critics would deplore not merely the style but the ethics.

"Ethics" and "style" were often used casually as if they were interchangeable, but most climbers who thought about the subject used "ethics" to denote questions of whether the rock was altered (as by a bolt or especially by enlarging holds) and "style" to denote questions of how much courage and calmness were required to cope with the mental problems created by leading difficult moves with less than perfect security. Ethics concerned actions that affected other climbers' enjoyment of the route. Style concerned questions of taste.

These viewpoints differed over time. To the first postwar generation, the climbers of the "conservative tradition," good style meant, among other things, providing ample protection at every difficult move so as to ensure the safety of both leader and followers. To the next generation, good style implied boldness. John Turner, who was renowned for using minimal protection and risking monstrous leader falls, was criticized by older leaders of his generation as climbing in poor style because they thought him unsafe. Yet, for exactly the same reasons, Turner has been hailed by one modern arbiter of taste in New England climbing, Al Rubin, for his "impeccable style" (Rubin's precise words). To protect inadequately was bad style to the former generation; to overprotect was bad style to the latter.

Climbers took these issues seriously. Sometimes very seriously. Often, as new standards of difficulty were introduced at a cliff, questions of acceptable ethics and style raged among climbers most active at the cliff. Sometimes a consensus might become widely established at one cliff—but it might differ markedly from the consensus reached at another.

An ethic was agreed upon at the Shawangunks during the 1970s that was very strict: no direct aid, no prior inspection on rappel, no placing of bolts, and (not quite universally accepted) no pitons. Meanwhile in New Hampshire during the 1970s a very different ethic evolved: bolts and pitons were quite acceptable, but still the climber who led "from the ground up," rather than placing protection on rappel beforehand, was regarded as having used better style. The acceptance or rejection of various techniques often seemed arbitrary. At a time when Shawangunk climbers frowned on bolts and pitons, they warmly embraced the use of gymnastic chalk; at the very same time period (the early 1970s), Cannon climbers regarded bolts and pitons as justifiable on their blank granite slabs but condemned chalk as a form of artificial aid that left ugly marks as well. Shawangunk ethics and style of the 1970s were generally thought to be as pure as those found anywhere; yet some climbers of that era regarded taking numerous falls as a point of poor style and Shawangunk climbers viewed multiple falls as a commonly accepted practice.

These points are described here in order to provide further perspective to the reader as we embark on the history of postwar rock climbing.

Again, these points should not be conceived only in terms of the leading edge of climbing at any given time. The leading edge understandably commands attention, but it is not necessarily the most important part of the climbing scene. Climbing is a young sport, and its historians have so far tended to write about it as if the only points of significance were the breakthroughs to each higher level of difficulty. In fact, from the standpoint of the social history of what is a social as well as an individualized activity, what climbing means to the majority of current climbers is at least as important at each stage as what the handful of top climbers was or was not able to achieve vis-à-vis their predecessors. The majority of climbers, as New England's climber-historian Al Rubin has maintained, "have been concerned with exploring their own personal frontiers or simply interested in enjoying exhilarating activity in beautiful surroundings." A British climber (employing British terminology) has cautioned us all not to forget the "average climber," pointing out:

> To the average climber, the ascent of the year is invariably one of his own, and not a 6b gritstone wall. And, while it is ludicrous to suggest that his climb should be publicized, it is equally ludicrous to ignore his ideals and aspirations. He is the majority of climbers.

What follows may too often ignore this warning and succumb to the temptation of focusing unduly on the leading edge, but the point should not be forgotten: climbing, whether on rock or ice or simply on wintry mountain ridges in that most demanding of seasons, has afforded and will always afford continuing challenge to northeasterners who follow in the footsteps of Robert and Miriam Underhill, of John Case, of Walter Howe and Thelma Bonney, and hundreds of anonymous spirits who have always sought and found adventure in the northeastern hills. ∎

Reference Note

Several climbers who were actively involved in World War II research and development of mountaineering equipment are prime sources on this subject: Robert Bates, H. Adams Carter, John Case, William P. House, and Bradford Washburn. The general development of climbing in the immediate postwar years unfolds in contemporary magazine and journal articles, the most useful being *Summit, Climbing, Off Belay,* the British *Mountain,* and the *American Alpine Journal.* An excellent historical treatment is, of course, Jones' *Climbing in North America,* referred to previously.

11: The Conservative Tradition— Rock: The 1950s and 1960s

ODDLY, THE IMPLICATIONS of nylon rope were not perceived at first, or at least not acted on. For over ten years after VJ Day, no one led climbs any harder than the best prewar routes. In fact, the postwar leaders did not even match the level of climbing that Fritz Wiessner had done in the 1930s, a hiatus of nearly a quarter century and a tribute to old Fritz, who had neither nylon rope nor cro-molly pitons, just skill, judgment, and courage. Until the late 1950s, the highest grade of difficulty led by anyone other than Wiessner (in the northeastern U.S.) was 5.7. Wiessner himself led the last 5.8: *Minniebelle,* a short, fierce crack put up at the Shawangunks in 1946 and scarcely if ever repeated for the next ten years—until the coming of John Turner and Jim McCarthy in the late 1950s.

Why it took so long to exploit the obvious advantage of nylon rope is another historical puzzle. Part of the explanation lies in the conservative temper of the postwar years. This was an era when social mores were dominated by veterans of World War II, most of whom vividly remembered the Great Depression of the 1930s. They had seen plenty of genuine risk and adventure in both cases, especially World War II. So they tended to seek security and play it safe. Their conservative temper showed in many ways: young men had crew cuts, young women wore skirts with hemlines well below the knees. They voted for Eisenhower, watched Ed Sullivan, listened to Perry Como, and never so much as swallowed a goldfish, let alone smoked pot. The climbers of the time, many of them returning from action with the fabled Tenth Mountain Division, enjoyed the camaraderie of climbing but frowned on unwise risk taking.

Further explanation of this puzzle may lie in a kind of perverse psychology that flowed from the first experience of a climbing generation with nylon rope. But this is speculation.

The reader will recall the prewar maxim of Geoffrey Winthrop Young: "The leader does not fall." With no confidence in hemp rope, leaders could not even *consider* the possibility of a fall. This restraint curbed their level of commitment, but one result was that they never, ever, thought about falling. It was not on their minds.

With nylon rope, postwar leaders *could* think about falling and they *did* think about falling. Now leaders realized they could place pitons at close intervals and rely on them and a good rope to ensure their safety. Instead of focusing on their own limits as climbers (what they could be sure they would not fall off of, what they could back down with assurance), postwar leaders concentrated on how to place pitons effectively and how to judge whether they would hold a fall. Gradually this kind of objective calculation replaced the prewar subjective issues of knowing your limits, understanding yourself rather than your equipment. A judgment of physical properties replaced a judgment of personal qualities.

It is interesting to observe that many prominent postwar climbers were engineers or physicists, that the outing clubs of MIT and Rensselaer Polytechnic Institute became influential spheres of climbers, and that IBM spawned an active rock climbing club. By contrast, few of the prewar leaders had scientific backgrounds. The technical questions of how much force could safely be exerted (by a fall) on a piton, a carabiner, the rope, or the climber's waist, gave a fascinating exercise to those who liked engineering problems. It was quantifiable, reducible to numbers, whereas the prewar leader's dependence on his climbing judgment seemed vague and indefinable, indeterminate.

The point is highlighted by an exchange on the subject of belaying that took place in 1950 and 1951. When Arnold Wexler, one of the prominent early postwar climbers, wrote an influential twenty-seven-page article for the *American Alpine Journal* in 1950 on "The Theory of Belaying," the pages bristled with diagrams, graphs, tables, and complex mathematical formulae. One passage read:

Hence equation (2) is used in equation (18) to yield

$$\frac{d^2x}{dt^2} + \frac{kgx}{WL} - g = 0 \tag{19}$$

whose solution is

$$x = \left(a_o - \frac{WL}{k}\right) \cos\left(t\sqrt{\frac{kg}{WL}}\right) + \frac{a_1}{\sqrt{\frac{kg}{WL}}} \sin\left(t\sqrt{\frac{kg}{WL}}\right) + \frac{WL}{k} \tag{20}$$

in which a_o and a_1 are constants of integration.
When t=0, then x=0 and therefore a_o=0. Likewise
when t=0, $\frac{dx}{dt}$=2gH and a_1=2gH. Equation (20) reduces to . . .

John Turner

THE FIFTIES AT A GLANCE

Principal climbing event: the conservatives' grip on the sport
Climbs of the Decade:—rock: *Recompense*
                        —ice: *Wallface* in winter
Hardest single climb: *Repentance*
Boldest lead: *Bloody Mary*
Emblematic item of gear: piton hammer and holster
Most important climber: John Turner
Most underrated: Ray D'Arcy
Most colorful: Rit Walling
Most colorful group: Hans Kraus's inner circle at the Gunks
Most prominent women: First half: Bonnie Prudden
                          Second half: Krist Raubenheimer
Child prodigy: Steve Jervis
Still-active father figure: Ken Henderson
Nice Guy Award: Jack Taylor
Most abrasive: William Lowell Putnam
Norman Clyde Award: Robert Kruszyna
Brainiest: Lester Germer
Couple of the Decade: Oh, there's a clear-cut choice, but they
    weren't married (to each other) so we shouldn't print their
    names
Person you'd most like to have climbed with: J. B. Gardner

King Kraus at court. Hans Kraus traverses on The Horseman, *1941 classic put in with Wiessner. During the 1950s Kraus became the dominant figure and arbiter of Gunks climbing style.*

When Hassler Whitney commented on Wexler's paper in the same journal the following year—implicitly speaking as a representative of the prewar leaders who relied on human judgment and not rope elasticities—his seven-page essay had not one formula. Brilliant mathematician that he was, Whitney pointed politely to an error in Wexler's analysis on one point, but confined that comment to a footnote. His main thrust was that no leader worthy of the name will fall; therefore fine points of just what a rope will or will not hold are not only largely irrelevant but also tend to distract the young climber from learning all those subtle mountaineering skills that a competent leader ought to master.

But Wexler, not Whitney, spoke for the new generation and to the one that followed. In the 1950s, whatever lip service conservative leaders gave to the Youngian maxim, they all knew they could fall—and they did fall.

A perceptive aphorism can be found in George MacDonald's children's story *The Princess and the Goblin,* when the heroine, panicking, flees from her house into the goblin-filled wood: "But that is the way fear serves us: it always takes the side of the thing that we are afraid of." Postwar rock leaders, now able to fall and therefore having falls on their mind and afraid of falls, become *more likely* to fall than their prewar predecessors for whom falling was simply not allowable. Perhaps this is why the standard of difficulty remained stagnant for the first postwar years.

Thus was born the "conservative tradition" in northeastern rock climbing. The quoted phrase is from a "Safety Code" circulated at the Shawangunks during the 1950s, when beginning climbers were cautioned: "Climb only with a recognized mountaineering organization of conservative tradition." In prewar centers—Boston, Connecticut, the Adirondacks, the crags near New York City—the conservative tradition was ascendant from the end of World War II until well into the 1950s and clung with tenacity but diminishing effect until the mid-1960s.

During those years the Shawangunks emerged as a major rock climbing center in the Northeast, and Hans Kraus as the dominant figure at the Shawangunks. Fritz Wiessner moved to Vermont in 1946, leaving his friend Kraus as undisputed master of the Gunks. For the next ten years the diminutive Austrian bestrode the towering cliffs like a colossus. "King Kraus" he was to some, "Papa" to others. Rarely has one man so dominated a major climbing area.

Gunks climbing centered on the mile-long cliff known as the Trapps and an adjoining area known as the Near Trapps, with occasional forays to the Sky-Top cliff over near the Smileys' Mohonk Mountain House. Along the base of the Trapps an old shale-surfaced carriage road built by the Smiley family at the turn of the century provided easy access to the cliffs. The hub of activity narrowed down to the south end of the Trapps, where one point became particularly well known: the Uberfall. This was where climbers descended after completing their climbs, rendezvoused for their next climbs, ate lunch between climbs, and left their packs. Gradually the Uberfall became the social center of the Shawangunks, the place where every northeastern climber—and many from all over the world—would sooner or later pass, a uniquely important physical spot in the social history of northeastern climbing. As the Gunks became popular and crowded, the Uberfall "scene" became at once its most loved and disliked feature: loved by those to whom it was a weekend home, but later disliked by those who deplored the crowds and carnival atmosphere that came to be associated with rock climbing at the Gunks as the years went by and the crowds increased.

On Saturday night the climbers would gather at a local inn run by a warm-hearted German couple, Otto and Margot Schlueter. Though the inn had a name, "Mountaincrest," to a generation of New York climbers it was "Schlueter's" and the only place to be on a Saturday night. While some few camped out in the woods behind the cliffs, most people slept at Schlueter's as well.

For the first postwar years, the New York Chapter of the AMC was basically the only group of climbers at the Gunks. The formal program of weekend climbing was under a Rock Climbing Committee. "Formal program" is a term chosen advisedly. Registration was required before the weekend, and the leaders would then assign all climbers, in advance, to designated rope teams for designated climbs. On a typical weekend there might be ten or twenty climbers. On the regularly scheduled training weekends, where novices were welcomed, as many as thirty or forty would show up, and the cliffs were then said to be crowded.

The AMC Rock Climbing Committee supervised this program. Kraus served on this committee but chose never to be chairman, though all the chairmen of that day deferred to his judgment and opinions. Under his overall sway, the leading committee members were at first drawn from the remaining prewar leaders like Percy Olton, David and Maria Millar, and Roger Wolcott. Under the watchful tutelage of these old masters, a new generation of leaders came up, among whom were George Smith, Frank Cary, Norton Smithe, and William Shockley.

The last-mentioned name is of special interest. Shockley had followed Wiessner up some of his harder postwar routes, like *Minniebelle* (5.8) and *Overhanging Layback* (5.7), and had himself led the first ascent of a large roof that became a classic of the Trapps: *Shockley's Ceiling* (rated 5.6, but thoroughly intimidating on first look). Shockley was a Bell Lab scientist who received the Nobel Prize for the transistor during those years. The climbers feted him at Schlueter's that Saturday night. He went on in later years to controversy for his racial views. But around northeastern climbers his name is still best known for *Shockley's Ceiling*.

Shockley and his contemporaries embodied all the desired qualities of early 1950s rock leaders. They were safe, sound, dependable leaders who paid a lot of attention to training beginners and bringing along new climbers, always being careful to inculcate them with the safety principles on which they had been trained. George Smith eventually published a primer on rock climbing that laid down all these principles. Norton Smithe and Shockley were relatively bold leaders for their time, but even with them the salient attribute was good judgment. Safety, not boldness, was the virtue of the age.

In the early 1950s, imbued with the postwar conservative outlook, the AMC's Rock Climbing Committee became increasingly concerned with safety. At the back of their minds was awareness that the Shawangunks cliffs were on private land. "We were scared silly that if somebody got hurt the land would be closed," recalled Kraus. Whether because of this fear or simply a general preoccupation with safety, the New York Appies embarked on a program designed to reduce the risk in this inherently risky sport.

Under the repeated prodding of Kraus, the Committee evolved a system of requiring leaders to be certified by a Qualifications Committee. For easier climbs, a blanket approval could be authorized, but to lead any climb of moderate or harder difficulty, you had to be approved for each climb individually. Only the most advanced and experienced leaders could be classed as "Unlimited Leaders," empowered to lead any climb they chose. To train upcoming climbers, the club set up stipulations, including a belay test, in which aspiring new climbers were required to catch a dead weight simulating a falling climber. Besides these rigid qualifications for their own members, the club drafted a "Safety Code" and sought its endorsement by other climbers at the Shawangunks. In various drafts of this Code and accompanying messages, the Rock Climbing Committee harped on such themes as:

- "Climb only with a recognized mountaineering organization of conservative tradition. . . . Avoid the extremist."
- "Follow the leader's orders implicitly."
- "No one should lead without having had sufficiently long and intensive experience."

COURTESY BONNIE PRUDDEN

Bonnie Prudden. Ex-chorus girl, budding TV personality, top-rank climber of her day, Bonnie Prudden rappels from her beloved cliffs.

- "One should lead only to 50% of one's ability."
- "This is a sport in which slow and steady progress goes much farther than flashy form."

To freewheeling young rock climbers of the late twentieth century it is hard to conceive how such a tightly disciplined system could gain acceptance in such an inherently individualistic and adventurous activity as rock climbing. The reason it worked as long as it did was a conjunction of several factors: the mood of the 1950s, already mentioned; the safety consciousness engendered by reliable ropes and pitons, also discussed; the relatively small number of climbers; and the fact that the few adventurous leaders of the time were given an outlet for their energies outside the official system.

Paradoxically, the designer of the last item was also the chief architect of the safety system itself: Hans Kraus. Kraus had never become fully a part of the AMC system, even though he dominated its affairs throughout the

CRAN BARROW

Krist Raubenheimer: One of the New York AMC's top leaders of the 1950s and 1960s was Krist Raubenheimer.

late 1940s and early 1950s. In 1950 he began to climb less and less with the club and developed his own small circle of ardent young disciples who were interested in harder climbs. Thus as the AMC retreated more and more into simply repeating the established easier climbs, "King Kraus" made it possible for the elect "princes and princesses of his personal court" to enjoy the challenge of good climbing at a higher level of difficulty.

Ken Prestrud may have been the ablest leader of Kraus's new circle, but by far the most interesting personality was Bonnie Prudden. Ex-chorus girl on Broadway and budding television star as physical fitness and exercise proponent, Bonnie and husband Dick Hirschland joined the Kraus circle in the late 1940s. During the early 1950s Dick dropped out, Bonnie got a divorce, and under Kraus's tutelage she blossomed into a top-notch climber, leading routes at the top of the standard of the day. In the postwar years it was rare indeed for a woman to rank right at the forefront of the prevailing standard. Though prewar predecessors like Betty Woolsey and Maria Millar and postwar leaders like Ruth Tallan and Krist Raubenheimer were immensely respected, they were not in a class with the best men leaders at the time. Bonnie Prudden was the only woman who climbed at the same level of difficulty as the best male climbers of her day until the 1980s.

In the early 1950s, Hans's circle climbed at a solid 5.7 standard. Because of Kraus's tolerant views on the use of aid, it is always difficult to sort out which of their harder climbs involved aid, and how much aid. Nevertheless, Kraus and his partners, especially Prestrud and Prudden, were (with Wiessner) unquestionably the top free-climbers of the early 1950s as well. Some of their more difficult Shawangunk routes of those years included:

- *Ken's Crack,* a short 5.7 test piece near the Uberfall, first done by Prestrud in 1951
- *Hans's Puss,* a long and intricate 5.7 characterized by wild exposure and airy belays, led by Kraus with Prudden as second, also in 1951
- *Bonnie's Roof,* a spectacular giant ceiling led by Prudden with one point of aid, Kraus seconding, in 1950—solid 5.7 free moves both below and above the roof, which was finally freed nine years later to make the climb a classic 5.8+
- *Gaston,* a very hard 5.7—some say a very solid 5.8—led by Prestrud with Lucien Warner as second in 1952
- *V-3,* a tricky 5.7, a collaboration of Kraus, Prudden, and Prestrud in 1954
- *Dry Martini* (originally *Drei Martini,* an indication of the condition of the first ascent party), moderate enough except for one desperate 5.7 move led by Kraus, with Warner and Prudden in uproarious attendance, in 1955.

The martini-loaded first ascent of the last-named climb, along with the complex marital patterns of some of the principals, suggested earlier, hint at the limited historical vision of some of the sketches of the Gunks scene which maintain that, prior to the coming of the Vulgarians in the late 1950s (chapter 13), rock climbing "had hitherto been as chaste and proper as lawn tennis" (to quote one 1983 article). Not so in Kraus's circle!

Meanwhile, back within the New York AMC system, the majority of climbers happily climbed away on the easier routes and enjoyed the sociability of Schlueter's on Saturday nights. Most of the climbing was at the 5.2 to 5.4 level. When a party headed for *Yellow Ridge* or *High Exposure*, it was a major undertaking and sometimes novice climbers would tag along to watch in awe from below.

In Boston the dominant group during the 1950s had many of the same qualities as that of the Gunks, except for the lack of a single colossus of Kraus's unique prestige.

In the first postwar decade, leadership within the Boston AMC rock climbers was gradually passed along from such prewar holdovers as Walter Howe, Irvin Davis, and Hec Towle to a new generation of leaders like John Perry, Bert Hirtle, Lyle Richardson, and the blithe spirit of the crowd, Jack Taylor.

This group evolved its own "conservative tradition" emphasizing that leaders should at all times thoroughly protect themselves and their followers with frequently placed pitons; that solo climbing was strictly forbidden; that beginners should undergo a lengthy apprenticeship of top-roped climbs on the short crags with which Boston is so richly endowed; that special invitations were required to advance to the larger cliffs of, first, Joe English and later, if approved, Whitehorse and Cathedral in New Hampshire; and that Cannon cliff was too rotten and dangerous for prudent climbers to risk, with the occasional exception of the *Whitney-Gilman* route. (In 1950 spontaneous rockfall off the Black Dike section of Cannon thundered down on an AMC party at the base of the cliff, breaking the leg of Gerry Barnes. This incident invested Cannon with an evil reputation. It was rarely climbed by the AMC thereafter until 1960. During a difficult rescue that year, Jack Taylor climbed a variation of the *Old Cannon* route of 1928 and came back bubbling with enthusiasm for the quality of the climbing. After that the bolder spirits in the AMC crowd resumed climbing on Cannon.) Until the 1970s Boston climbers seldom went to the Shawangunks.

"The emphasis in training," recalled one Boston leader of that era, "was on climbing well, not how hard you could." To climbers of the 1970s and 1980s the phrase "climbing well" would mean doing increasingly difficult climbs. Not so to those of the 1950s and 1960s. To them it meant climbing with good technique and proper concern for the safety of the party. The result of this philosophy was a friendly spirit of cooperation and camaraderie rather than competition among the climbers, but unquestionably it also dampened the climbing standards and discouraged the spirit of initiative and risk taking on rock.

Inevitably, however, individuals came up through the system who could not repress a streak of boldness and adventure. Even this group could not escape the dominant conservatism of the times and did not push standards beyond the 5.7 level. Nevertheless, they did explore their own new routes and did some adventurous pioneering on previously unexplored (or at least long neglected) crags, some of which remained rarely visited even after the sport became so much more popular in the 1970s and 1980s—cliffs like those on Mount Garfield, Mount Lowell, Devil's Slide, other White Mountains

J. B. Gardner. Connecticut's leading climber of the early postwar years, shown here on a route at the Sleeping Giant. Note footgear: specialized climbing boots lay far in the future.

obscuranti, and Maine's Katahdin and Tumbledown Mountain. The chief new faces in this group were Robert Kruszyna, John Post, Charles Fay, and Earle Whipple, with a crucial role being played by the ever effervescent Jack Taylor, who was a long-established "conservative tradition" leader when the new faces began to emerge but who encouraged and joined in on their bolder ventures.

Still, Boston climbing remained fundamentally conservative throughout the 1950s. The system was not quite so tightly controlled as New York's, in that no special certification was required to lead individual routes, merely a general certification of competence to lead in general. Nevertheless, progress was slow for aspiring climbers who were effectively forbidden to go up to the north country climbing areas until their long apprenticeship on Boston area crags was faithfully completed.

Connecticut climbers sailed through the conservative tradition era with far less formal apparatus or stifling spirit. The reason is largely attributable to the principal Connecticut climber of the times, J. B. Gardner. A graduate of MIT's climbing program in the late 1940s, Gardner moved to Connecticut and soon became the most proficient and prominent climber on the small crags of that state, and a well-known figure at the Gunks, New Hampshire, and Katahdin as well. Gardner was technically in a class with Kraus and the best Boston climbers but had no taste for regimenting and certifying less gifted Connecticut climbers. Under his leadership a circle of adventurous leaders developed and explored new routes throughout their own state as well as farther afield. It was in Connecticut during the 1940s, under Gardner, that a very young Jack Taylor learned to climb, before he moved to Boston to play the pivotal role there described above and in chapter 13. Later came Harold May, John Woodworth, Bill Schmidt, and Whit Stueck. During the late 1950s the rising stars were John Reppy and Ron Bell. Almost more than any other prominent postwar climber, Gardner disdained the ego-boosting tradition of naming and recording first ascents. On the contrary, he fostered a spirit within his circle of deliberately keeping quiet about where and what they climbed, with the idea of preserving for later climbers the thrill of exploration that they enjoyed. As a result, history cannot record specific new routes by this group, but enough is known of their prowess to report that they were climbing at a technical standard roughly equivalent to that of the best New York and Boston-based leaders but with neither the formal system nor the accompanying acrimony that characterized those areas.

Several northeastern colleges indulged in rock climbing during the 1950s, but they too hewed to a suitably conservative line.

Yale climbers carried on a parallel but sometimes overlapping activity vis-à-vis the Connecticut AMC group. These Yalies of the early postwar years exhaustively explored the Sleeping Giant cliffs, until a climbing death there in 1953 led to official closure of the cliffs to climbers. After that the sons of Eli turned attention to the more distant Connecticut crags. At first Ragged Mountain, all of twenty miles from New Haven, seemed like "the new Siberia" to the disgruntled collegians, who regarded it as an inferior locale to their now-forbidden favorite, the Giant, also known as Mount Carmel. Penned one Biblically inspired Yale climber in 1955: "Now abideth Sanford, Waterville, and Ragged and the greatest of these . . . is still less than Carmel." Little did they realize that in the early 1960s Yale climbers would transform Ragged into a major climbing area.

Another college where rock climbing flourished during the 1950s was Dartmouth. The Dartmouth Mountaineering Club enjoyed more official encouragement than most college groups, a rock climbing class was offered for credit as early as the late 1940s, and Bartlett Tower was almost daily festooned with aspiring campus climbers. A wealth of nearby cliffs was found and mined, most of them unknown to other climbers; they were "Dartmouth preserves." Dartmouth climbing always had more of an all-around mountaineering emphasis, as compared with the specialization in short, hard rock climbs that was catching on elsewhere. As a result, many of the outstanding Dartmouth climbers of this era moved on to the high mountains for their later careers and did not figure prominently in the Northeast. Barry Corbet, a rising star of the 1950s and a member of the 1963 American Everest expedition, spoke for the Dartmouth outlook when he lamented:

> It must soon become evident that climbing during the school year is only a means, for the end cannot be found here. The mountaineer needs mountains, else his sport degrades into specialized rock climbing. At this point we like to say "Go West, young man," for here is found the true satisfaction of mountaineering. And there only can a mountaineer be born.

The Harvard Mountaineering Club oscillated in emphasis between a Hanoverian accent on all-around mountaineering and MIT-style focus on pure rock, depending on who were the dominant undergraduates. In the former category, Harvard continued to breed some of America's top expeditionary mountaineers, from Jim Maxwell in the 1940s to Boyd Everett in the 1950s. Specialists in short, hard rock routes emerged from the same club, however, one of whom, Kevin Bein, became a major presence in northeastern rock climbing for twenty years. Somewhere in between—highly competent rock climbers who took their skills to the high mountains—were David Roberts, Hank Abrams, and numerous others from Harvard.

Pure northeastern rock climbing found its most compatible academic home at MIT. Intrigued with the technical problems, both of the rock itself and of the protective mechanisms (rope, pitons, carabiners, belaying systems), the budding engineers of MITOC haunted the Quincy Quarries midweek and the Gunks on weekends, generating a steady flow of good climbers plus a handful even better who climbed at the forefront of the day's standard. In the early 1950s Dave Bernays not only climbed but put in routes as hard as anyone, as did Ray D'Arcy in the middle and late 1950s and Willy Crowther in the late 1950s and early 1960s. MITOC also produced some wild and woolly "characters," among whom the most notorious was Ritner Walling, who combined in one raucous personality the eclectic skills of a first-class rock climber, resourceful winter climber, daredevil downhill skier, cool river-runner, formidable beer-swiller, and madcap pilot whose aerial exploits included flying through the narrow "Gunsight Notch" in the Tetons and buzzing the shelters in Tuckerman Ravine to the consternation of campers present and the outrage of the Appalachian Mountain Club and the White Mountain National Forest.

Rensselaer Polytechnic Institute (RPI) was another technical school that bred a batallion of able rock climbers. During the late 1940s RPI climbers began to frequent cliffs near their Albany-Troy-Schenectady home base. Fritz Wiessner took an interest in encouraging them and introduced them to the Shawangunks, where they gradually became a regular part of the scene. In January 1950 the Rensselaer Mountaineering Club was formally organized.

MITOC provided leadership for a broader group of collegian climbers under the umbrella organization of the Intercollegiate Outing Clubs of America (IOCA). The non-Ivy League colleges, many of whom bred too few climbers to maintain their own mountaineering clubs, could band together under IOCA and thereby participate in a vigorous climbing program. Those most involved included RPI and Syracuse, but MITOC was always dominant. Throughout the late 1950s and all of the 1960s, Gardner Perry III ("GP-3" they called him) was the atlas of the whole, organizing weekends, setting up beginner training programs, and personally driving the MITOC hearse, loaded with climbers and gear, to and from climbing areas from the Shawangunks to Katahdin. IOCA climbing gave full opportunity to college women as well as men, unlike the men's colleges heretofore mentioned. In the 1960s, as we shall see, some superb climbers emerged from the IOCA group and contributed to the rapid advance in technical standards, but for most of the 1950s and 1960s alike, for the great majority of IOCA climbers, the conservative tradition remained ascendant. The climbing pace was relaxed, noncompetitive, and moderate in difficulty.

Elsewhere throughout the region, rock climbing carried on with a low profile, its spirit dominated by the conservative mood of the times, its technical accomplishments limited accordingly, and its participation considerably smaller than at the Gunks, Boston, and Connecticut. In the Adirondacks, for example, no local circle of active climbers developed during the 1950s, though Jim Goodwin continued his occasional climbs, emphasizing a tone of wilderness exploration rather than technical gymnastics.

Change lurked beneath the surface, however. The impulse toward adventure and innovation continually pressed against the confines of the 1950s spirit. At the Shawangunks during that decade, in Boston after 1960, and elsewhere throughout the region during the 1960s, new forces broke out. The day of the conservative tradition came to a close. After that, things would never be the same. ■

Reference Note

No published accounts of postwar northeastern rock climbing accurately reflect the complex, interesting, and often controversial character of the pre-1960 years. This history is partially revealed (and partially obscured?) by records of various AMC rock climbing groups, IOCA's rock climbing wing, IOCAlum newsletters, records of individual college outing clubs, the Vulgarians' accounts in the form of historical sections in the various Shawangunks guidebooks, and conversations and correspondence with dozens of climbers who lived through the period. In our detailed source references at Dartmouth, the authors mention sixty-two different individuals who were helpful to us in recalling the era.

12: The Conservative Tradition—
Ice: The 1950s and 1960s

ROPED ICE CLIMBING went through a long twilight during the 1940s and 1950s and 1960s. This was not just an extension of the conservative tradition to the winter season. Most summertime rock climbers disdained ice climbing as outrageously unpleasant, perhaps to be endured only as training for dealing with the big mountains, but surely no fun. For the tiny bands who undertook the rigors of cutting steps up the slippery slopes before 1970, a conspicuous lack of progress in technical standards was noteworthy between 1940 and 1969.

Mount Washington's Huntington Ravine continued to be the sole significant locale. For the ice climbers of those years, there were scattered local haunts, but only one premier location—"the Ravine"—and its six classic gullies saw a small but steady stream of traffic. Pinnacle Gully was the tough-

Dave Bernays. A bold and innovative winter climber of the early postwar years was Dave Bernays, who first shone as a precocious high school student in the Adirondacks and later at MIT.

ANDREW GRISCOM

est route in the Northeast, maybe the whole country. Way back in second place in popularity was the Willey Slide in Crawford Notch, considered much easier and therefore suitable for training beginners.

Isolated coteries formed the postwar ice climbing community, each with its inner core of experienced leaders and outer circle of occasional participants, each group with its favorite local ice floes and its annual pilgrimages to Huntington Ravine. From Boston came at least four distinct clusters: Harvard's aspiring mountaineers who sharpened their skills for distant ranges by practicing on Mount Washington; MIT climbers, from the brilliant and innovative David Bernays in the early 1950s through a line of gifted successors—Ritner Walling, Leif Norman-Patterson, and Henry Kendall; mainstream AMC rock climbers; and several fringe AMC climbers, some of whom were especially bold winter mountaineers for that conservative era: John Griffin, Bob Hall, Geoff Wood, John Porter, David Isles. Connecticut climbers knew the mysteries of dark, twisting, hemlock-shaded Race Brook in the Taconic Range. Here—and to Huntington—came a small but able succession of ice men led by Harold May, Whit Stueck, John Woodworth, and Ron Bell. New York City ice climbing revolved around Boyd Everett, a quiet, cerebral investment analyst who departed Wall Street for a month each summer to lead a series of stunningly successful expeditions to the largest mountains on the continent, establishing two new routes on Mount McKinley, one on Logan, and one on Saint Elias. New Yorkers had their nearby areas that occasionally froze up sufficiently, like the floes in the Catskills' Deep Notch. But Everett and his circle regarded the total alpine experience of Huntington Ravine as valuable training, so they developed a tolerance for long-distance driving ordeals on two-day weekends that made the actual climbing seem mild. Among the more active New York Appies who joined Everett on both his summer expeditions and winter weekend epics were Ted Church, Art Fitch, Mike Hyjek, Chuck Loucks, and Ed Nester. The Adirondacks had its own small circle of postwar ice climbers, starting with Dave Bernays before he went off to MIT, Donald Le Beau, Bud Smith, and a trickle of others down through the 1960s. They went largely to the Colden Dike in Avalanche Pass, the "Big Slab" at Chapel Pond (adjacent to the summertime rock route, *Bob's Knob*), and the roadside ice in Cascade Pass. To picturesque Smugglers Notch came a small cadre from Burlington, Vermont, led first by David Cass and Philip Koch, cousins, and gradually widening during the 1960s to include Chuck Bond, Bob Olsen, Chet Callahan, and Keith Thibault. Dartmouth had its hidden ice in the hills near Hanover and no shortage of outstanding mountaineers practicing there and in Huntington Ravine. In the 1960s two of these, Dennis Eberyl and David Seidman, went on to pull off some major first ascents on Alaskan peaks. Every once in a while a party from one of these various coteries would make the long trip north and climb Katahdin's snow-filled Chimney, thereby acquiring great prestige in winter climbing circles.

Ice climbing in the step-chopping era was not without its perverse attractions. The small corps of devoted initiates developed a special pride in the toughness of their chosen punishment. It was unquestionably some sort of accomplishment to hang in there for hours, wind and snow blowing mercilessly, bodies half frozen from cold and the enforced inactivity of belaying a leader chopping upwards of fifty steps and handholds per pitch. Each gully in Huntington was considered a full day's climb. Bivouac gear was taken—and sometimes used. The satisfaction in enduring and sur-

HENRY W. KENDALL

Hugo Stadtmuller. Shown here on his first winter ascent of Cathedral's Standard *route, Hugo Stadtmuller brought a bolder vision to New England winter climbing in the 1960s.*

Stadtmuller on Odell's. This picture classically portrays the ice climbing scene preceding the revolution in techniques of 1969. Hugo Stadtmuller leads, a group of his friends belay and watch from below.

Bob Proudman. Rugged woodsman from AMC's White Mountains' Trail Crew, Bob Proudman also pioneered in early winter ascents and "alpine adventures."

mounting these arduous conditions made up for the lack of stimulating technical difficulty. Then too, there was (and is) a special beauty and wildness to the ice-bound heights of Huntington Ravine, Smugglers Notch, and Avalanche Pass; the true secrets of such places seemed accessible only to the ice climbers.

To withstand the conditions of their work, they dressed warmly, if not stylishly. Net underwear was often supplemented by a full union suit of wool. Heavy wool shirts, pants, and socks were mandatory. Over these went windbreaker and the obligatory baggy windpants (often olive drab Army surplus). On long belays a down parka was often donned. Keeping feet warm was a trial: the superwarm but clumsy rubber Mickey Mouse boots were common ice climbing footgear, though many expedition aspirants wore double or triple leather boots, while some confirmed New Englanders climbed in winterized Limmers.

With relatively little communication between these groups or even awareness of each other's existence, these proud squads of hard men (and *very* few women in those days) carried the banner of ice climbing all through the long Dark Ages of the sport until the revolution in equipment, technique, and standards that suddenly burst at the end of the 1960s.

The ice revolution of 1969 seemed to explode out of nowhere, but in truth a growing number of harbingers of change were prowling around the fringes of the scene during the 1960s and even back in the 1950s. Bernays climbed New Hampshire's Whitehorse Ledge, and in the Adirondacks Wallface, Rainbow Falls on Gothics, and routes near Cascade Lake that were all far ahead of their time. In the early 1960s alpine veteran Hugo Stadtmuller moved to New England and brought a bolder vision to winter climbing. With MIT's Henry Kendall and the AMC's John Griffin, he began doing serious mixed routes, the most notable being a 1964 ascent of Cathedral Ledge via the iced-up *Standard*. Kendall and Stadtmuller also did a winter ascent of Cannon's *Whitney-Gilman* in 1964, though this was much more rock than ice. In 1965 a soldier named Dugal Thomas made a solo ascent of the North Face of Gothics, a remarkably daring adventure. In the late 1960s several climbers began to anticipate the future with visionary assaults on Cannon's huge ice-encrusted routes. The driving force was a short, peppery, lion-hearted cleric from Uruguay studying at Cornell named Jorge Urioste. Others included AMC's Bob Hall, Paul Doyle, Joe Boden; Cornell's Rich Mathies; and AMC north country employees like Bob Proudman and Mark Lawrence of the AMC Trail Crew and the Damp brothers of the AMC hut crews. Urioste pioneered in first winter ascents of *Cannonade* and *Old Cannon*, the latter a four-day siege under extreme conditions. Proudman and Lawrence pulled a major plum with a winter ascent of the long and exposed *Sam's Swan Song*. In 1969, over in Smugglers Notch, Dave Cass and Phil Koch climbed a couple of routes that were a step above the prevailing standard there.

These prerevolution climbs were not difficult by post-1969 standards, but in bad conditions they could be serious enough. In fact, risk and potential tragedy always stalked the sport, reaching out to snuff out even its most able protagonists. Pinnacle Gully claimed the lives of Harvard's Craig Merrihue and Dan Doody in 1964 and the brilliant Hugo Stadtmuller and John Griffin in 1965. In 1969 Boyd Everett led an expedition to the Himalayan giant Dhaulagiri, taking Dave Seidman in the party. There, seven thousand miles from Huntington Ravine and on the eve of exciting changes in their sport, Everett and Seidman were buried in a monstrous ice avalanche. Years of conservative tradition they might have been, but "the sterner and more primitive discipline" of ice exacted its cruel toll. ∎

Reference Note

See note for chapter 11.

13: Young Turks, Old Bootleggers, Vulgarians, and a Boston Tea Party

THE CONSERVATIVE TRADITION had two distinct aspects: a set of rules governing who could climb what and where, and a restraint on the level of difficulty of what anyone climbed. The former was the only conscious objective of the conservatives. The latter was merely a consequence that flowed from the spirit in which the former was applied. That is, no one specifically said thou shalt not climb harder than 5.7. But the temper of the times frowned on spectacular exploits or risk taking, so as a practical matter no one wanted to try harder than 5.7. Not until the formal rules were upset did standards of difficulty rise.

The overthrow of the old order occurred first at the Shawangunks. The restrictive safety program adopted by the AMC, at Hans Kraus's repeated prodding, began to meet mounting resistance even in the early 1950s from at least three distinct sources:

1. A growing volume of young college climbers, most of them loosely affiliated under the IOCA umbrella. The most active college climbing club at the Shawangunks was MITOC, led by a succession of strong personalities and excellent climbers—Bernays, D'Arcy, Walling, Crowther, and the IOCA master of ceremonies, Gardner Perry III. These and other college climbers largely disregarded the AMC's program. "This [AMC Safety] Code," wrote the Yale Mountaineering Club president, Earl Mosberg, "has all the force of the recent loyalty oaths; anyone can sign it with a smile."

2. Several aggressive and eager young leaders within the AMC itself, who found the qualifications system excessively restrictive. Among the most active New York Appie climbers were Ted Church, Krist Raubenheimer, and Bob Larsen—all excellent climbers and good club members but increasingly frustrated by attempts to tell them what they should or shouldn't lead. Their cause was championed by the prestigious leader of the Connecticut AMC rock climbers, J. B. Gardner, who counseled his New York colleagues:

> Who is going to give a darn what you or I or whoever else makes codes thinks about a certain person's climbing

Lester Germer. World War I aviator, distinguished physicist—and, late in life, rene-gade rock climber who broke all the rules and exasperated the Establishment of the conservative tradition, Lester Germer walked his own way for a quarter century of northeastern climbing.

credits? If Joe Blow climbs the "slippery eel" in a rainstorm, that proves he is good. Nuts to us!

3. A small number of fringe AMC members who declined to abide by the system and became known as "bootleggers." Kraus's circle of followers (Prestrud, Prudden, et al.) were the most prominent of these.

Another bootlegger of special interest and importance was the inimitable, indomitable, and (to the exasperated AMC Committee) incurable Lester Germer. A renowned World War I fighter pilot, Germer had gone on to a distinguished career in physics that very nearly won *him* a Nobel Prize; Germer and a colleague, Clinton J. Davisson, made discoveries important to the development of the electron microscope, and Davisson was awarded the 1937 Nobel Prize in physics. (One Nobel winner (Shockley) and one near miss (Germer) among the small circle of New York climbers—plus a Nobel later awarded to Henry Kendall, who was active at this time (1950s) in New Hampshire climbing—strikingly attest the appeal of the postwar phase of the sport to those with scientific bent, as mentioned earlier.) Dr. Germer had settled down to a professional career at Bell Labs in northern New Jersey and, in 1945 at the age of forty-nine, launched a side interest in rock climbing. By the early 1950s, Germer was climbing widely all over the Northeast, but with a relaxed, casual style that never sat well with the safety-conscious New York Appies. He was repeatedly turned down for Unlimited Leader by the Qualifications Committee—once with the comment: "Not passed. Likes people too much and is too enthusiastic"—but continued to show up at the Gunks and climb what he pleased with whoever was willing to join him.

In the first half of the 1950s, the college climbers, the AMC's own Young Turks, and old Lester found themselves in increasing conflict with the Appies' safety system, and the cliffs were more and more plagued with dissension. The old Appie leaders chided both their own members and the college youths whenever they thought they observed unsafe practices. The rebels chafed under such constraints.

Finally in 1955 Norton Smithe became chairman of the Rock Climbing Committee. Although a part of the system, Smithe had always been something of an adventurous leader himself. As Chairman, Smithe negotiated with consummate diplomacy a truce between the old guard and the Young Turks. A conciliatory Qualifications Committee was persuaded to bestow Unlimited Leadership status on Ted Church, Krist Raubenheimer, and Bob Larsen. By 1957 all three were actually members of the Rock Climbing Committee and, on Larsen's motion, the committee voted what it never would have considered five years earlier: "that Club leaders who have the ability to lead hard climbs be encouraged to do so at every opportunity and also be encouraged to take some of the better Club members up these climbs."

After this change, the AMC ceased to harass the college climbers. Not even Smithe's diplomacy, however, could win over the old guard to accept the perpetual renegade. "Lester Germer," mused one Appie leader, "is past reforming." Undaunted, this genial gentleman continued to climb, gradually over the years becoming a fixture at the Gunks, perhaps its most generally recognized and best-loved face—"a one-man climbing school," it was later said. Long after old guard and Young Turk alike had largely retired from the scene, old Lester continued to climb at his beloved Gunks, continued to horrify those who had any view to proper safety procedures, and continued to have an unblemished accident-free record (he had never taken even a leader fall) for twenty-six years until he died of an instantaneous

Vulgarian protest. More raucous and more vivid than Lester Germer, the Vulgarians raised the banner of revolt against the conservative tradition—and in the process did some superb climbing. In this widely circulated photograph, which became almost a symbol of Vulgarian protest, a prominent Vulgarian ascends Shockley's Ceiling *in an outfit not approved by the conservative tradition.*

FROM *CLIMBING IN NORTH AMERICA* BY CHRIS JONES

heart attack at the cliffs, leading beginners on a 5.5 one week short of his seventy-fifth birthday.

Smithe's smoothly negotiated peace lasted only a couple of years. By the mid-1950s the Gunks scene had become much more crowded and fluid than in the days when the AMC's system had been designed. The college climbers were now as numerous as the AMC, loosely organized under their own IOCA "ARC" (Advanced Rock Climbers) system, casually presided over by MITOC's Gardner Perry. Beyond this competing "system," a growing number of wholly unaffiliated climbers were there every weekend. By 1956 a young AMC climber named Art Gran, who had come up through the ranks, finally grew impatient with the safety procedures and restrictions and broke with the club. In 1957 Gran began to associate himself with a small band of freewheeling, untrained, but immensely talented young climbers from the City College of New York. As the CCNY group developed confidence in their climbing prowess, they also grew more and more openly contemptuous of and eventually outright hostile toward the AMC. Gradually their affiliation with CCNY waned, new faces were added, their collective personality became more vivid, and they proclaimed themselves the "Vulgarians," in raucous defiance of the more polished manners and reverent climbing tradition of the AMC.

The Vulgarians worked hard at becoming one of the more colorful circles that ever whirled through the northeastern climbing orbit. Brash, boisterous, and ever eager to shock, they exalted bad manners to the level of an art form. They held wild parties below or above or even on the cliffs; climbed nude; staged nighttime auto joy rides on the Smileys' carriage roads plus a "Vulgarian Grand Prix" around the public highways that circumnavigated the Trapps; invaded Appie campgrounds with their all-night orgies; sometimes got carried away and did damage to Smiley property, overturned an Appie car, or urinated off the roof on Appies as they emerged from a local restaurant. They also did superb climbing.

The cast of leading Vulgarians was a kaleidoscope of constant change, and it is difficult to single out who the leading figures were. Claude Suhl, Roman Sadowy, Al DeMaria, and Bill Goldner were certainly among the abler climbers, as well as the most ill-mannered ruffians. Although at first an all-male cast, some females became accepted in their circle, competent as climbers and reasonably vulgar as well; among these were Elaine Mathews, Gerd Thuestad, and Muriel Mayo. One versatile young woman managed to marry, in swift succession, one Appie, one Vulgarian, and Bonnie Prudden's discarded mate. Probably the most gifted as a climber and most ingeniously vulgar as a Vulgarian was the square-built, strong and loud Rabelaisian figure of Dave Craft. A unique contribution came from the off-color satirical pen of Joe Kelsey, who produced a mock "Accidents in Shawangunk Mountaineering" (a takeoff on the official "Accidents in North American Mountaineering"); a supplement to Art Gran's guidebook, with outrageous, hilarious, and purely fictitious route descriptions; and ultimately several issues of an underground magazine, the *Vulgarian Digest*. Art Gran maintained an uneasy relationship with the group: though he was at first something of a mentor and climbing leader, he became increasingly the target of jibes rather than himself an instigator.

Until the Vulgarian era the various climbing circles at the Gunks were benignly neglected by the owners of the land, the Smiley family. As the stresses grew harder to ignore, first with the coming of more college climbers and then with the antics of the Vulgarians, the Smileys finally grew concerned that this increasingly effervescent weekend activity was associated with a sport that seemed potentially dangerous and could lead to accidents or death on Smiley property. In 1959 that long-feared event occurred: a Yale climber took a long leader fall on *High Corner* and was fatally injured. (Ironically the youth was wearing a hard hat, the symbol of safe climbing to so many conservatives of that time and later.)

Even before this tragedy the Smileys had begun to move. Representatives of the family approached the climbers they found most approachable—the AMC, not the Vulgarians—and proposed the introduction of restrictions on the numbers of climbers, to be effected by a permit for climbing on Smiley land. To obtain a permit, the Smileys innocently suggested (ignorant of the AMC's unsatisfactory experience of just a few years earlier), each climber should be asked to sign a Safety Code.

The old issue of a Safety Code brought out all the wrong instincts on both sides. The AMC gleefully dusted off their old drafts and came forward with just the document which the Smileys had suggested. On September 1, 1959, a formal permit system went into effect, along with a new "Mohonk Safety Code." But if such procedures had been offensive to the mild and respectable dissenters of the early 1950s, their reception among the Vulgarians was scarcely likely to be warm. The system never got off the ground. There were a couple of dissension-filled years again, during which efforts were made to require the new Code's acceptance. Ex-rebels Ted Church and Krist Raubenheimer now found themselves unexpectedly leading the conservatives—but not Bob Larsen, who went over to the Vulgarians. The permit system for climbing on Smiley land was established, but it became largely a formality and did not restrain either numbers or behavior.

Time more than diplomacy healed these wounds. By the early 1960s, the AMC effectively abandoned its ambitions of governing the mores of the Shawangunks. As the more controversial Appie leaders climbed less, new faces took over leadership of the group, now shrivelled in importance to a relatively small if still visible portion of the Gunks' climbing population. These new club leaders—Mike Hyjek, Chuck Loucks, Arthur Fitch— were more interested in climbing than in controversy. The Vulgarians also mellowed. As the bad little boys matured, they became possibly less interesting, certainly less prominent at the cliffs. Some faded from the scene entirely. Others settled in the area and deteriorated into respectability. One veteran of the old wild parties was elected mayor of a nearby town; others became major property owners in the area; and that once dread marauder of the

Vulgarian night, Dave Craft, became maitre d' of a local restaurant, more often seen bird watching than climbing.

By this time a new generation of climbers of outstanding ability had usurped the Uberfall and largely ignored the old issues. The college climbers were now very active, and many new climbers were unaffiliated with any organized group, whether of "conservative tradition" or radical. Though they neither followed the 1950s safety procedures nor ostentatiously displayed bad manners, they were in fact obviously climbing with reasonable safety, happy enjoyment, and impressive skill. The old issues were never resolved; they simply faded away.

The Appie-Vulgarian feud was a stage in the evolution of Shawangunk climbing, but it has received vastly more attention than it deserved. The Vulgarians have received proper credit for their riotous vulgarity; more credit than they deserve for overthrowing the Establishment (the conservative tradition was merely making one last and clearly foredoomed stand, the far more difficult revolution having been accomplished already by the Appie Young Turks, the college climbers, and Lester Germer); and not nearly enough credit for their fine climbing, which will be described in the next chapter.

The social history of the breakup of the conservative tradition was mirrored in Boston, but in a different form and considerably later. The old system was accepted throughout the 1950s, perhaps because its constraints had never been as tight in Boston as they had in New York.

In 1960, however, in response to mounting safety concerns, the Appalachian Mountain Club—this time the "mother church" at club headquarters on Boston's Beacon Hill, not just the New York Chapter's Rock Climbing Committee—launched an ambitiously conceived program for ensuring safety through the formal certification of leaders in all phases of mountaineering. A blue-ribbon Mountain Leadership Safety Committee was established. Many of the leading Boston-based climbers of the time were influential on this committee. Robert and Miriam Underhill were persuaded to lend their names and immense prestige to the committee's work. The chairman was the strong and experienced Harvard mountaineer William Lowell Putnam III. Veteran of the first full ascent of Damnation Gully (chapter 6) in 1943 and a hero of wartime exploits in Italy with the Tenth Mountain Division, Putnam was a commanding personality and resourceful mountaineer with a long list of first ascents in the Canadian Rockies. Though not previously active in the AMC climbing circle, Putnam was not a man to hold back when he and others thought strong action was

HENRY BARBER

Appies of the 1960s. This group of AMC climbers shows the equipment, clothing, and personal style of their era, remote from today's styles and technical advances in equipment.

needed. The Mountain Leadership Safety Committee soon developed an elaborate grading system for certification of leaders in rock climbing, winter climbing, general hiking, and all-around mountaineering. Specified skills were listed as requisites for certification at each level of leadership. Here was embodied all the safety consciousness and passion for system and rules of the conservative tradition. With characteristic energy and force, Putnam moved to implement the new system.

An explosion lit up the sky over Beacon Hill. The most active rock climbers in the club at the time included some personalities almost as strong-willed and incandescent as Putnam, notably Robert Kruszyna, John Post, and Charles Fay. They heatedly objected to Putnam's Committee telling them who was qualified to do what climbing. In the ardor of their dudgeon, they recalled the proud tradition of Massachusetts' Sons of Liberty. In an explosion of tempers, bitterly denouncing the "regimentation inherent in any such regulatory programs," Kruszyna led a mass exodus of most of the club's best rock climbers completely out of the club. The good-humored Jack Taylor sought to moderate the dispute without success. Letters and telephone calls flew through the surcharged air around Beacon Hill and interminable meetings sought to meld the objectives of both groups, until the weary Taylor lamented:

> I have never heard so many complaints nor spent so much time talking about a subject as I have about this one. . . . I find little enough time now to climb.

The result was that Boston AMC rock climbers were left in a relatively leaderless state for a couple of years, while the Kruszyna crowd, now operating independently, continued to climb at a very active and competent standard.

Gradually a new generation of AMC-bred leaders emerged, led by Wayne Kellner, William Phillips, and others. The new faces retained much of the stringent system under which they were introduced to the sport, though with a milder and friendlier spirit than had prevailed before. Boston AMC rock climbing regained the 5.7 plateau on which the Kruszyna-Taylor generation had operated before the uprising of 1960. Nevertheless, the system continued to function as a restraining force on Boston-based rock climbing until the late 1960s.

The conservative tradition in Boston eventually faded in much the same way as it had earlier at the Shawangunks. The same liberalizing forces were at work around the Quincy Quarries and Joe English as at the Uberfall. Hordes of new climbers entered the sport—college youths, people who had learned to climb elsewhere, and other unaffiliated "independents"—who were blissfully unaware of the old issues and who largely ignored the system. They climbed with evident pleasure and reasonable safety, without the encumbrances of excessive system. Bolder climbers within the AMC itself began to break through to higher standards, displaying such control and skill in the process that application of the old rules seemed silly.

The Mountain Leadership Safety Committee's elaborate system of certification continued to enjoy some homage within the club. One product of the Committee was a week-long "Mountain Leadership Workshop" designed to train hiking leaders in safe summer trips in the Presidential Range and comparable terrain. This workshop was aimed primarily at leaders of summer camps and others who brought large groups of inexperienced hikers into the White Mountains. Almost alone of the Putnam Committee's once far-flung apparatus, this workshop continued to function effectively into the late twentieth century. The rest of the safety and certification system, however, failed to survive a much-publicized accident in Wyoming's

Teton Range, in which tragedy struck a visiting AMC party ineptly led by a fully certified leader. That incident snuffed out whatever flickering credibility the system had retained among technical climbers. After that, in New England as in the Gunks, the conservative tradition gradually wasted away rather than being overturned in any one cataclysm.

As the formal system of regimentation withered, the horizons opened up in rock climbing. Again things happened first at the Shawangunks, later elsewhere. We turn in the next few chapters to a period of creative intensity during which the full implications of nylon rope and improved pitons were realized at last and the spirit of the conservative tradition, as well as its apparatus, was swept away in a burst of magnificent climbing. ■

Reference Note
See note for chapter 11.

Chasing Ghosts on the Armadillo

THE ARMADILLO IS a gigantic, fluted triangular buttress incongruously fastened to the very top of the 2,300-foot wall above Chimney Pond. The *base* of this feature is about level with the *top* of the second highest peak in Maine, Katahdin's lofty neighbor, Hamlin. From there, at 4,700 feet, the Armadillo's triangular front soars upward 300 vertical feet, ending in an airy apex from which a knife-edge arête (much more truly "knife-edge" than the nearby ridge over which the hiker's trail of that name promenades) leads another 200 feet to the summit plateau. Below the triangle, the mountainside sweeps down another 1,800 feet to Chimney Pond, that jewel of a mountain tarn nestled in the great glacial basin directly beneath the summit of Katahdin.

One-third of the way up, the Armadillo triangle is crossed by a horizontal grassy ledge about 10 feet wide. Perched precariously on this ledge, a slender detached fin of rock leans against the face in a second, smaller triangle-within-a-triangle that rises another 100 feet. From the top of this fin—a most exposed place to stand—a jam crack leads straight up the last 100 feet to the apex of the main Armadillo triangle.

All of this is set square in the middle of the vast amphitheater known as Katahdin's South Basin. The spires of Pamola and Chimney peaks on the east, Baxter and South peaks on the southwest, and the Cathedrals on the north rim the towering walls of this magnificent arena.

The Armadillo was first climbed in 1935, a very early year for such exposed and bold climbing. A party of fifteen Appalachian Mountain Club rock climbers from Boston and New York spent a week at Chimney Pond. One day, Herbert C. (Hec) Towle led a group of five on the first ascent. Although the team looked at the direct route up the fin and jam crack, they decided not to attempt it and worked out a line going farther to the right. Two days later a mass assault force of twelve climbers repeated the route, with Roger Wolcott in the lead and four women achieving the first female ascents. The difficulty of their route in modern jargon was about 5.5—modest by today's standards but quite respectable at the time.

"First time man was ever here!" This caption was proudly penned in Walter Howe's album of snapshots under this photo, following the first ascent of this route on the Armadillo at Katahdin.

WALTER HOWE COLLECTION

In 1954 as many as three new routes were put up the buttress. Two were inaugurated on the same day, August 26. One party, led by Bob Kruszyna, worked out a line that included a long, frightfully exposed traverse on the crux pitch. An even more difficult if not quite so airy route was climbed by John Reppy, John Shagrue, and Bert Arsego. Both of these climbs were about 5.6 in difficulty.

Today's standard route—straight up the detached flake and 5.7 crack above it—was pioneered in the early 1950s. Who done it? The heroes of this stunning achievement remain shrouded in mystery. In a 1983 article in *Summit*, Katahdin ranger Ben Townsend guessed that it was not climbed until 1972. However, our contacts turned up a definite ascent in 1951—see chapter 20. But was it the first? Whoever was first performed at the forefront of

American technical standards in the early 1950s. It was not until the end of that decade that anyone in New England climbed harder.

But now to our own story—mere mortals chasing ghosts of earlier giants up cracks and chimneys on the Northeast's most spectacular rock wall.

In 1985 we journeyed north to Katahdin with three friends, John DeLeo, Ken Query, and Brad Ogden. Our mission was to explore and sort out the various routes on the Armadillo. This project soon grasped the undivided attention of all five of us plus several Baxter State Park rangers (Esther Hendrickson, Brendan Curran, and Lester Kenway), who watched and encouraged our efforts from our base at Chimney Pond.

John DeLeo drafted the original write-up of our experiences, and Ken Query critiqued it, so this account is theirs as much as ours. Their permission to reproduce it here is gratefully acknowledged.

At the base of the Armadillo triangle, we maneuvered up and through the first real technical pitch of our climb, an enormous chimney rated about 5.5, the size of which was not fully realized until we actually stood at its bottom. This chimney appeared as a thin layback crack from Chimney Pond but proved to be at least 6 to 8 feet wide at the base, tapering to 4 feet wide at the top, some 90 feet above. We have reached this chimney only after two and a half hours of bushwhacking through dew-laden brush and exposed third- and fourth-class scrambling over steeply vegetated sections and solid slabs. These labors brought us to the spot where the 1935 team began their ambitious climb of the Armadillo buttress.

Our mission was to attempt to follow this original route. Finding an old piton in the chimney helped to reassure us that other climbing parties had come and gone before. From the top of the chimney, on the upper terrace that cuts across the base of the Armadillo, we traversed 80 feet to the right (north). At this point discussion sprang up about where the route went from here. Although we had completed just one pitch and an 80-foot traverse, we had already used up almost five sentences of the six-sentence paragraph that described the 1935 route. We peered upward and debated where Towle and party went.

What is now the standard route for the Armadillo ascends the detached flake to the left at this point. However, our route description seemed to encourage our moving up more to the right, to the north. At first appearance, this part of the cliff—rather steep and apparently blank—offered more potential for pioneering and excitement than any of us was willing to undertake. It made us wonder about the stamina and fortitude of the 1935 party. Upon examination, however, we found a break in the wall: a flake leaning away from the buttress provided an eighteen-inch space that allowed the leader to half-layback, half-chimney, or squirm upwards, depending on how secure he or she felt. Protection was out of the question because of the width of the crack—we simply did not have anything that big.

The summit of the flake, some 50 feet higher, provided a platform to resume the continual debate: "Where to from here?" The primary question in the leader's mind in this kind of exploratory climbing was, "Will I be able to down-climb what I just came up?" Suspense began to animate the followers clumped and tied together at the belay spot as the lead climber went out of sight. A reassuring cry from above soon had us hopeful again: the leader shouted down that he had just found the remains of an old piton about 15 feet up and to the left of the top of the flake. He gladly clipped into this remnant, and not just for historical reasons. Although it did not attach him more firmly to the rock, it provided a certain sense of relief: he was still on route and was at least clipped into something. His confidence was buoyed again when he found another old pin 15 feet above the last. Within a few moves he was anchored into yet another old pin on what appeared to be a proper belay ledge.

While belaying, he began to wonder how much time had passed since the last party had been on this route. The lush but fragile vegetation—truly alpine at this altitude of nearly 5,000 feet—hinted that we were the first to pass this way in a long while. One old pin the leader had clipped into slipped easily out of the crack when tugged. We were all excited about climbing a route that had been nearly forgotten, buried in the archives of climbing journals. Since there is no climbing guide to the Katahdin area, except for the fragmentary log kept at the Chimney Pond ranger cabin, these routes could have remained unclimbed for many years.

At the belay ledge, once everyone had arrived, discussion resumed. We were just about out of route description and only two pitches up the climb. Above we could see that at least three or four more pitches would be necessary to gain the apex above the Armadillo triangle, after which another three or four leads of class 4 and 5 climbing on the Armadillo ridge would take us to the summit hiking trail. Almost 2,000 feet beneath our feet, Chimney Pond glistened in the sun.

After more discussion and the discovery of more pitons of varying ages, we decided we were at a junction of three routes: the 1935 route and both of the 1954 routes. Our primary goal was to stay on the 1935 line for as long as our route-finding ability allowed. We continued up and right (north) for another pitch, about 5.4. It was at this belay that our party diverged from the 1935 route. We followed a series of vertical cracks straight up for two pitches to the ridge above. At first glance this course seemed to follow the route description and it looked climbable, but once committed to the first of these two pitches we found the climbing more difficult and sustained (5.6), although most pleasant.

Our mistake was not fully realized until the entire party had reached the top of the buttress. We found no old pitons on these pitches, although Reppy's 1954 route description indicated that his party removed its pitons while climbing to the top of the buttress. From here looking back, we could see grassy terraces that continued further to the right (north and east), which seemed to fit the 1935 route description.

The remaining three or four pitches of class 4 and 5 climbing along one of the most alpine ridges in the East, the party agreed, offered as classic a ridge as anyone would find in the Tetons or the Cascades. It was a delightful situation: high in a glacial cirque surrounded by other steep ridges and gulleys hundreds of feet below on either side, overlooking sparkling Chimney Pond.

Alpine climbing is generally not considered a spectator sport. It is a sport in which one's performance is measured by personal experience mirrored in intrinsic rewards that flow through an 11-mm nylon umbilical cord to one's climbing partner. However, while climbing on this final ridge we were scrutinized by spectators' eyes. The cirque became an arena. Hikers making their way back and forth to the summit cairn queued up along the Knife Edge and on the Cathedrals. We all agreed that it was a unique and foreign experience.

At 1:30 P.M. we were eating lunch on the summit hiking trail, reflecting on the tenacity and boldness of the 1935 climbing party and on the excellent eye of John Reppy, who picked out such a fine line. We felt that we had just taken a trip back through time and rediscovered two classic climbs that deserved to be dusted off and put back in the northeastern climbing repertory. However, we must admit that we did not climb these routes in their original style. Hemp rope was replaced with nylon; sneakers or lugged Vibram soles gave way to state-of-the-art Fires; boldness and courage were replaced with a large rack of sophisticated modern hardware. There is an old saying among mountaineers—or if there isn't, there should be—that goes, "We carried our courage in our rucksacks."

The following day we regained the base of the Armadillo to find the Kruszyna route of 1954. According to the description, the route made a high traverse of the Armadillo buttress. The preceding day we noticed several pins that sketched a route off in the right direction. At the first belay above the upper terrace that skirts the base of the Armadillo, we continued straight up a layback and eased left (south) on a ramp via layback and friction technique (5.5) until we reached the next belay ledge. Several old pins materialized along the way, and several more appeared at the obvious belay site: there was no question that we were on the Kruszyna route. The route was now supposed to traverse across the face on a small ledge. To our excitement, there it was. This traverse is perhaps the most exhilarating traverse in the East. Thousands of feet drop under your heels as you make your way delicately across, protected by two old pins—placed in 1954?—along the way. The traverse spans about 60 feet (technically 5.5, but psychologically 5.wild!) and ends at the top of the vertical crack of today's standard Armadillo route. A final 5.4 pitch takes one to that fantastic airy fourth-class ridge along the top of the Armadillo leading to the summit hiking trail.

As we were happily eating lunch on top, we talked with great admiration of the climbers of this 1954 party who had put such a fine route up the Armadillo. We concluded that those guys had guts!

On another day, three of our group did the standard route: straight up the detached flake, then up the 5.7 jam crack above. No finer setting can exist in the Northeast. Here is one of the region's finest routes, yet no one knows who first climbed it!

One other classic ridge climb we managed to fit in was the Flatiron, the smaller triangular buttress to the right (north) of the Armadillo (its two pitches rated 5.8 and 5.9). This climb is highlighted by a Yosemite-like, 150-foot sustained vertical crack that varies in width from two to ten inches.

When we started our adventure we never expected to find such climbing treasures in such a classic alpine setting, with technically moderate but respectable climbing, wildly exposed class 3 and 4 scrambling, loose rock, and mountain weather. All too often climbing magazines tout only the most recent first ascents, with photos of climbers in action on the current edge of the climbing standard. If a route is not at least 5.12 today (5.10 yesterday, 5.14 tomorrow), it drops into obscurity in the climbing press. Ours was a venture of rediscovery. We wanted to salute, to pay tribute to the climbers of these early ascents on Katahdin. ■

14: Breakthrough on Rock: 1957–1966

W HEN NORTHEASTERN ROCK climbers finally began to climb harder, they never looked back. Standards of difficulty rose relentlessly. During the years of the conservative tradition before 1960, northeastern climbing standards had lagged behind those of Europe (especially Germany's Dresden) and even behind those of Colorado and California, where 5.9 was established during the early 1950s. When the 5.7 barrier fell on northeastern rock in the late 1950s, however, breakthroughs to new levels came tumbling through thick and fast for the next fifteen years until by the mid-1970s the toughest routes at the Shawangunks ranked among the very hardest in North America.

Whatever the shortcomings of the "great men" theory of history in other fields, it is impossible to resist its allure when describing the advance in technical standards of rock climbing. When a climb is done that is harder than anything done before, it is one individual who leads that climb. Increasingly since the late 1960s, the more difficult routes may be team efforts in which two or more climbers take turns attempting the hardest moves, but at any given moment, one climber is in the lead and everything depends on that one climber. The legs and arms of one frail mortal, together with his or her courage, intelligence, and creative imagination, make all the difference in achieving what has never been achieved before.

During the middle and late 1950s, several northeastern climbers were getting very good. Connecticut's John Reppy was blossoming under the encouragement of J. B. Gardner. Gardner himself was at the top of his form and ready to push the prevailing standard. Reppy recalled serious attempts he and Gardner made during the 1950s to free-climb Gunks routes like *Roseland* and *Directissima*, 5.9s later done by Jim McCarthy. Among the college climbers, Willy Crowther suddenly emerged into the front rank, egged on by Gardner Perry, Ray D'Arcy, and other MITOC enthusiasts. The best Vulgarians, notably Dave Craft, Phil Jacobus, and the brothers Jim and Pete Geiser, were ready for higher challenges. Even more eager was the original mentor of the Vulgarians and lately the butt of their harsh humor, the abrasive, egotistical, but extremely able Art Gran. But of them all, two names stand out as primarily responsible for the breakthroughs into the world beyond 5.7: John Turner and James P. McCarthy.

Turner caught fire first and blazed brightest for a short time (see chapter 17). But the most potent force in northeastern rock climbing for a decade beginning in 1957 was undeniably McCarthy.

During these years the Shawangunks bustled onto the Northeast's center stage, a position of prominence held without the remotest challenge from 1960 until the late 1970s. It was Shawangunk rock climbers of the late 1950s, 1960s, and early 1970s who were doing exciting new things, not just in advancing technical standards but in establishing a code of free-climbing

COURTESY JIM MCCARTHY   COURTESY JIM MCCARTHY

Jim McCarthy. Leading the way to higher levels of difficulty at the Shawangunks during the late 1950s and early 1960s was New York trial lawyer, Jim McCarthy, shown here on a route at Connecticut's Ragged Mountain.

ethics, style, and environmental concern, and in the process having a wonderful time in an area of exquisite natural beauty.

If Turner was an isolated comet flashing across northeastern skies and then disappearing, the other key figure never showed any such wraithlike elusiveness. James P. McCarthy occupied the limelight from the beginning and stubbornly held that role for at least one and maybe two decades. Out of Princeton University, class of 1955, McCarthy learned to climb with the Princeton Mountaineering Club and went on climbing through law school and a career as a New York City trial lawyer. At a crucial stage of his development, he came under the tutelage of Hans Kraus, but it was not long before pupil passed master. Then his partners were drawn from whoever could manage to follow his difficult leads, mostly Vulgarians. He was not a natural talent nor given to airy flights of imagination, and his routes are more noted for their harsh difficulties than for aesthetic qualities. An overpowering competitive disposition brought him to the top. "Mr. Competition" one Shawangunk climber called him. "Even a conversation with McCarthy is a competitive event," declared another. A tough, chunky, combative Irishman, McCarthy was driven by a strong desire to excel and a self-punishing tolerance for the physical and mental discipline and training required to become what he became—the best climber in the Northeast, incomparably so for the first half of the 1960s, sharing that claim only with Turner for a few years before and with two or three others for a few years thereafter. Indeed, he clung at or near the top until past forty, an astonishing testimony to his climbing mastery as well as his obdurate will and steadfast competitiveness. Like the bulldog he almost resembled, once McCarthy sunk in, he hung on.

In 1957 McCarthy climbed the first pitch of Wiessner's classic *Yellow Ridge*, seconded by Appie-turned-Vulgarian Bob Larsen and the Kraus protégé Ken Prestrud. Wiessner's route then traverses far to the left to avoid a big overhanging zone of rock directly above the first pitch. But on this day in 1957, McCarthy had other ideas. Climbing boldly up to an unpromising alcove, he found himself crouched below that characteristic Shawangunk problem: a gigantic overhang. McCarthy committed himself out on small holds and, with a surge of optimism and power, worked his way up and over the top. Proximity to Wiessner's classic suggested the unlikely name for this bold lead: *Yellow Belly*.

This climb was harder than anything previously done at the Gunks, harder than even Wiessner's legendary *Minniebelle* and as hard as any of Fritz's prewar Connecticut test pieces. At the time, some of McCarthy's contemporaries were more impressed with other McCarthy accomplishments, like the nearby *Fat Stick,* also done in 1957. But McCarthy's recollection is clear: "For me, the psychological breakthrough was *Yellow Belly.*" An admiring Gran declared: "In 1957 this was the hardest climb on the cliffs." Indeed it was the hardest in the Northeast. Though today's rating system was unknown then, modern climbers usually call it 5.8, though some have said 5.9. Although much harder climbs were done within a few years, *Yellow Belly* was historic in that here was the time and place where the death knell of the conservative tradition was sounded, the old restraints broken, and the era of advancing standards launched.

It is a pleasing historical fact that the seconds on this occasion provided, in Larsen and Prestrud, representation of three different groupings from the old strife-torn years of the conservative tradition—the Appies, Vulgarians, and Kraus's chosen circle of independents. Pleasing, but not immensely significant; the man at the front was not really a part of any of these traditions. That is almost always the way with climbing breakthroughs. The individuals who achieve them are often new faces who are not imprisoned by old perceptions or old loyalties.

In 1958 McCarthy established several other 5.8s: *Snooky's Return, Blistered Toe,* and another climb that bordered on 5.9, *Birdland.* His seconds now were increasingly from the Vulgarians—Dave Craft, Jim Geiser, Jim Andress, and others.

Where Turner had shone in isolated brilliance in the north country, McCarthy was surrounded by eager competitors at the Gunks. Turner himself was around, though the two never climbed together ("although we watched each other a great deal and spent many evenings together in bars and campsites," recalled Turner). The raucous ranks of the Vulgarians teemed with talented climbers. But the two who came closest, most consistently, to matching McCarthy's exploits were ex-Appie, ex-Vulgarian, ex-college (CCNY) climber Art Gran and MITOC's Willy Crowther. Gran was even less a "natural" than McCarthy but was driven to the fore by a brash egotism and discordant extrovertish temperament. His harsh personality effectively concealed a more sensitive side to his nature that nurtured a deep love of climbing as an art form, a quality that fitfully shone through in passages of his 1964 guidebook to the Gunks (the first published guidebook to the area) and that Turner noted when he observed: "[Gran] was always keenly aware of the aesthetics of a climb as something related to but separate from its difficulty." Crowther was even more attuned to the artistry of rock climbing, as richly attested by the airy classicism of his best routes—*The Arrow* (5.8), *The Spring* (5.9), *Moonlight* (5.6), *Hawk* (5.5), Whitehorse's *Sliding Board* (5.7). Both Gran and Crowther were slightly built, but the divergence in personality could not have been more marked: Gran loud, abrasive, everybody's favorite target for jibes and ridicule; Crowther quiet, a natural leader, everybody's favorite climbing partner.

Within a year of McCarthy's breakthrough to 5.8, these two and others were right behind. In 1959 Gran pioneered some very solid 5.8s of his own, notably *Outer Space,* with Vulgarian Jim Geiser, and *Boldville,* with MITOC renegade Rit Walling. In that year Crowther put up *Sky Top Route,* the difficulty of which was at first underrated by guidebook authors but which has since been acknowledged as solid 5.8. Dave Craft and the other Geiser brother, Pete, put in the awkwardly abstruse *Inverted Layback* in 1959; though later regarded as at least 5.8 if not 5.9, there is some question as to whether the hardest moves were done free on the first ascent. Indeed, questions of historical fact about these stormy Vulgarian years becloud the record on several fronts. During the 1958–1959 period, two superb new 5.8s were the fierce and continuously overhanging *Double Crack* and the subtle face climb with the appropriate ballet allusion in its name, *Pas de Deux.* In his guidebook, Art Gran claimed the first free ascents of both these routes, but subsequent doubters credited Jim Geiser. From their known accomplishments on other routes at the time, either was capable of such splendid climbing.

When the dust settled from this first breakthrough to 5.8 in the late 1950s, McCarthy's *Birdland* was, as Gran pronounced it, "probably the most difficult route of its class." But it remained the hardest for less than two years. In 1960 McCarthy broke through again.

In the spring of 1960, McCarthy headed up to one of the most forbidding sections of the cliff, where hitherto the only routes had been done with extensive artificial aids. With him that day and keeping him loose and laughing were two Vulgarians, Claude Suhl and Roman Sadowy. The line he chose climbed thin cracks to an overhanging corner. Here McCarthy swung out to the right and around the overhang, a move harder than any of his previous climbs—in modern parlance, 5.9 had solidly arrived at the Gunks. Above that corner, a steep crack continued up, still at a difficulty of 5.9, then the route went up over two more roofs, one of which was again 5.9. The demands of this climb were far above those of the previous two years. The climb was given the terse and distinctively Vulgarian name *MF,* which some have wistfully explained stands for "McCarthy's Folly." *MF* was, Gran admitted, "a modern classic." Though the first universally acclaimed 5.9 at the Shawangunks, it has remained ever since the classic of its grade, "the" 5.9 to do at the Shawangunks. The unrelenting standard of the middle section of the climb, the aesthetic quality of the climbing, and the impressive location on that steep wall combine to enhance its historical importance.

McCarthy added other hard routes in 1960, of which *Roseland, Land's End,* and the one-pitch test piece *Apoplexy* are all regarded now as 5.9, though none of them quite as hard as *MF.* As before, neither Art Gran nor Willy Crowther was far behind. By the end of 1960 Gran had climbed *Triangle,* a borderline 5.9, and the next year Crowther pushed up *Three Vultures,* a route that the Vulgarians at first discounted (the first guidebooks called it 5.7!), but that has since been accorded a full 5.9 rating. One of the Vulgarians, Phil Jacobus, led the short tenuous face climb *Jacob's Ladder* in 1960; though

COURTESY RICK WILCOX

Matinee. *Visiting Californian Yvon Chouinard established the Shawangunks' hardest single climb in 1961 with his free ascent of the first pitch of* Matinee, *a solid 5.10. The route remains popular with today's climbers, one of whom approaches the crux in this scene.*

this climb has since been rated 5.10, its crux was brief and near the ground; in 1960 it was felt to be at least on a par with the longer hardest climbs (5.9), though less substantial because of its small size.

As may be apparent, rating climbs is no exact science. In the first two guidebooks, Gran's of 1964 and Williams' of 1972, a high standard governed ratings, and a Gunks 5.8 might easily equate with a 5.9 elsewhere. In Williams' 1980 guide, wholesale upgrading of climbs attempted to correct this imbalance. Thus several former 5.8s mentioned above—*Yellow Belly, Birdland, Inverted Layback, Three Vultures* (the last a 5.7 in the early books)—were accorded a 5.9 rating in 1980. In Todd Swain's 1986 guidebook, *Yellow Belly* and *Birdland* were reduced to "5.8 plus," while the other two were kept at 5.9. Many other ratings wavered over the years.

Regardless of precise ratings, however, it was clear that by 1960 McCarthy and his pack of pursuers had brought Shawangunks climbing to the level achieved by Turner in the previous two years at Pok-o-moonshine in the Adirondacks and Cathedral Ledge in New Hampshire.

Nor did McCarthy rest on his laurels. The very next year he tackled two of the well-known aid routes near the Uberfall, the showcase adjoining crack systems known as *Retribution* and *Nosedive*. Both were regarded as still harder than *MF*, and *Retribution* has since been consistently accepted as the Northeast's first 5.10, with *Nosedive* at first regarded as hard 5.9, later as 5.10. Another climb approaching this new standard that McCarthy climbed in 1961 was *Tough Shift*. A still more solid claim to 5.10 was established later that year when visiting Californian Yvon Chouinard free-climbed the first pitch of *Matinee*. In 1963 McCarthy freed the second pitch of what was regarded then, and for several years, as the hardest multipitch climb in the East.

In the space of five years, the standard of difficulty in northeastern rock had gone from 5.7 through both 5.8 and 5.9 to a very solid 5.10. Eastern rock climbing standards had approached those of America's other leading rock climbing areas in California and Colorado. McCarthy and Gran achieved national recognition individually, the former becoming a leading figure in the American Alpine Club. In the process they brought respectability to the Shawangunks in the eyes of the California and Colorado climbers, many of whom now made pilgrimages to the hitherto little-heralded New York scene.

It was a time of prolific new-route development at the Gunks. In the five years 1960 to 1964 McCarthy alone put up at least thirty new routes in the 5.7 to 5.10 class. Gran and the Vulgarians were scarcely less active, but it is of McCarthy that the story is told of the day when he and Claude Suhl were roping up at the bottom of one climb when McCarthy noted another ceiling

COURTESY DICK WILLIAMS

Dick Williams. Competitive gymnast who developed a lifelong commitment to high-level rock climbing, Dick Williams brought a fluid and dynamic athleticism to the new levels of difficulty attained in the 1960s.

with a crack in it nearby. The story, as related in the climbers' newsletter *The Eastern Trade,* alleges that the following exchange ensued:

McCarthy: "Wow, man! Do you suppose that's been done?"

Suhl (consulting guidebook): "Yeah, Jim. It's been done."

McCarthy: "Who did it?"

Suhl: "You did it, Jim. Two years ago."

McCarthy: "Does it say how hard it was?"

With the establishment of 5.10, McCarthy pulled away from his old rival Gran and most of the old Vulgarians as well. In the early 1960s new faces arrived who were less constrained by the old perceptions of the possible and prepared to leap into the new standards. One, Steve Larsen, climbed at a remarkable level for his time. His short fierce leads, such as *Tweedle Dum,* were clearly ahead of their time, though never widely heralded, perhaps because they were short and never became popular test pieces.

Among the talented climbers who rose to new heights during the early 1960s was that amiable, ill-fated troubadour, John Hudson. He combined the unkempt plebianism of the Vulgarian-Beat Generation with something of the airy vision and poetry of the coming hippie movement, the whole suffused with a pleasant easy-going disposition and a raw talent for difficult and daring climbs that was without equal. Hudson seconded the first free ascent of *Matinee* and is credited with the first free ascent of the improbable overhang at the Uberfall sometimes known as the *Trashcan Boulder Problem* and sometimes as the *John Hudson Boulder Problem,* rated 5.11 minus. Hudson did this route in 1963, though whether on the lead or on top-rope is uncertainly remembered. This affable outcast was lost in an avalanche in the Andes in 1969.

The newcomer who emerged as McCarthy's chief rival by the mid-1960s, however, was Dick Williams, a competitive gymnast in his school years and a lithe and agile performer on difficult rock. In 1961 Williams had astonished his Vulgarian peers by pulling off the second ascent of Chouinard's awe-inspiring *Matinee* at a time when even McCarthy had not yet done that celebrated first pitch. If it was McCarthy who established 5.10, it was Williams who was, by 1964 to 1966, most prolific in establishing new routes at the 5.7 to 5.10 level. Indeed, Williams did some shorter top-rope problems of even more exacting difficulty, such as *Mental Block,* which may qualify as the first led 5.11 at the Shawangunks, though its length and marginal rating deprived it of recognition either at the time or in later historical assessments. Williams' gymnastic background and natural athleticism brought a fluid, dynamic, and exciting dimension to the top grades that the dogged bulldozing strength of McCarthy had lacked. Among Williams' outstanding lines of that period are several that have become classics at the Gunks: the barbarously exposed high roof of *Modern Times* (5.8 plus), on which he was seconded by Craft, still climbing well; the adjoining line he created with Californian Chouinard, *Psychedelic* (5.8 or 5.9); the popular short-but-savage *Double Clutch* (5.9 plus), which he put in with John Hudson and Pete Geiser; and a route he did with McCarthy as second in 1964, *Frustration Syndrome* (5.10), which was fully as hard as any big route on the cliffs at that time.

During these years the best climbers often collaborated on difficult new routes. Outstanding examples of joint efforts include *Never Never Land* (5.9 plus), first free-climbed in 1964 by a team of McCarthy, Williams, Craft, and visiting Coloradoan George Hurley; *Realm of the Fifth Class Climber* (5.9), established by Williams, McCarthy, Gran, and none other than Hans Kraus; and two climbs whose names showcased their distinguished coadjuvancy: *MacReppy* (5.8), by McCarthy and Connecticut ace John Reppy; and *Mac-Kor-Wick* (5.8), on which McCarthy and Williams (sometimes nicknamed "Wick") watched the outstanding Colorado climber Layton Kor do a brilliant lead.

During this period a code of ethics and style in free climbing gradually strengthened at the Shawangunks. Many aid routes had been done at these cliffs, routes of such intimidating steepness that their first-ascent parties made extensive use of pitons and etriers, or "stirrups," as they were often called then. Aid routes continued to be done throughout the 1960s, but McCarthy, Gran, and the other dominant leaders made a careful distinction between "aid" and "free." The highest accolades increasingly were reserved for the free-climber. Indeed, many of the "new" routes mentioned above were actually old aid routes climbed for the first time without aid—"first free ascents."

The ethical and stylistic standards for a free ascent were very high: not only was it unacceptable to pull up on a piton or sling, but most leaders felt it was equally inexcusable to rest even temporarily by artificial means. The idea was that it was just you and the rock. The rope, pitons, carabiners, et al. were only there for protection in case of a fall, *not* to be used in any way for either progress up the rock or resting en route. It was also regarded as poor style to do a climb with a top-rope first: the entire climb, especially the hardest moves, should be done on the lead starting from the bottom. On this score Crowther was not as "pure" as his Vulgarian contemporaries. Weaned on top-roping at Quincy Quarries, Crowther brought this tactic to the Gunks at first. The splendid final move on *The Arrow,* for example, was rehearsed on top-rope, then led. But Crowther increasingly held to demanding standards of free climbing as the 1960s progressed.

It was also still relatively uncommon for leaders to fall when attempting new routes. While leader falls were acceptable, they were rare, and the usual plan was to climb even a hard new route without taking a fall on the crux.

In evolving this code, the Shawangunks were accepting what was largely already established in northeastern rock climbing circles. However, as standards rose to more difficult levels, the enforcement of good style was not automatic elsewhere. Sometimes—even occasionally at the Gunks—climbers might feel that a top-rope or a wee rest on aid might be justifiable in cases of extreme difficulty. The Gunks' ideals of ethics and style were rising during the mid-1960s and were destined to reach, during the next decade, a level of "purity" that became famous or infamous in other climbing circles. The seeds of the "Great Debate" of the 1980s were already being sown. ∎

Reference Note

The guidebooks for the Shawangunks—Arthur Gran's (1964) and Richard C. Williams' (1972, 1980, and 1991)—are valuable not only for the historical essays in each, but even more for the first ascent data given for each climb. Some inconsistencies and errors are inevitable, but they are surprisingly few. See also relevant passages in Dumais' *Shawangunk Rock Climbing,* Jones' *Climbing in North America,* and John Harlin III, *The Climber's Guide to North America: East Coast Rock Climbs* (Denver: Chockstone Press, 1986). Contemporary notices of climbing news appeared occasionally in *Summit* magazine and later more consistently in *Climbing, Mountain,* and *Off Belay.* The authors benefited from talks with many of the leading and minor climbers of this period. Special thanks are due to Thom E. Scheuer for arranging conversations with various groups on numerous occasions.

15: On Beyond 5.10: 1967–1973

T HE YEARS 1964 to 1966 were a period of consolidation of the new
standards at the Gunks. Nothing much harder than 1963's *Matinee*
was achieved during these years. In 1967 came the next giant steps,
this time from two new and disparate sources.

McCarthy had naturally attracted the top young climbers who sought
to make a name for themselves by climbing with him at the leading edge of
the sport. In 1966 a twenty-two-year-old mathematician named Rich Goldstone appeared. As a teenage hopeful in New York City in 1960, Goldstone
had originally applied to the conservative Appies to learn how to climb.
However, he had actually mastered his skills when attending the unlikely
climbing locale of the University of Chicago, mainly in frequent trips to Wis-
consin's short, demanding Devil's Lake cliffs. Back in New York after gradu-
ating, Goldstone's obvious talents soon brought him to McCarthy's attention and the two paired up to explore the possibilities of free-climbing some
of the largest roofs on the cliffs.

Unlike the relaxed and raucous Vulgarian partners of yore, Goldstone
was a serious young man, earnestly dedicated to raising his climbing to the
highest possible level. With this end constantly in view, he opened Mc-
Carthy's eyes to some new approaches. On weekday evenings in New York
he faithfully worked out at a gymnasium, systematically developing
strength, balance, and endurance. At the cliffs between climbs, disdaining
the Vulgarians' eager rush to the local bars, he endlessly practiced the hardest moves on boulder problems along the carriage road. Others, including
McCarthy, had exercised and bouldered, but Goldstone pursued such practices with dedication bordering on fanaticism—and soon had McCarthy
doing so too. Goldstone also introduced an important and occasionally
controversial item of gear to the climbers' rack: gymnastic chalk. On hot
days the adverse effects of perspiration could be significantly reduced by the
liberal dusting of chalk on the climber's fingers.

With zealous exercise, bouldering, and chalk, Goldstone and McCarthy
prepared themselves to lay siege to the frowning overhangs along that steep
section of the Traps where *MF* had been found and which gradually

acquired the general name of "the McCarthy Wall." Here Goldstone introduced McCarthy to still another weapon in the relentless pursuit of higher
standards: an acceptance of the inevitability of falling—and repeated falling
if necessary—to master an exceptionally difficult lead. The two climbers
would alternate at the lead, hanging on until even their extraordinary
strength could no longer endure, then (perhaps after sustaining a well-
protected fall or two) would switch places, the belayer resting while the
other leader worked on the moves. In this determined manner, reminiscent of
the siege tactics employed on great Himalayan peaks, the required sequence
of holds and moves would be slowly and methodically mastered, until finally—
with Goldstone usually in the lead at the final stage—several routes of the
most extreme difficulty were accomplished. The outstanding climbs of this
new approach, both completed in 1967, were *Coexistence* and the appropriately named *Try Again*. Both have been rated 5.10, but the clear message
that buzzed around the Shawangunks in 1967 was that these routes belonged
in a special category, then referred to simply as "the hard 5.10s." The 1986
guidebook called *Coexistence* 5.10 plus.

Siege tactics were only beginning. As Goldstone and McCarthy were
dangling on the huge roofs of the McCarthy Wall, they were occasionally
amused by glimpses or reports of an awkward, long-armed, bespectacled
and introverted physicist from Washington, D.C., who was making the five-
hundred-mile round trip almost every weekend and taking almost as long to
siege 5.7s as they were on the "hard 5.10s"—and falling much more regularly. A bit later they chuckled to hear this clownish creature had now advanced to 5.8, falling still more, but eventually getting up. Soon he was working on 5.9s, and Goldstone and McCarthy stopped laughing. Then came the
rumor that the upstart was working on *Foops*.

Foops is the unpretentious name for a historic piece of Shawangunk
rock. Located in an exceedingly prominent position at the base of the usual
descent route for the Sky-Top cliff, it is an 8-foot ceiling 80 feet above the
ground, split by a crack. McCarthy and a Princeton buddy had first aided
that crack in 1955. No one had seriously thought of climbing it free until the
peculiar physicist from Washington, D.C., started to work on it in the spring
of 1967.

John Stannard had begun climbing with IOCA when doing graduate
work at Syracuse University in 1964. Progressing slowly in ability, he began
to improve when Willy Crowther started climbing with him. His studies
completed and working in Washington, Stannard committed himself to a
single-minded devotion to rock climbing. Like Goldstone, Stannard also
trained hard and worked incessantly on boulder problems. At the office he

Foops

Jim McCarthy

THE SIXTIES AT A GLANCE

Principal climbing event: breakthroughs in sheer difficulty (early sixties, rock; late sixties, ice)

Climbs of the Decade:—rock: *Foops*
　　　　　　　　　　　　—ice: *Cathedral Standard*

Hardest single climb: Boulder problem on *Doug's Roof* by John Gill as he passed through

Boldest lead: *Old Cannon* in winter

Emblematic item of gear: Royal Robbins' blue boots

Most important climber: Jim McCarthy

Most underrated: Gary Brown

Most colorful: Dave Craft

Most colorful group: the Vulgarians (almost as colorful as they've been telling everybody, especially themselves, ever since)

Most prominent woman: Cherry Merritt (Austin)

Child prodigies: Kevin Bein, Rick Wilcox

Still-active father figure: Lester Germer

Best-looking: Elaine Mathews

Brainiest: John Stannard

Nice Guy Award: Chuck Loucks

Vanishing act: (Climber prominent in this decade, gone completely by the next): Art Gran

Norman Clyde Award: the Damp brothers

Couple of the Decade: Patty and Willy Crowther

Person you'd most like to have climbed with: John Hudson

HENRY BARBER

Foops. A significant breakthrough to higher levels of difficulty was the widely heralded ascent of the giant roof on Foops, *by John Stannard in 1967. Here another of the superstars of that era, Steve Wunsch, repeats the crux.*

would periodically chin up on door frames or hang from his long arms for extended periods, to the puzzlement of office mates. At Washington's Carderock he worked out a difficult boulder problem to the roof of the park's outhouse, only to be discovered there by the police one day and promptly booked for "Improper Use of Comfort Station." At every off hour during the week he climbed at local crags like Carderock, while on weekends he sometimes headed for West Virginia's Seneca Rock, but more often for the Gunks—and by the spring of 1967 most often for the 8-foot ceiling of *Foops*.

Gradually, and taking repeated falls in the process, Stannard thoroughly mastered and memorized the precise combination of holds required to inch out the crack and get one hand on the lip, so that these terribly difficult moves no longer fully taxed his strength. Repeatedly he committed himself to holds at the lip, only to fall off as his strength gave out before he could pull up to higher holds. At the time, old aid pitons filled up the first crack above the lip, making it unusable, so Stannard was forced to lunge for a much higher (and less ample) hold than later used. The patience of a battery of seconds was worn thin catching his numerous falls, but a growing audience realized that the man was serious about persevering and that one day it might happen. Late in the spring of 1967, it did happen. Stannard climbed *Foops*, a route of significantly greater difficulty than anything else in the Northeast, even harder than the "hard 5.10s" just being conquered by McCarthy and Goldstone. In modern parlance, the grade of 5.11 was born.

Stannard quickly showed that this achievement was no fluke. Later in 1967, employing the same siege tactics, he free-climbed *Directississima*, an unrelentingly steep direct variation of *High Exposure*, rated 5.10 but placed by most contemporaries in the same category with *Coexistence* and *Try Again* among the "hard 5.10s" of the time. The next year he added two more 5.11s, *Comedy in Three Acts* and *Swing Time*. The next year it was *Generation Gap* and *Low Exposure*. In 1970 and 1971, in a supreme effort, he worked out the most difficult line yet, a long and continuously overhanging crack at an outlying crag, which he affectionately dubbed *Persistent*, memorializing the single most outstanding trait required for its first ascent.

History has placed Stannard in the forefront of northeastern rock climbers beginning with the ascent of *Foops*. It should be observed, however, that for a few years following the "hard 5.10s" of 1967 and 1968—at first Stannard declined to designate any of his climbs 5.11—Shawangunks climbers enjoyed debating whether Stannard or Goldstone was Number One. In 1970 the latter put up a short thin face called *Farewell to Fingers* which may have been as hard as *Foops* or *Persistent*. Some called it the hardest 15 feet of rock climbing in North America at the time it was done, and it certainly demonstrated that Goldstone's skills were not limited to huge overhangs. Stannard himself always felt that Goldstone's bouldering skill was unexcelled. He once wrote a friend:

> *Coexistence* would probably never have been freed at all if McCarthy had not made the fatal error of getting Rich to try climbing with a rope. If anyone manages to convince Rich the cliff is just a boulder problem, we are going to be in even deeper trouble.

However, Stannard's role in later breakthroughs has tended to give his name more prominence even in the earlier period, and certainly suggests that even then he was the one who was in league with the future.

Stannard's arrival at the top of the standard shook the Vulgarian Establishment, if that seeming contradiction in terms can be used to describe the circle of climbers who had grown accustomed to being the dominant clique at the leading edge. While McCarthy had belonged to no one, Gran had been rudely thrust from the inner circle, and Goldstone had neither interest in nor talent for vulgarity, nevertheless, these three and virtually all the other top climbers at the cliffs (Crowther excepted) had been most often in the company of the Vulgarians and employed them as seconds. When Hudson and Williams matured, vulgarity had been largely displaced by good climbing, but they were glad to be admitted to the same in-group.

Stannard was an outsider, a graduate of the IOCA system. Moreover, he drew his seconds from an emerging group of very able ex-IOCA climbers, some of whom actually succeeded in following his extreme leads (though at first not *Foops* or *Persistent*). Crowther, Stannard's one-time mentor, followed on the first ascent of *Criss*. On *Directississima* and *Generation Gap* it was the high-strung, athletic, brilliant but moody and ultimately suicidal Howie Davis. On *Comedy in Three Acts* it was Gary Brown, unprepossessing in appearance but endowed with uncanny strength and endurance in extremis. On the giant roof of *Fat City* (5.10) in 1968, Brown clung to the minutest of holds and drove in a piton. For years thereafter, Gunks hard men, barely able to stay on the holds long enough to clip into Brown's piton, shook their heads in disbelief as to how anyone could have stayed there long enough to drive it in. Brown's lead of *New Frontier* in 1969 also displayed extraordinary strength and boldness. Brown, Davis, and Crowther, all from the IOCA circle, were all worthy seconds on the new frontiers Stannard was exploring.

More significant than the unorthodoxy of Stannard's social background was his ultrapersistence in siege tactics. He may have begun with the least natural talent of any of the pantheon of great Shawangunk figures. "New things are done," he once mused, "by simply trying them again and again until one succeeds." During the early 1970s the American Alpine Club asked Shawangunk climbers to participate in a carefully documented test of ropes. Among the data to be recorded were the number of leader falls for each rope and various other events. Of sixteen climbers participating, eleven reported fewer than five leader falls. Stannard reported 168 leader falls. The other four, also 5.10 leaders, reported from 10 to 49.

This acceptance of the inevitability of multiple falls was the direction in which lay the future of higher standards in rock climbing. Goldstone, McCarthy, and Williams before them had been tending in that direction, but Stannard flew past them into the future. Up there in the new world of "elevated aerial bouldering" (as New Hampshire's climber Ed Webster later termed it) was the ultimate recognition of the implications inherent in that nylon rope on which Bob Bates had rappelled out of the Washington, D.C., office building a quarter century before: if the rope was strong enough to hold repeated falls, why not climb right to the edge of the humanly possible, master each delicate move at the limit, fall off as often as needful to determine just where that limit lay, and slowly progress through a sequence of one extreme move after another until a long chain of barely possible moves could be strung together to get up a section of rock previously regarded as unthinkable. When Stannard climbed *Foops,* observed John Harlin III, "it set people to rethinking what, in fact, *was* possible." The road opened not merely to 5.11 but to the constantly receding horizon of the possible.

Nevertheless, after the breakthroughs of 1967 and 1968 the dizzying pace of advancing standards momentarily slackened. The Shawangunks climbing community paused to catch its collective breath after the string of feats McCarthy had set off ten years before. Like the period 1964 to 1966, it was a time for consolidation. But while no new breakthroughs were achieved during the years 1969 to 1972, it was a period of great creativity in other ways—as we shall see in the next chapter.

By 1972 the hiatus in advancing standards had lasted long enough. By now many climbers were masters of 5.10. A teenage whiz or two had been over the Goldstone-McCarthy "hard 5.10s." No one had yet repeated *Foops,* but Dennis Merritt and Connecticut star Sam Streibert were working on it and getting very close. Throughout the community, standards had been rising everywhere but at the leading edge. The pressures were building for a new breakthrough.

In 1972 the paths of four men converged to set the stage for a new advance:

- John Stannard was ready to carry the standards up another notch. Throughout his involvement in the events of 1969–1972, he had never ceased hard climbing.
- Steve Wunsch had made a reputation as one of Colorado's top climbers when he switched his primary allegiance to the East and the Gunks. An inspirational talent, capable of rising to incredible peaks of performance, Wunsch's brilliant personal style neatly complemented the more pedestrian, more persistent approach of Stannard's.
- John Bragg was a very large and strong climber, a blond Adonis from Harvard. In 1972 he had made little impression on the climbing world, but with his great size, strength, endurance, and calmness in extremity, he steadily and unspectacularly improved until very nearly on a par with the more celebrated pair. If the bearded, alienated Wunsch was clearly a product of the 1960s, Bragg could have been a varsity gridiron hero from the 1950s—in fact, he was an All-American swimmer at Harvard and not

HENRY BARBER

Open Cockpit. *Wunsch climbs his celebrated thin crack climb, first free-climbed in 1973.*

Kansas City. *Another 1973 classic,* Kansas City, *climbed here by John Stannard, was first climbed free by John Bragg. Stannard, Wunsch, and Bragg constituted the chief agents of change during the early 1970s at the Shawangunks.*

HENRY BARBER

in the HMC as an undergraduate. In succeeding years, unlike Stannard and Wunsch, Bragg applied his developing talents to the realm of ice and of large-scale alpinism and moved into the forefront of world-class mountaineering, of which more in later chapters.

- Henry Barber was the least continuously active at the Shawangunks. At nineteen the youngest of the four, Barber was a hot young Boston climber, eager, on the make, and on the verge of becoming possibly the greatest rock climber in the world. If Wunsch belonged to the 1960s and Bragg to the 1950s, Barber presaged the overtly self-promoting young-men-in-a-hurry of the 1980s. In 1972 he was just beginning to make waves all over the Northeast. He began climbing at the Shawangunks often that year, usually teaming up with the other three, but not present as consistently due to his feverish activity elsewhere, of which more—much more—in chapter 18.

In 1972 two events set these four on a new advance in standards. With Merritt and Streibert reputed to be very close to mastering *Foops,* Barber made one of his patented sudden sorties from Boston and picked off the coveted second ascent of that historic roof. It had taken almost five years since Stannard's first, an unusually long time for such a celebrated plum to ripen, and a tribute to how far ahead of his time Stannard had been in 1967. Barber's climb, taken with Wunsch's second ascent of *Persistent,* in effect raised the curtain on a new epic period at the Gunks.

Near the end of 1972 Williams brought out a new guidebook. In it were still listed some thirty-three aid routes. (The 1972 guidebook actually listed thirty-eight aid routes; it turned out, however, that five of these had previously been done free.) Aware that aid climbing had traditionally involved copious placement and removal of pitons, Stannard regarded this publicizing of so much aid as a direct threat to the success of the clean climbing movement (chapter 16), not to mention a challenge to his free-climbing skills.

Speedily, with the happy compliance of Wunsch, Bragg, and (when he was in town) Barber, Stannard began a systematic campaign to eradicate aid from the Shawangunk scene. In 1973 all but five of the thirty-three were freed. Some turned out to go free at a relatively moderate level (5.9 being moderate in this league), but over half of them proved to be 5.11 or harder and tasked the finest efforts of the front four. At least half a dozen were significantly harder than *Foops.* Stannard was almost invariably involved in these supreme efforts, with either Bragg or Wunsch or both. In two cases, however, Stannard was unable to complete the crux moves first, and these two routes have been regarded as the most noteworthy of all the great climbs of 1973:

Open Cockpit, the quintessential thin crack climb, which fell to Wunsch's superb form, and *Kansas City,* the biggest roof yet done, surmounted in one Herculean burst by Bragg. *Open Cockpit* is rated 5.11 plus and considered a true classic of the cliff. *Kansas City* was rated even harder: 5.12 minus.

With the fall of *Kansas City,* only five aid routes remained unsolved. The next year Stannard climbed *Kama Sutra* (5.12 minus) and the following year *Wasp Stop* (5.11 plus), leaving only one long continuously overhanging climb expressively called *Happiness Is a 110° Wall* and two gigantic roofs, *Poops* and *Twilight Zone.*

The big climb of 1974, however, was an obscure line, never in the guidebooks in the old days because it was located off the beaten track. Way

Supercrack. *Considered a major breakthrough in its time,* Supercrack *was first climbed by Wunsch in 1974. It has remained a test piece for succeeding generations of climbers, including this one here.*

down along the Sky-Top cliff was a detached pinnacle 40 feet high. Its outer face was split by a single narrow crack from bottom to top, cutting through a single eighteen-inch overhang less than halfway up. As standards rose, all the top climbers had gone after this crack. It became a gathering place for the climbing elite who aspired to pull off this brightest plum of the area, the single most desired fruit in the orchard. The front four were often there; so were Kevin Bein and his followers, many visiting celebrities, and a host of old and new faces, all conscious of the prestige that would go to the conqueror of this 40 feet of vertical rock. Even before anyone was close to climbing it, the route had its name: *Supercrack*.

Finally one spring day in 1974, a group foregathered and, with the usual siege tactics, placed a few pieces of protection as far as the small roof. Wunsch was there and, as a stylist without peer, was aware that to tie in with the rope already through protection would mar the purity of an ascent. When his turn came that day, Wunsch pulled the rope through, tied in on the ground, and in one brilliant effort, with no falls, moving fluidly and confidently, placing the rope in the existing protection below the roof and placing his own protection above—where the difficulty did *not* ease off—Steve Wunsch climbed *Supercrack*.

In 1974 *Supercrack* was probably the hardest climb in North America, possibly even the world. The Gunks community originally proclaimed it 5.13, though when that grade became a reality in the 1980s, mostly in locales other than the Gunks at first, *Supercrack* was politely scaled back to 5.12. But it should be noted that almost three years passed before two visitors from California (where vertical cracks are a regular diet) worked to exhaustion for four days before managing the second ascent of those 40 feet. For ten years after Wunsch's exploit, the number of ascents was severely limited. Anyone claiming one was regarded as a true master of the craft. Top climbers would willingly devote days to that little crack on the obscure pinnacle. Its stature in climbing legend may be compared only with Stannard's *Foops* (1967), Turner's *Repentance* (1958), Wiessner's *Minniebelle* (1946), Kraus's *High Exposure* (1941), the *Whitney-Gilman* (1929)—and one yet to be heard from in the north country, Jimmy Dunn's *The Prow* (1977).

(Lists like this are diverting to construct but inevitably provoke more discussion than they resolve. The seven cited here are selected not so much as the hardest of their time—*High Exposure* and *The Prow* were not, *Minniebelle* was no harder than Wiessner's Connecticut routes a decade earlier—but because of the towering respect which these seven routes almost uniquely commanded at the time they were done and the legendary mystique they preserved for many years thereafter. Wiessner's Connecticut routes were the hardest in the Northeast for twenty years but almost unknown to the climbing community. McCarthy's routes of the 1957 to 1967 period were held in awe, but no single route stands out head and shoulders above the rest. The same may be said of Henry Barber's routes of 1971 to 1974. For those who like the symmetry of "Ten Best" lists, start with the seven listed, add one of Wiessner's (*Vector?*), one of McCarthy's (*MF?*), and one of Barber's (*Jane?*)—then regret omissions like *Vandals* (a 1980s route not yet in sufficient perspective), *Kansas City* (too soon overshadowed by *Supercrack*), *Coexistence* (placed in the shade by *Foops*), *Old Cannon* (eclipsed by the *Whitney-Gilman*), and maybe Helburn's 1919 ascent of Katahdin's Chimney.)

The achievements of Stannard, Wunsch, Bragg, and Barber at the Gunks in 1972 and 1973 are justly renowned but have tended to unduly eclipse other remarkable climbers of those years. The continued excellence of climbing by Goldstone, McCarthy, and Williams during the early 1970s should not be obscured by the greater brilliance of the front four. Indeed, McCarthy was often included in group sieges of the harder routes, and not just because the others immensely respected what the aging warrior had contributed in earlier breakthroughs. One unkind wag commented that the stages of McCarthy's climbing career could be likened to the Stuart dynasty in seventeenth-century England: when he opened up 5.9 and 5.10 with *MF* and *Retribution*, he was James I; when he did *Coexistence* he was James II; when he joined Stannard and company to attempt the 5.11s and 5.12s of the early 1970s, he was the Old Pretender. Yet Stannard and the others held him in the highest esteem even then.

Of others, a very young Rich Romano was perhaps outstanding. Of the twenty-eight aid climbs freed in 1973, Stannard was on the first ascent party for twenty-three, Barber for eleven, Bragg for eight, Wunsch for three, and six other names once each. It is noteworthy, however, that the apparent leader was Stannard on sixteen of the twenty-eight, Barber on eight, Wunsch on two, Bragg on one—and the unheralded Romano on one. More about this boy wonder in chapter 23.

The rest of the 1970s was another period of consolidation at the Gunks. Nothing harder than *Supercrack* was climbed, but a growing number of able young climbers performed at the 5.11 level with occasional spurts into the heady realm of 5.12. What they did, and how they did it, led directly to the exciting and controversial developments of the 1980s. ∎

Reference Note

See note for chapter 14. For a full account of *Supercrack's* special place in climbing history, see Alison Osius, "Super Crack," *Climbing*, August-September 1991, pp. 76–77.

16: Clean Climbing

T HE PURSUIT OF difficulty at the highest levels is by no means all there is to the story of rock climbing. One of the most interesting and creative periods of Shawangunks climbing was 1969 to 1972. As mentioned, this was *not* a period of advancing technical standards. It was a breathing spell, a time for consolidation, when the advances of the leading edge percolated down into the consciousness of the entire Shawangunks community. But it was also a time of environmental awakening.

These were years when rock climbing's popularity first began to explode. The Shawangunk cliffs, which had seemed crowded with forty climbers in the 1950s or perhaps eighty as late as 1968, began to see crowds of two hundred or more on popular weekends. The Uberfall became a social scene bustling with activity—climbers preparing for climbs, eating lunch, exchanging climbing stories or tips on how to do a favorite route, and diligently bouldering or top-roping on every nearby piece of rock. The standard multipitch routes in both easy and intermediate grades teemed with traffic all weekend long. Often a party would set off in search of an unoccupied climb of a given difficulty level and walk along the base of the cliff for hundreds of feet before finding one available. Prior to the late 1960s Gunks climbing was a spring and fall phenomenon, with little activity in summer (when climbers went West and the local weather was too hot) and no climbing at all during the winter. During the 1969–1972 years the traditional summer hiatus all but disappeared, while Stannard and Goldstone and, at first, no more than a half dozen other equally dedicated if less well known climbers began to climb on winter weekends as well. By the mid-1970s Shawangunks climbing was a year-round activity, and growing numbers could be found even on weekdays.

Though more populous, the Gunks climbers retained a sense of community during that 1969 to 1972 period. The regulars all knew each other still and shared a common love of the cliffs and adherence to a free-climbing ethic. Several distinct circles existed, but old animosities had melted.

- The New York AMC was still there, though no longer an important force. Its own numbers remained about the same, but the rest of the population had swelled so much that the Appies were little noticed, save for their quaintly archaic clipboards, sign-out procedures, and training sessions, now viewed with more amusement than resentment by the rest.

- Vulgarians were still around but not so vulgar. While Williams and others who joined that clique considered themselves card-carrying Vulgarians, they really came primarily to climb, not to party.

- A new and younger contingent calling themselves the Degenerates inherited the mantle of wild parties and vulgarity, but they too were fundamentally more interested in good climbing. Many of the Degenerates contrived to elude the discomforts of full-time employment and thereby climbed almost every day. They were perhaps the first full-time Gunks climbers, or "climbing bums" (after the fashion of earlier "ski bums"), setting the precedent for a group of still better climbers who became "regulars" in 1973, of whom more later.

- The college climbers under IOCA contributed a numerous throng, for whom Willy Crowther was spiritual leader or "good shepherd."

- An independent crew of collegians, some of them loosely affiliated with Harvard, provided some individuals who merit special note, including Al Rubin, who climbed all over the Northeast for more than twenty years and became the unofficial historian of northeastern rock climbing with his historical essays in several guidebooks; Dennis Merritt, who was one of the outstanding free-climbers of the day; Cherry Austin, probably one of the two best women climbers of the early 1970s (the other being Patty Crowther, Willy's wife); and two who soon occupied a unique niche in Shawangunk climbing, Kevin Bein and Barbara Devine, of whom more in chapters 22 and 23.

- Smaller circles included a contingent of IBM climbers; the Boston AMC, which now resumed regular weekends at the Gunks; a new generation of able Connecticut hard men, only loosely tied to Connecticut's AMC Chapter and preferring to call themselves the Mud and Slush (parodying Britain's celebrated Rock and Ice); a smattering of regular Canadian visitors; and, for the first time, some local talent from New Paltz High School.

- A few eccentric individuals became ubiquitous Uberfall irregulars, including the aging Lester Germer until his death in 1971 and some very able climbers who seemed to fit into no group but were always there, like the blond Turk Dennis Memhit, the dark Greek Demetri Kolocotronis, Rod Swarz, and Morrie Jaffe.

- Lending a distinctive touch was the occasional glimpse, treasured by the Gunks regulars, of Hans Kraus and Fritz Wiessner walking slowly together along the carriage road, heads bowed, hands behind their backs, seeming incredibly short of stature and large of spirit, two gnomes from the mythology of the Shawangunk past.

Everyone was climbing better. Though attention is usually lavished on what happens at the leading edge of climbing achievements, the real story of 1969–1972 was what took place on down the line below Olympus, among the mere mortals. Within the clubs, college groups, and independents alike, just about everyone slowly extended their horizons to higher personal standards. The old 5.6 leaders began to lead 5.7s or even an occasional exhilarating 5.8. Duffers who for years had struggled on 5.4s found themselves surmounting 5.5s and 5.6s, maybe even 5.7s. Beginners didn't always have to start on 5.2s anymore. In the spring of 1968 a fifteen-year-old kid led the 5.10 roof on *Retribution,* barely mastered by McCarthy just seven years before. By 1972 that now ex-fifteen-year-old's fifteen-year-old kid brother, not to mention several other teenage whizzes, were quite regularly leading 5.10s and not attracting special attention. Oldsters—not just Wiessner—were doing 5.7s and 5.8s; seventy-year-old Lou Lutz climbed *The Arrow* and *Pas de Deux.* A lot of women were climbing at levels once attained only by Bonnie Prudden and Krist Raubenheimer, with Cherry Austin and Patty Crowther merely one step ahead of the rest. Even within the conservative fortress of the AMC, where 5.7 had long been the ceiling for all but one or two individuals, club leaders began to do a dignified 5.8 now and then.

This general advance was not, of course, due to any sudden rise in the agility or muscularity of Americans but rather to (as at the leading edge in the previous decade) changes in perception and confidence. The breakthroughs at the top sent an inspiring message down through the ranks. Veterans of the sport redefined their personal limits, but much more of the change was due to the rapid turnover in climbing population. The more confident attitudes and improved climbing displayed during the 1969–1972 years were not so much the result of the same climbers changing their minds as of new climbers coming in who saw possibilities in a different light. Old inhibitions left the sport with those who dropped out. Undoubtedly the social context of the late 1960s played a role in how climbers looked at what they could and couldn't do. The mood of the 1950s had not encouraged boldness, but in the turbulence of the new social unrest, constraints fell.

With the Degenerates climbing all week long and others pushing the season into the winter months, the responsibility of land management grew more taxing. In 1963 the Smiley family and interested conservationists created The Mohonk Trust (later Mohonk Preserve) as a nonprofit educational agency to manage a large tract of Shawangunk ridge, including the Trapps and most of the Near Trapps. Every weekend during the late 1960s, a TMT ranger named Joe Donahue parked a pickup truck on the carriage road near the Uberfall, becoming the most widely known personality of anyone at the cliffs, save possibly Lester Germer. Besides selling climbing permits, Donahue carried on a side business of his own in climbing equipment, which he sold directly out of the back of his truck. The arrangement was convenient for the climbers. On one occasion a leader on a nearby aid climb, *Stirrup Trouble,* finding himself in urgent need of a piton of a particular size, called to a friend at the Uberfall ("Quick, I need a ⅝-inch angle!"), who stepped to Donahue's truck, purchased the needed pin, and raced to the base of *Stirrup Trouble,* where the leader had lowered a coil of rope and a carabiner to transport the desperately desired item to where it was put into action within a minute or two of purchase.

When Donahue's side business was terminated (The Mohonk Trust eventually deeming it inappropriate), the business opportunities in this growing market were not long neglected. Up until now the venerable old musty New York walk-up store, Camp and Trail Outfitters, had been the single source of supply in the New York area. In 1967 AMC climber Leon R. Greenman opened a new store in the city and rapidly surpassed his competition. His ascendency with Shawangunk climbers was brief, however. In 1970 a consortium of Gunks climbers opened a store called Rock and Snow in New Paltz, the little town nearest the cliffs, and installed Dick Williams as manager. Hiring a succession of popular climbers to work behind the counter, Williams built Rock and Snow into by far the most patronized climbing shop of the area, a frequent gathering place for climbers on late Sunday afternoons or whenever it rained.

Donahue was replaced by a faintly more formal administrative system. However, constructive relations with the climbing community were assured by The Mohonk Trust's addition in 1972 of a rock climber to its Board of Trustees, of ex-Appie climber Bradley J. Snyder as top staff assistant under Daniel Smiley and ex-Vulgarian Thom Scheuer as Chief Ranger. In the next few years the low-key, immensely popular Scheuer succeeded Lester Germer as the one universally recognized figure at the cliffs. Under him, a succession of seasonal rangers was hired. Often dedicated Gunks climbers themselves— Ron Matous, Rick Perch, and Todd Swain, to mention examples—these seasonal rangers also enjoyed excellent rapport with the regulars. One key to the tranquility of these halcyon years at the Shawangunks was the remarkably sympathetic relationship between the climbers and the landowners' agents.

The most significant development of the years 1969 to 1972, however, had nothing to do with land management, business trends, or more difficult climbing. It was the clean climbing movement, the environmental awakening under which the entire Shawangunk community discontinued the use of pitons in favor of artificial chockstones, or climbing "nuts."

Climbing nuts were first regularly used in Great Britain; originally they were literally machine nuts employed by nonaffluent British climbers in place of the pitons they could not afford. When John Reppy returned from a visit to England in the early 1960s, he brought back nuts and used them in Connecticut, but the novelty did not catch on. In the mid-1960s California's climbing guru Royal Robbins began using them. Boston's climber-craftsman Steve Arsenault began designing and making his own nuts in 1966. At about the same time, several Gunks regulars began trying them out: IOCA's Willy Crowther, Vulgarian Dave Craft, and the popular Appie leader Chuck Loucks. Jim McCarthy used them as early as 1967. The motive for these early experimenters was largely curiosity and the entertaining novelty the new toy afforded. "Most of us early nutters," recalled Robbins, "appreciated that climbing is *more fun* using nuts, because they require more skill and care" (italics in original).

But by the end of the 1960s another force entered the picture. This was the time of the hippie revolt, back-to-nature enthusiasm, Earth Day, and a strong surge of environmental consciousness. About 1969 and 1970, hikers and backcountry managers were growing concerned over the impact of the backpacking boom, caretakers and ranger-naturalists were being hired to protect the backcountry, trail erosion was being resisted and a broad education campaign launched to protect the mountains from being loved to death. As more climbers swarmed to the Gunks, the impact on approach and descent trails began to disturb the regulars as well as The Mohonk Trust.

Most of all, climbers began to notice piton scars. In the early days pitons made of soft iron bent with the contours of the rock, could not often be removed and reused, and consequently were left in place. With the widespread adoption of cro-molly during the 1960s, climbers began more and more to place and remove their own pitons. Indeed, it became a requisite skill for a good leader that he/she could place good protection and the mark of a good second that he/she could remove it, even when this meant dangling awkwardly with one hand from small holds on overhanging rock. Ironically, removing the pitons was originally considered environmentally enlightened, as it allowed later parties to experience the unmodified rock. Using soft iron pins and leaving them behind was disdained as an example of European-style littering.

With heightened environmental concern, climbers now noticed that the technique of removing pitons—banging them from side to side until

Nuts replace pitons. This March 1973 issue of the climbing magazine Summit *cap-tured the chief development of the early 1970s throughout American climbing: the conversion from traditional pitons to the newer forms of protection, beginning with climbing nuts.*

loose—severely scarred the rock. Where pitons were repeatedly placed and removed, the crack would widen and be chipped away at the lip. Warned one Gunks regular:

> Their "hard" steel pitons are just that: hard on the rock. They
> chew to pieces the edges and interiors of cracks wherever
> they are repeatedly placed and removed. . . . Moreover, the
> scars that continual piton placement and removal make
> are ugly.

Fearing the long-term result on the integrity of the beautiful Shawangunk rock, some climbers began to worry. Wrote Stannard:

> All the climbs up through 5.5 are literally being pulled
> apart. Another two years of this and all these climbs will be
> nothing but a sequence of piton holes and broken rock.

In time these trends might have slowly generated a shift from pitons to nuts. However, in the spirit of the environmentally concerned times, some climbers felt that a slow evolution would take too long. One man was particularly alarmed: John Stannard. With the same dedication and perserverance that had carried him into 5.11 in 1967–1968, Stannard threw his energies, intelligence, and prestige as the area's top climber into a campaign to promote "clean climbing." His fervor and commitment to this cause were singular. He began climbing exclusively with nuts; began systematically doing a climb or two with every Gunks regular he could meet, so as to show them personally how well nuts worked; launched a newsletter (*The Eastern Trade*) to spread the message; conducted demonstration tests of how much force could be held with nuts; personally produced a special brand of soft-iron pitons, tinted the same color as Shawangunk rock, which he placed as permanent or "resident" pitons at key spots where everyone agreed piton protection was needed; and carried on a far-flung correspondence promoting the cause. Besides the campaign to end the use of pitons, Stannard also participated in efforts to halt trail erosion at the cliffs and would get up early every Sunday morning to patrol the nearby roadsides with a garbage bag and pick up every scrap of litter. His dedication was perceived as peculiar by the rest of the climbing community, but because he was the man who had freed *Foops* his impact was enormous.

Others joined in. Rock and Snow kept a book of "all-nut" ascents, and climbers vied to make "first all-nut ascents" of each route. After a while Rock and Snow simply refused to stock pitons. The Mohonk Trust, under the leadership of a trustee who had briefly rock climbed with the New York Appies in the 1940s and 1950s, LaVerne Thompson, began a series of meetings with concerned climbers with a view toward developing a consensus on needed environmental measures. On April 22, 1972, Thompson met with Stannard, McCarthy, and two Appie leaders. This was the prelude to a series of three larger "town meetings," the first on May 13, 1972, to which thirty to forty climbers were invited, the list carefully drawn to ensure representation from all the most active circles, with three or four Mohonk Trustees present. The meetings were presided over, in turn, by Stannard, Rutgers Outing Club faculty adviser Robert Markley, and Appie Chuck Loucks. Volunteer work projects were organized by the climbers themselves, with the support of the Trust, to combat trail erosion. AMC's professional White Mountains trail crew came down to give technical advice. A measure of the broad support of all climbers is the fact that one 1972 work weekend featured four projects and the climbers in charge were drawn from four different climbing circles—the Appies, the Vulgarians, the Degenerates, and IBM. This spirit of community interest was in marked contrast to the divisive spirit of the 1950s: where the old Vulgarians had rebelled against Smiley-AMC overtures then, their spiritual heirs as bad boys (and girls) of the cliffs, the Degenerates, were as zealous as anyone in watching over the integrity of their beloved cliffs, working on trails, climbing without pitons. Every significant circle of climbers supported the clean climbing movement, Stannard diligently cultivating leaders in each group who would set an example for their peers. From Vermont the man who had originally opened up the Shawangunks to rock climbing, Fritz Wiessner, bestowed his prestigious blessing, writing Stannard:

> I am delighted that you continue with your good work on promoting nuts and limiting piton use. . . . I think that the progress in climbing ethics is very encouraging and ensures the protection of the hills and mountains we love.

The revolution was over remarkably quickly. Climbing historian Chris Jones notes:

> The turnabout in attitudes toward pitons came faster in the Shawangunks than in California. While Valley climbers carried pitons "just in case," Easterners were totally committed to the cause.

In 1969 virtually everyone at the Gunks climbed with pitons; walking along the carriage road at the Trapps, one would hear the ring of hammer on steel all up and down the cliffs. By 1972 virtually no one ever placed a piton; a serene quiet reigned over the cliffs, in spite of the greater numbers. The conversion from pitons to nuts was complete. ∎

Reference Note

An indispensable aid to study of the "clean climbing" movement of the 1969–1972 years is *The Eastern Trade*, a newsletter issued by John Stannard between October 1971 and Spring 1978; and the file of papers kept by him and donated to the Mohonk Preserve, which generously allowed the authors to peruse it.

The Rack and the Theory of the Expanding Universe

THE 1980S SPAWNED a bewildering cornucopia of new devices for protecting climbers. It was the Decade of Pro, as the paraphernalia came to be known. There were not just nuts or stoppers or hexes. There were also Friends and cams and tricams. There were also TCUs and RPs. There were also Pollocks and Bugaboos and Fifis. There were also Stones and Rocks and Balls. There were also Camalots and Fish Hooks and Big Bros. There were also Screamers and Shunts and Dog Bones.

Back in the 1960s, when we learned rockcraft, there were pitons. Period. Early in the 1970s came the sudden conversion from pitons to nuts (chapter 16), but at first there weren't a whole lot of nuts to choose from. Our personal racks dropped pitons fast, but as the 1980s progressed, neither our inclination nor our budget tempted us to try all the proliferating new species of pro. We continued to climb with a rack of perhaps a dozen assorted old nuts proven to be useful and loyal.

Most 1980s climbers, however, took full advantage of the wide range of available pro. Almost all the new leaders were doing harder climbs than we and were raised to a style that believed wholeheartedly in protecting all these hard moves. So we found a growing disparity between the size of our rack and those of all our friends, especially our new friends (and their new Friends). In contrast to our modest, meager dozen, most other racks we saw glistened with serried rank on rank of well-ordered pieces of metal. For every conceivable crack or incipient concavity in the cliff, a precisely tailored piece of pro could unfailingly be plucked from the assembled troops. On one level we were impressed and envious; on another, uninterested.

On more than one occasion, when we'd greet a young friend and decide to do a climb together, he might say something like: "Want to bring your rack, my rope?" Then he'd see our little squad of a dozen old faithful nuts come out of the pack and he'd suddenly remember a reason not to use his rope. "Why don't we take *my* rack, your rope?" (Of course, that might give him further concern when he saw our rope. . .)

All this by way of background to make a point: the growth in "The Rack" did not start in the 1980s.

When we were starting research for this history in the early 1980s, we arranged to do a number of climbs with Jack Taylor (see chapters 11 and 13), in order to learn some of the original routes of his era and otherwise pick over his memories of forty years on northeastern rock. On one occasion, Jack led one rope while one of us led another on adjacent climbs. At the top, he looked over at us and our twelve-nut rack and exclaimed: "Jeez, you carry a lot of stuff!"

Taylor belonged to the era when protection was largely a function of the mental discipline and long-accumulated self-knowledge of the leader. His generation believed in well-anchored belays and protection where necessary, but the definition of "necessary" wasn't the same as it became in the 1980s. In fairness to the later generation, Taylor and friends were not doing the desperately difficult, dead-vertical terrors to which the 1980s generation routinely aspired. Taylor himself told us he couldn't possibly do anything harder than 5.7—"Look," said he once, flexing his biceps, "no muscles!" But right up to his limit, he had the assured knowledge of what he could and couldn't do that made protection almost optional.

We recall his showing us a 5.6 friction climb on Whitehorse Ledge. At his indicating the general direction to lead, one of us led the first pitch. It was very low angle and had no cracks in which to place pro. We reached the end of the rope and still no cracks, not even a bush, in fact nothing to belay from. We called down to Jack in mild desperation. He called up: "Sit. Just sit down." Looking around we saw a slightly depressed spot that we decided to call a seat. We felt, though, that Jack didn't quite understand our problem. However, he soon started up and took over the next pitches, the hardest involving a long runout to a crux move. Jack calmly ran out 60 feet of rope till he got to the move, then decided the weighty camera around his neck was a liability, whereupon he down-climbed all 60 feet of friction (friction being one of the harder kinds of climbing to reverse), gave us his camera, re-climbed the 60 feet, placed one nut (of his half-dozen or so) and walked airily through the crux. Of the four of us on two ropes that day, Jack was the only one who remained perfectly relaxed throughout this entire procedure.

There's more to tell about the history of The Rack. Taylor's was not the first northeastern climbing generation, neither did the growing size of The Rack begin with ours.

On another occasion, Hassler Whitney agreed to a date with us to show us some of his original routes on the Sleeping Giant from his student days at Yale. Now Whitney was an undergraduate at New Haven from 1924 to 1928, and our date was in 1982. More than fifty years had passed since Whitney had climbed at the Giant. Fifty years: think of that a minute, reader. Where were you fifty years ago today?

On the appointed morning, we convened at the parking lot, us with our modest dozen-nuts rack and a young Connecticut climber who was also interested in learning about the early history of the state's climbing, who naturally sported an enormous rack with array after array of various sophisticated protection devices. Then Whitney drove up and stepped out ready to climb, carrying just one thing: his lunch, in a little brown bag. So much for The Rack in the 1920s.

There's more yet. When we walked along the base of the cliff, Whitney looked up, announced that he thought one of his old routes went up here— and thereupon started up! We looked at our young friend, he at us: should we rope up? Should we put on our specialized climbing boots? (Whitney was wearing old sneakers.) If we rope up, should we belay? If we belay, should we place pro? Meanwhile, the seventy-six-year-old Whitney was proceeding steadily up through rock of roughly 5.3 difficulty.

Eventually he halted at the base of a move, and when joined by us (*and* our ropes, *and* our racks, *and* his lunch), he explained that this next move was not one that he would do unroped. So he agreed to be tied in while one of us led the move (perhaps 5.5) and belayed from just above, still 30 feet below the top of the cliff. Whitney followed effortlessly and, on surmounting that move, promptly untied and continued to the top where he awaited our eventual arrival, slowed as we were by ropes, protection, belaying procedures, and the like.

All part of the education of a climbing historian—and a further indication of the changing role of The Rack in climbing history. ∎

North country wilderness. This lonely party on the Adirondacks' remote Wall-face in 1965 experiences the quiet in the north country characteristic of the years before 1970. Note extensive wilderness in background.

17: Quiet in the North Country: Before 1970

F OR MANY YEARS after the Shawangunks had become a crowded bustling scene, the rock cliffs of the north country remained quiet and lonely places. If you came to climb at the Gunks, you were in the society of other climbers all day. Rare was the belay stance from which several other parties were not visible along the cliffs. If you went north before 1970, you embarked on a different world, rarely anyone else in sight, a feeling of exploration and commitment, an aura of mountaineering rather than "just" rock climbing, a sense of being thrown on your own resources to find the route, watch for bad weather, and handle any crisis as you might in the wilds of the Canadian Rockies. Of course, as later climbers realized, neither Cathedral Ledge nor even Cannon cliff was Mount Robson, and the road was always nearby. But the spirit of adventure and self-reliance was palpable for the small bands who chose to climb in the north country during the 1950s and 1960s.

In 1945, just as World War II ended, Herb and Jan Conn showed up at Cannon cliffs. Cousins, the Conns had summered in North Woodstock during the 1930s. There they explored the White Mountains and scrambled happily along the rocky contours of Lost River, "one of the spots which spurred our love of the physical contortions involved in both climbing and caving." Living in Washington, D.C., during the war, they learned to rock climb properly at the Potomac cliffs. When they arrived at Cannon on August 23, 1945, armed with sneakers, borrowed gear, and a single 120-foot rope, the young and inexperienced pair knew only of rumors that a route went up the main face. No one else was around. They headed straight for the central and highest part of the cliff, anxious to avoid "that deflating self-accusation which we might feel later, that we had 'avoided the face'"—little realizing that the likes of Underhill, Whitney, and Wiessner had settled for less intimidating routes on either side. The route they climbed wove through difficult and dangerously disintegrating rock, with "magnificent exposure, the bleak granite slabs that seemed so smooth and forbidding, and the worrisome feeling of becoming more and more extended as we climbed higher." They emerged on top at dusk, having climbed a route of

TRUDY HEALY

far greater difficulty than those of their illustrious predecessors. (Much of the original *Conncourse* has changed through rockfall, but some sections were fully 5.7 if not harder; some of the route follows the very popular later 5.8 route known as *Moby Grape*.) Like the novice kids they were, Herb and Jan Conn roamed the souvenir shops of Franconia Notch next day looking for postcard pictures of the cliff to send to their friends, but were disgusted to find only the usual tourist shots of the Old Man of the Mountain. In drizzling rain, with an indifferent world of nature and people alike ignoring the extraordinary feat they had just achieved, they hiked up to Greenleaf hut for a chilly night and next day, soaking wet, boarded a bus for Boston, cutting a sorry spectacle for two people who had just pulled off by far the longest and possibly also the most difficult climb in New Hampshire before the coming of John Turner in the late 1950s. The Conns never climbed much in the Northeast, a loss to the region, as their climbing skill, mild and cheerful personalities, and voluminous fund of good climbing songs never really entered this region's legacy. They shortly moved to South Dakota, where they took up such interesting pursuits as living in a cave, Herb earning his living cleaning the faces of the Mount Rushmore Presidents, Jan playing flute in a local symphony orchestra, and both earning renown among cavers for exploring and mapping the fifth longest cave in the world.

The Conns' spirit of solitary exploration was often the lot of north country climbers for the next quarter century. Another Potomac-based team probed new routes on Katahdin in 1945. Over in the Adirondacks, high-schooler David Bernays inherited the mantle of Jim Goodwin in escapades on wilderness cliffs like Wallface, summer and winter. Later, the dedicated Adirondack outdoorswoman Trudy Healy and climbers from Penn State followed in his footsteps. Harvard mountaineers found rock routes up the crumbling cliffs in Vermont's Lake Willoughby region. Two Vermont "locals," Roger Damon and Dan Brodein of St. Johnsbury, climbed all over Vermont and New Hampshire crags. A couple of European climbers transplanted to the Mount Mansfield area—Helmut Lenes of Burlington and Adi Yoerg of Stowe—dabbled independently but each with professional skill on Vermont rock. Dartmouth's aspiring mountaineers knew a dozen small cliffs that no one else knew of, much less climbed. Boston-based climbers continued to visit Whitehorse and Cathedral with some regularity but largely avoided Cannon for nearly a decade after an accident due to spontaneous rockfall in 1952. Within the AMC group, the Kruszyna-Fay-Taylor crowd explored many outlying crags, some involving long trailless approaches. So did Earle Whipple, sometimes with AMC and sometimes with Harvard climbers. In the 1960s, after the Kruszyna crowd pulled out of the AMC (chapter 13), a secondary wavelet of AMC mountaineers-rather-than-rock-climbers plied the north country cliffs—a clique that included Paul Doyle as leader, Bob Hall, who cultivated a taste for big cliffs like Cannon and Katahdin's north basin wall, and high-living, hard-drinking maverick Geoff Wood. Whipple produced a guide to Cannon climbs in the form of an *Appalachia* article in 1965, and Hall updated it in 1971–72. From MITOC came the boldest innovators in north country climbing of the 1950s (not counting John Turner): Dave Bernays (once he reached college age and came to Cambridge) and Ray D'Arcy, backed by willing accomplices like Rit Walling, Stan Hart, Harry King, and the soon-to-emerge Willy Crowther. Connecticut climbers, led by J. B. Gardner and John Reppy, were also active in explorations off the beaten track. In the late 1960s, the AMC's Trail Crew spawned adventurous cragsmen, including the later Trails Supervisor, Bob Proudman. A brace of New Hampshire brothers, Jeff and Andy Damp, was active for a time. In North Conway a father-son team, Joe and Phil Ostroski, opened the region's first primitive guide service and climbing school in 1965.

Among these disparate circles, all small and isolated from one another, nothing much harder than 5.7 was done. But technical difficulty was not the point. In the spirit of those times, adventure and commitment provided the spice that Shawangunk climbers of that time were finding in breaking through to 5.8 and 5.9 and 5.10. "The routes were all so fearsome then," recalled Kurt Winkler, who began as a Trail Crew climber in the late 1960s. Even repeating long-established routes felt like exploration, with no guidebook and no one else around to consult. As compared with Quincy or New Paltz, the routes seemed toweringly high and long. Proudman called any route on Cannon "an alpine adventure." A newcomer at Cathedral in the late 1960s, Joe Cote, recalled:

> When I started out, there were no books and hardly any climbers—you had to take a chance and learn everything by yourself, a thrilling feeling of discovery which I think is now lost.

In the quiet pre-1970 years two isolated phenomena swept through the north country. Neither started trends, yet both left noteworthy legacies.

John Turner was a renegade Englishman who had climbed at a high standard in Britain before coming to MIT for a year's study. To avoid military draft, he moved to Montreal in 1956 and stayed six years. At this time he waged a series of lightning raids on U.S. climbing areas, during which he electrified

John Turner. This elegant fox hunter of the 1980s would scarcely be taken for the hard-living high-climbing rebel of the late 1950s who pioneered the hardest climbs of the day at the Adirondacks' Pok-o-moonshine and New Hampshire's Cathedral Ledge. It is the same man, however: John Turner, then living in Montreal, now returned to his native Britain and "a more suitable occupation for elderly persons."

ALAN ADRIAN

those few climbers who caught glimpses of what he was up to. Of modest height, unprepossessing airs, and coke-bottle-thick spectacles, Turner trained hard to develop extraordinary upper-body strength, his huge chest and long arms contrasting oddly with a narrow waist and spindly legs. "His shoulders started at his ear lobes," recalled one northeastern climber who watched him in action at Cathedral Ledge. "A gorilla with glasses," was another's assessment.

But strength was only the beginning of Turner's equipment for revolutionary rock climbing. More important was a singular boldness and willingness to push himself to the limit—precisely the point the conservative tradition had counseled against. Sometimes he pushed beyond that limit: his long leader falls became legends and spawned the nickname "Tumbledown Turner." To the reigning conservative tradition he was "foolish and dangerous," but he in turn saw their conservatism as "a dead hand on the development of climbing in the North East at that time." As for his reluctance to use much protection:

> I sometimes was viewed askance by the traditionalists who whacked in a statutory peg every eight feet and were frequently to be seen virtually immobilized either by rope

drag at the top of a pitch or by an inertia of assorted ironmongery at the bottom.

While Turner climbed at the Shawangunks, Joe English, Smugglers
Notch, Whitehorse Ledge, and the Chapel Pond area, his important contributions were made at two north country cliffs: the Adirondacks' hitherto
unexplored Pok-o-moonshine and New Hampshire's Cathedral Ledge.

In 1957 Turner put in two routes at Pok-o-moonshine that were no
harder than the prevailing northeastern standard but that were of remarkably fine quality: *Catharsis* (5.6) and *FM* (5.7), both of which have remained
among the most favored routes at the cliff. In 1958, however, he broke into
higher levels of difficulty. That year he put in *Discord,* the first 5.8 at Poko.
And on June 29, 1958, he appeared at Cathedral Ledge with Art Gran and
climbed *Repentance.*

Given its early date and bold style, *Repentance* must rank as one of the
tours de force in northeastern climbing history. The route follows a wide,
flaring, ugly crack and chimney system, dark, dank, mossy, with a steep, awkward and intimidating crux section at the start of the second pitch. This passage was much harder than the prevailing 5.7 standard of New Hampshire
climbing: posterity has called it "5.9 plus" or even "borderline 5.10." Subsequent ascents enjoyed the protection of a bolt (later an oversized piton) at
the crux, but Turner led that section relying on a much lower piton. The
performance was slightly flawed by his stepping on that piton, but that was
before he reached the real difficulties and was of trivial significance. The
later superstar Henry Barber exclaimed on this lack of protection as much
as on the difficulty: "The honesty of Turner: *Repentance* with a piton!" Later
that summer Gran repeated the lead. After that, however, twelve years
elapsed before another free ascent, an extraordinary interval for such a
line. During that period the route acquired the mystique of legend, was regarded as unclimbable, and boundlessly augmented Turner's prestige.

(The rumor that Gran led *Repentance* the very next day is discounted by
Turner himself: "After the climb we drank a lot of beer in the American
Legion, Berlin, NH, and were certainly in no condition to repeat it the next
day." Indeed, Gran's abrasive personality and aptitude for controversy led
some climbers to question whether he ever led it. However, Turner believed
he was fully capable of doing so and accepts Gran's lead; and there is no objective reason to doubt that he did. If true, it adds immensely to Gran's
credit as a high-level climber and does little to diminish the subsequent legend of *Repentance.*)

The following year Turner put in three more routes of very nearly the

S. PETER LEWIS

Recompense. *One of the all-time classic routes on New Hampshire rock, Cathedral's* Recompense *was also one of the most difficult when John Turner first climbed it in 1959. Modern climber Marc Chauvin here leads the celebrated airy crux.*

same difficulty. Two at the Poko cliff, *Bloody Mary* and *Positive Thinking*, were also 5.9, steep, exposed, and poorly protected. Again, years passed before their second ascents. The other 1959 5.9 was *Recompense* at Cathedral. If aesthetics and the enjoyment afforded later climbers are the criteria, *Recompense* was an even greater contribution than *Repentance*. An elegant line, its crux occurs on the fourth pitch, a long series of laybacks and stems over a beautiful arching crack near the top, several hundred feet of airy space above the Cathedral pines. To this day, many north country climbers regard *Recompense* as "the" climb to do at Cathedral, probably its finest line. On these 1959 climbs his seconds were drawn mostly from Canadian climbing friends.

Elsewhere around the region Turner appeared at unpredictable intervals. He climbed a couple of cracks on the Washbowl cliffs near Chapel Pond, created a dramatic variation on a popular Shawangunks route, *Thin*

Slabs, and was rumored elsewhere. Wherever he went, his routes featured difficulty and boldness. An expression grew among north country climbers that there were 5.8s and Turner 5.8s, with the unspoken implication (often accompanied by raised eyebrows and a despairing shrug) that the latter involved more difficulty and boldness than most leaders preferred.

Turner was unquestionably ahead of his time, not only for the raw difficulty and daring of his routes but also for the impeccable style in which they were dispatched. As compared with McCarthy, however, he was not so influential. At Poko and Cathedral his routes were the only ones of anything like that level of difficulty, and more than ten years elapsed before local climbers regained and surpassed his standard, whereas McCarthy was pursued by a clamorous pack of able aspirants at the Shawangunks. Turner's distinction is not in his effect on the sport so much as the solitary splendor of his brilliance. By 1962 he was back in England, doing little climbing thereafter. In later years, at a time when McCarthy was still climbing at a respectable standard at the Gunks, Turner settled into the pursuit of fox-hunting "as a more suitable occupation for elderly persons." But his memory remained indelibly etched on New England granite in the soaring elegance of *Recompense* and that ugly, dark, dank, flaring phantasm of *Repentance.*

The second north country phenomenon of the pre-1970 years was the application of Yosemite-style big wall direct-aid techniques to New Hampshire's cliffs.

Until the 1960s northeastern climbers, beginning with Hans Kraus in the 1940s, had used aid as an occasional resort on short climbs where technical difficulties seemed insurmountable, but by the 1960s McCarthy and his henchmen were busily eliminating most of the aid from Shawangunk rock. The intimidating granite walls of the north country seemed fair game for aid still, however.

To the left of the *Conncourse,* Cannon's cliff soared upward in a series of huge gray-green arches, "a vast wall where only a fly could stick," as the Conns had declared. Up this towering blankness, the fertile imagination of Connecticut's John Reppy conceived the possibility of a line, given the patience for extensive nailing and the cool-headedness to work all day in the most airy and exposed setting obtainable in the Northeast. In 1964 Reppy persuaded McCarthy and Dick Williams to join him in an attempt. Plagued by bad weather and inexperience in the arts of big walls, they failed. But now Williams was intrigued. Later that year he returned with Dave Craft and Ants Leemets. Again weather was uncooperative. The north country was teaching the Shawangunk regulars what the mountain setting implied.

The following September (1965), Yosemite's renowned Yvon Chouinard was in the East. Seizing his opportunity to enlist one of the most seasoned big wall climbers in the world, Williams conscripted Chouinard and Art Gran for a renewed attempt. The Vulgarians trooped north en masse to provide support and encouragement—and a big party the night before, which left all three aspirants in marginal condition for such an undertaking. ("It was a big event, I'm telling you," recalled Williams.) Hangovers notwithstanding, Williams, Chouinard, and Gran, all sharing leads, worked their way high up the wall by dusk Saturday. On a tiny ledge they bivouacked. After a breakfast of a single can of sardines, in which Williams

PAUL ROSS

Arsenault on aid. Self-trained Steve Arsenault pioneered in establishing major direct aid routes all over the Northeast. Here he works his way up Cathedral Direct.

couldn't bring himself to partake, they completed the Northeast's first claim to a Yosemite-style big wall, calling it the *VMC Direct* (for Vulgarian Mountain Club).

The disappointed Reppy soon perceived an adjacent line. Returning the following year with Yalemen Sam Streibert and Bob Crawford, he pioneered his own big wall route, *YMC Dike.*

This brief flirtation with advanced aid techniques produced the Northeast's one true master of that art before the heightened ethic of free climbing rendered it largely obsolete. Steve Arsenault, who blossomed in 1967 and 1968, marched to his own drummer. In contrast to the Yale-Harvard-

RICHARD AREY

Joe Cote. The north country's first near-full-time "regular," Joe Cote made a significant impact on the pattern of future northeastern climbing, and in the process established many of today's popular classics, including the Mines of Moria, *shown here.*

PAUL ROSS

Princeton backgrounds of so many prominent eastern climbers of the day—even the Vulgarians were mostly college men, though not Ivy League—Arsenault was a self-made, largely self-taught master craftsman. He started to climb with the Boston AMC, but his earnest enthusiasm and evident raw talent proved passports to the society of the best climbers in the East. Willy Crowther saw him in action on the crags around Boston and became an early mentor. When he went to the Shawangunks, the Vulgarians instantly accepted him as one of theirs. Yet he also matched smoothly with Ivy League partners like Yale's Streibert. Although as good a free-climber as almost anyone, Arsenault's interest was stirred by the intricacies of sophisticated direct aid, which he applied first to a variety of short Boston area climbs, notably on Crow Hill. In 1967 and 1968 he moved up to the blanker sections of Cathedral Ledge. Here he nailed up such uncompromising lines as *White Eye* (with Streibert), *Intimidation* (with Kevin Bein and Bruce Beck), *Solitude Crack* (with Beck), and *Mordor Wall* (with Joe Cote for the bottom pitches, finishing roped-solo on the top). His most important route was *The Pendulum* (with Paul Doyle), which involved a sensational pendulum swing out from under a huge roof to a crack system on the left. Arsenault's classic Cathedral aid routes were destined for the fate that befell almost all aid routes: to serve as vehicles for the hard free climbing of the 1970s. But when they were first done, they were stunning achievements.

In 1968 Arsenault went off to Vietnam, but his place at Cathedral was immediately filled by an equally devoted climber, Joe Cote. A student at the University of New Hampshire, Cote became the first true "regular" in the north country, in the sense of a climber who was there every weekend, climbing everything that had been done, diligently searching the cliff for new lines—in short, who treated the hitherto intimidating vertical monolith of Cathedral in the casual manner with which Shawangunk "regulars" had treated their smaller cliffs since the time of Hans Kraus. Cote was a talented craftsman at both free and aid climbing, if not a path-breaker in technical difficulty or new methods. He regarded Turner's *Repentance* as "unclimbable." His historic contribution lay in his concentration on Cathedral as no one had done before, and as hundreds would do in the next generation. He showed the way. Largely by his impetus, the number of routes on Cathedral jumped from sixteen in 1968 to fifty-five in 1971. In 1969 Cote brought out a small guidebook to Cathedral climbs, the first published guidebook for a north country cliff.

Cote's arrival as a "regular" signaled the end of the long years of quiet in the north country. Beginning in 1970 new forces converged on

Cathedral and Cannon that rapidly brought north country climbing back into the prominence it had enjoyed in the prewar days of Underhill and Wiessner. ∎

Reference Note

North country climbing in the years between 1950 and 1970 is best documented for New Hampshire, in the magazine articles cited in the Note for chapter 3 (Kruszyna, Rubin, Macklin) and Al Rubin's historical essay in the Ross-Ellms guide. The original account of the first ascent of *Conncourse* was Herb Conn's "A New Rock Climb on Cannon Mountain," *Appalachia*, December 1946, pp. 264–266. See also the two compilations of Cannon route descriptions published in *Appalachia* before there were any Cannon guidebooks: Earle R. Whipple, "Climbing Routes on Cannon Cliff," June 1965, pp. 518–538; and Robert B. Hall, "Rock Climbs on Cannon Cliff, Part 1," June 1971, pp. 145–165, and "Rock Climbs on Cannon Cliff, Part 2," June 1972, pp. 103–113. For the Adirondacks, sources include James A. Goodwin's chapter, "Rock Climbing in the Adirondacks," in Grace Hudowalski, ed., *The Adirondack High Peaks and the Forty Sixers* (Albany: The Peters Print, 1970), pp. 134–143; Trudy Healy, *A Climber's Guide to the Adirondacks* (Adirondack Mountain Club, 1967); and Don Mellor, *Climbing in the Adirondacks*.

18: Streibert and Barber

TWO CHANGES WRENCHED the north country climbing scene beginning in 1970. One was the coming of higher standards of difficulty. The second was in the long run a more profound change: the birth and development of a social and institutional setting that gave north country climbing its own distinctive stamp.

The disparity in technical standards that had opened up between Shawangunk conglomerate and White Mountain granite between 1957 and 1970—despite the head start Turner had given the latter—was remarkable. Although the cliffs of New Paltz and of North Conway were but an easy day's drive apart, McCarthy and his retinue had taken Gunks climbing progressively through 5.8, 5.9, 5.10, and 5.11, yet still no one had repeated Turner's 5.9 *Repentance*. Obviously this gulf could not long remain unbridged.

STEVE ARSENAULT

Sam Streibert. For many years, summer and winter, and at many different cliffs throughout the Northeast, Sam Streibert maintained a significant niche at the cutting edge of climbing—yet rarely received the acclaim his sustained excellence deserved.

In southern New England, the Gunks' example of more difficult free climbing began to be heeded earlier. In the early 1960s MITOC climbers and other Bostonians began doing 5.9 and 5.10 at Quincy Quarries and other local crags, but almost invariably on a top-rope. Over in Connecticut Reppy was ready to push the standards, and he found a capable co-conspirator in the best of the Yale undergraduates, Sam Streibert. Streibert, it turned out, was to play a key role not only in Connecticut but all over New England, especially the north country.

Handsome and clean-cut, slightly aristocratic in bearing, Theodore P. ("Sam") Streibert came to Yale via Hotchkiss School, already a splendid athlete and competitive high-jumper. Family vacations in Europe exposed him to the Alps as a boy and kindled an affinity for mountains that proved enduring. He showed an extraordinary talent for climbing that enabled him to rise quickly and remain at the top levels of difficulty in the sport for twenty years. Though Streibert learned to climb at Yale and with IOCA (he was yet another to whom Willy Crowther was an important influence at an early stage of his development), his first major alliance was with the older John Reppy, then on Yale's faculty. In the early 1960s Reppy and Streibert began systematically to develop the climbing potential of Ragged Mountain. In 1964 they put up Connecticut's first recorded 5.9, *Shadow Wall* at Ragged. Though this was four years behind McCarthy's *MF*, and even later than *Matinee* (5.10), it showed that the mania for sheer technical difficulty was beginning to spread east of the Hudson River.

One mark of the progress in rock climbing throughout the region was the publication in 1964, almost simultaneously, of the first three guidebooks to rock climbs: Gran's for the Shawangunks; Crowther's for Quincy Quarries; and Reppy's and Streibert's for Ragged. A measure of where the activity was most intense is that the Ragged guide listed 54 routes, the Quincy one gave 60, that for the Gunks 249. The absence of any published guide for north country rock was conspicuous.

In 1970 north country standards finally moved to catch up. At Cannon cliff two Boston-based climbers, George Eypper and Larry Winship, put up two bold crack climbs, going free at 5.9. Gunks regular Kevin Bein, then climbing a lot in the north, dazzled everyone with the first wholly free ascent of Turner's *Repentance*. Joe Cote was steadily climbing harder, though still relying on aid for most new routes.

The key figure in bringing the gospel of hard free climbing to New Hampshire was Sam Streibert. Even as a young college climber, Streibert had been strongly pulled in the direction of the north country, joining Reppy and Harold May on the impressive Cathedral 5.8 *Three Birches* in 1963 and pioneering on the intricate route-finding for what became one of New Hampshire's most popular climbs, the misnamed but magnificent *Sam's Swan Song*. (Though Streibert pushed the critical bottom pitches of *Sam's Swan Song*, it was left to Phil Nelson and Alan Wedgewood, with visiting Britishers Michael and Sally Westmacott, to finish the first complete ascent of this classic. Nelson was climbing well in those years. He also led the first ascents of the great *Reppy's Crack* (5.8) and *Duet* (5.7), both also on Cannon. His best climbs always seemed to have someone else's name on them—*Sam's, Reppy's*.)

Starting in 1970, Streibert raised the ante. Teamed at first with visiting Colorado hard man Mike Stultz and subsequently with Dennis Merritt, Streibert demonstrated what could be achieved by combining ability with the determination to keep trying difficult problems with Stannardian persistence. In 1970 he and Stultz mastered a couple of extremely bold Cathedral routes in the 5.8 to 5.9 class and came very close to freeing *Repentance*. In the spring of 1971, Streibert and Merritt succeeded, after long effort, in freeing *Intimidation*, one of Arsenault's Cathedral aid routes and the first solid 5.10 to be climbed in the north country. Cote responded to the challenge of better free climbing and, in the fall of that year, contributed two superb 5.10s, one of which, *The Book of Solemnity*, climbed with Arsenault, was destined to become (once enough 5.10 climbers were bred) one of the most popular routes on the cliff (though later downgraded to 5.9+).

Elsewhere the team of Streibert and Merritt was hot in 1971, and their example expanded the horizons of climbers all over New England. On Crow Hill, near Boston, they free-climbed another Arsenault aid route, *Cromagnon Crack*, the first 5.10 in that area. At Connecticut's Ragged, they established that state's first 5.10, freeing *Aid Crack*. In the Gunks, Streibert and Merritt worked hard on pulling off the second ascent of *Foops* that fall, but as mentioned in chapter 15, they had not quite succeeded when that plum fell to Henry Barber in early 1972.

In July 1974 Streibert and Bob Anderson brought 5.11 to Cannon. They did so with flair on an all-free ascent of the *VMC Direct*, that historic nine-pitch aid route that Williams, Chouinard, and Gran had struggled up less than ten years before. With its length and sustained severity, it was a true tour de force, pulled off in impeccable style.

The range of Streibert's path-breaking contributions was remarkable. The same individual who first established new standards on Connecticut's short (sub-100-foot) traprock cliffs in 1964 also pioneered on Cannon's enormous (supra-1,000-foot) granite wall in 1974—we shall meet him again in chapter 21 creating new standards in ice climbing in the early 1970s.

Henry Barber. Hot Henry surmounts a characteristic extreme Shawangunks problem.

HEATHER HURLBUT

But Streibert never attained quite the prestige in the northeastern climbing community that his contributions merited. The reason was probably that his brightness was dimmed by the sudden outburst of a star whose brilliance placed all others in the shade.

Henry Barber completed the updating of north country standards that Cote and Streibert had begun. That—and much more.

A sportswriter once said of a flamboyant and controversial owner of the Washington Redskins: "George Preston Marshall slipped into town last night at the head of a seventy-six-piece brass band." In much this spirit Henry Barber stole onto the center stage of northeastern rock climbing. Wherever "Hot Henry" went, climbers knew it.

Barber was a lanky, awkward, raw-boned, brash and headstrong teenager whose relentless energy failed to find adequate outlets in baseball or schoolboy fistfights, until at age sixteen he began climbing with the Boston AMC. Where other top-grade climbers of his time enjoyed disparaging the AMC climbers, Barber never did, remembering his start there as "the best thing that ever happened to me." Rapidly going through early

At home in a vertical world. Barber exploring new ground on the Spider's Web in the Adirondacks.

mentors like D. Byers and George Meyers (before the latter moved to Yosemite), he soon branched out on his own with a string of younger partners—Oriel Sole Costa, Rick Hatch, Ajax Greene, Steve Hendricks, Chip Lee.

Barber had everything going for him. To begin with, he had a natural aptitude for climbing: "the single most talented climber I've ever seen," Mc-Carthy called him. His most visible trait was the phenomenal energy. Where other young hotshots might preen at the local bar after climbing a route at the top of the standard, Barber would exhaust his seconds by climbing three or four such routes in a day—then hit the bars most of the night and be up at dawn to climb the next day. Alone of the 1970s star climbers (Rich

COURTESY HENRY BARBER

Another impossible route. In 1971 a fellow climber bet a six-pack of beer that Recluse *could not be climbed free. Above: Barber completes the first free ascent and claims his reward.*

COURTESY DON MELLOR

Romano excepted), Barber did not follow a regimen of exercise and specialized training. Instead (like Romano) he simply climbed all the time—he trained to climb by climbing. In his early days Barber had converted his family's basement into a training gymnasium, doing chin-ups on paint stirrers nailed to the wall and building a "Foops machine" on which to practice the moves he'd need for the second ascent of Stannard's classic. But after 1971 he ignored training and simply climbed full time. In 1971 he climbed 260 days of the year; in 1972, 350; in 1973, 350. His response to competition was electric. He loved the limelight.

Barber's biggest weapon, however, was neither his talent nor his energy. It was his confidence. The venerated British alpinist Geoffrey Winthrop Young had identified the three requirements for achieving the highest standard of difficulty in rock climbing as "physique, confidence and endurance." If Goldstone had demonstrated the advantages of a splendid physique, and Stannard had shown what inexhaustible reserves of endurance could do, Barber now arrived to show what power lay in unlimited, unquenchable confidence. "An instant's failure of will or confidence," Young had warned, "will disturb the delicate adjustments of balance as fatally as a broken leg." Barber uniquely possessed that unshakable will and confidence. He firmly believed, when approaching a previously unclimbed problem, that he was the man who could do it. In the most precarious situations, approaching a seemingly insurmountable roof or blank face, his last piece of protection far below him, he never wavered in that quiet belief that he would find a way up. As Carlyle said of Robespierre: "Doubt dwelt not in him."

In 1972, his apprenticeship completed, Barber pulled off the first of what became his trademark: a concentrated blitz of a single climbing area, during which he left all onlookers breathless and drastically altered the local standard. In 1972 it was Cathedral Ledge. In a whirlwind of free climbing, mostly with Bob Anderson as partner, Barber put up eleven new routes in that year, nine of them at a level of 5.9 or higher, including the cliff's first 5.11, *Lichen Delight*. The upper left section of the cliff was so thoroughly saturated with his new routes that it became known as the "Barber Shop." Many of these lines were old aid routes nailed by Cote and others. Barber's demonstration of what could be climbed free gave the first major impetus to a movement away from aid in the north country, though New Hampshire climbers never did renounce aid as devoutly as did their counterparts at the Shawangunks.

Wherever Barber went, he created new standards. At Whitehorse, he put in the first 5.10, *Beelzebub*. At Cannon, he put in the first 5.10, *Whaleback*

Henry Barber, one of the most influential climbers of the 1970s, raised climbing standards and style throughout New England and the world.

JOHN CLEARE

Crack. Down at Crow Hill, he put in the first 5.11 in Massachusetts, *Jane.* At Ragged, he put in what was seen at the time as Connecticut's first 5.10, *Subline,* though subsequent second thoughts upgraded the Streibert-Merritt masterpiece, *Aid Crack,* from 5.9 to 5.10, upstaging Barber this once. All of these "firsts" were done in 1972 and all with Bob Anderson as his partner. Obviously Anderson was climbing very well too, a fact often overlooked—it was a quality of Barber that he put everyone around him in the shade.

One of Barber's most important contributions to the changing character of the sport was the transformation of the nature and purpose of Boston area practice climbing. Hitherto, Boston climbers had congregated on weekday evenings or nontraveling weekends at Quincy Quarries, Black and White rocks, and other crags where they climbed in miniature the same kinds of climbs, and at approximately the same levels of difficulty, to which they were accustomed when they went to the Gunks or the north country. Barber led a movement toward bouldering on several man-made stone walls—a 13- to 17-foot-high overpass near Kenmore Square on which more than thirty distinct routes were developed in the early 1970s; a similar construction in Olmstead Park; the Waban Arches, supporting a viaduct for the Chestnut Hill Reservoir; Echo Bridge, another part of that viaduct; and Charlesgate, a retaining wall for an overpass leading to one of the bridges over the Charles River. These were lower than Quincy or Black and White and (to say the least) not aesthetically situated. But the level of difficulty was miles harder. At Kenmore Square, with few exceptions, routes started at 5.9 and included at least three at 5.11. Barber's message was that the path to higher standards elsewhere lay in diligently practicing the most difficult moves imaginable at home, regardless of aesthetic considerations. After 1971 ambitious Boston area tigers logged more hours at Kenmore Square and the Waban Arches than at Quincy or Black and White (though less zealous climbers understandably preferred the old haunts). Barber had more to do with this change than any other individual.

After 1972 Barber widened his theater of operations until it took in the whole planet, as he systematically descended upon Yosemite Valley, England's crags, Australia, Africa, the Soviet Union, and various other spots, significantly altering standards wherever he went. An aura of competitive superiority—a "fastest gun in the west" syndrome—grew up about him. He became the first major American "rock star," featured on nationwide television specials and a familiar face in climbing magazines and posters. Young climbers of the mid-1970s had to climb in white painter's pants because that's what Hot Henry wore. He became the first northeastern climber to make a living as a climber, combining lecture fees and endorsements with serving as representative for climbing outfitters. Perhaps even more significant was his influence on climbing ethics and style. Following the lead of John Stannard and Steve Wunsch, he became an uncompromising proponent of free climbing, disdaining any form of aid. As the region's most prominent superclimber, he powerfully pulled an entire generation of climbers in the direction of high standards of ethics and style, though, as we shall see, other influences outweighed even his in the north country.

For a few years after he became a world-renowned star, Barber continued to climb frequently in the Northeast. In 1973 he was active at the Shawangunks with Stannard, Wunsch, and Bragg (chapter 15). Throughout the mid-1970s he was a presence in the New Hampshire climbing scene, residing (when not globe-trotting) in the nearby town of Conway. In 1977 he took an interest in a cliff in the Adirondacks and in a single season, in the words of that area's guidebook editor, "brought our free-climbing here near the level of New Hampshire's."

This celebrity's public career received a severe jolt from an incident on Africa's Kilimanjaro. His climbing partner was badly injured, rescued through a supreme effort on his own and Barber's part, but then left to be evacuated and to recuperate in a primitive African hospital without as much attention and solace from Barber as he felt was appropriate. Embittered, the partner wrote magazine articles and a fictionalized book about the incident, painting Barber in a most unflattering light. In a short space of time, Barber went from being the darling of the climbing world to an object of scorn in the eyes of many critics. With his brassy candor and undisguised egotism, Barber had been respected and imitated but never loved. Critics were quick to jump on the fallen idol. Within a year or two this young-man-in-a-hurry who had welcomed the limelight retreated from the public stage almost completely. Though he continued to climb, he avoided publicity, never reported first ascents, and deliberately withdrew from the competition at the cutting edge of the sport.

It had been a glorious five years or so, though. Barber compares with Underhill, Wiessner, Kraus, McCarthy, Stannard, and possibly Streibert for his impact on northeastern rock climbing. Of the others, only Wiessner climbed as widely throughout the region. In terms of impact on the sport, as noted in chapter 7, Wiessner was too far ahead of American standards to elicit emulation. But Barber was always one step ahead of a crowd of hot young climbers in each area, so he drew them after him like hounds to a fox. His impact on climbing standards was therefore probably greater than anyone's. One of his contemporaries went so far as to say that Barber had "a greater influence than any climber who ever lived," obviously a judgment difficult to defend, but which was based on the observation that Barber came along at a time when standards were ready to rise (to catch up with the Shawangunks), so when he showed the way, everyone came along. Once everyone caught up to his level, further progress inevitably slowed, making Barber perhaps "the last great name in North American rock climbing," to cite another contemporary judgment. Again *that* is difficult to defend, but it is based on the theory that further advances will inevitably occur so slowly, or at least so spasmodically, that no one will ever stand out ahead of the pack nor raise an entire region's sights so dramatically as did Henry Barber in 1972. ▪

Reference Note

Sam Streibert is credited copiously in the first ascent data and history sections of several area guidebooks but is otherwise not much described in printed sources. Henry Barber, on the other hand, is the subject of many interviews and articles, as well as the full-length biography by Chip Lee, *On Edge: The Life and Climbs of Henry Barber* (Boston: AMC Books, 1982). A representative magazine interview at the height of his fame was Demetri Kolocotronis, "Hot Henry," *Climbing*, May-June 1974, pp. 2–5.

19: North Conway Renaissance: 1970–1979

W HEN JOE COTE became the first Cathedral "regular" in 1969, he proved to be a pioneer for a profound change in the north country. This change ran deeper than simply the higher technical standards that came with Streibert and Barber.

Into the "quiet village" of North Conway—which the nineteenth century poet laureate of the White Mountains, Thomas Starr King, had called "a little quotation from Arcadia, or a suburb of Paradise"—came new people, new institutions, new ideas. Skiing and general summer tourism had

Rebirth of the mountain guide profession. One significant result of the North Conway renaissance was the emergence of a regular profession of mountain guiding for the first time since the nineteenth century. The new breed of climbing guides included (standing) Jimmy Dunn (left), Rick Wilcox (fourth from left), Alain Comeau (fifth from left), and (sitting) Joe Lentini (third from left).

found a home in North Conway. During the 1960s both had expanded steadily. But after 1970 the rate of growth turned radically upward. Starr King's Arcadia headed toward the status of a major recreational resort. Along with population growth and a proliferation of tourist attractions, a hothouse residential and commercial development caught fire. Second homes, condominiums, chalets, and all the accompanying trappings of the movement toward weekend-and-vacation housing and sharper-image life styles spread throughout the little hamlet and its nearby neighbors and crawled up the hillsides on every hand. Stores crowded North Conway's main street, then spilled southward in a classic "strip" along what had once been a lonely wooded highway, Route 16. Where formerly had roamed the black bear and the white-tailed deer, now sprang forth Beef and Ski Restaurant, Sandwich World, and McDonald's (of course); Haircraft, the Tub Shop, and the Yellow Balloon; and "factory outlets" for a wide variety of products. By 1985 the suburb of Paradise was called "an alpine version of Filene's Basement."

Northeastern climbing before 1970 had never found congenial company in the fast track of commercial development. Climbers were notoriously *un*fashionable, social outcasts, an *un*profitable business market, their only specialized stores being quaint, *un*businesslike (albeit much-loved) holes in the wall like New York's musty Camp and Trail Outfitters and the Boston area's cluttered Climbers Corner. In 1970 the image began to change. That was the year Rock and Snow opened in New Paltz to serve Shawangunk climbers. Far more significant, however, was the following year's opening of an Eastern Mountain Sports branch in North Conway.

The mother Eastern Mountain Sports had opened in the Boston area (Wellesley) in 1967. Sensing an opportunity that others had not taken, EMS hired Tom Lyman to organize a "Climbing School," which operated at first out of the Boston store under the name of "North American Mountaineering."

The idea of a climbing school was a significant departure in northeastern climbing. At the Shawangunks, the top climbers frowned on commercial activity in rock climbing as a matter of lofty principle. Stannard and his contemporaries waged a vigorous fight to maintain a spirit of casual amateurism in a sport that was in the process of change. Shawangunk climbers actively discouraged media coverage of climbing, declined invitations to appear in television commercials, turned a collective cold shoulder on professional guiding. Throughout the 1970s only a handful of Shawangunk climbers guided for pay and most of them operated sub rosa; their peers looked down on such activities. These policies were commended by The Mohonk Trust. In the north country Joe and Phil Ostroski had started a climbing school and guide service in 1965, but it had never been a thriving success.

Lyman's Climbing School started slowly but solidly. Among his first guides were two young men destined for major roles in northeastern climbing: Kevin Bein, age twenty-one in 1970, who was soon to leave EMS for New Paltz, becoming indelibly associated with the Shawangunks; and Rick Wilcox, age twenty-two, who became a key figure, perhaps *the* key figure in the north country.

On June 10, 1971, EMS opened a branch in North Conway, within sight of Cathedral and Whitehorse ledges. Lyman's Climbing School was installed there and began more aggressive operations at both cliffs. Though only twenty-three now, Rick Wilcox was given the responsibility of managing the store.

Richard French Wilcox, Jr. had learned to climb with the Boston AMC as a high-schooler during the mid-1960s. With precocious talent, he soon found its conservative tradition unduly restraining. In 1967 he went to the University of Massachusetts and began climbing with some bolder spirits

S. PETER LEWIS

"The guy who's pulled the scene together." Rick Wilcox, shown here on Cannon, combined talents as a climber and businessman with a friendly personality to become the key figure in the revitalized North Conway scene.

Henry Barber

THE SEVENTIES AT A GLANCE

Principal climbing event: rediscovery of New Hampshire
Climbs of the Decade:—rock: *The Prow*
                 —ice: *The Black Dike*
Hardest single climb: *Supercrack*
Boldest lead: *Armageddon*
Most improbable coup by a nobody: *Doug's Roof*
Emblematic item of gear: — rock: the pitonless, hammerless rack
                           — ice: the drooped pick and second
                                       tool
Most important climber: Henry Barber
Most underrated: — rock: Bob Anderson
                 — ice: Ed Nester
Most colorful: Howard Peterson
Most colorful group: the Degenerates
Most prominent woman: Barbara Devine
Child prodigy: Ajax Greene
Still-active father figures: Fritz Wiessner and Hans Kraus
Best-looking: John Bragg
Brainiest: Kevin Bein
Nice Guy Award: Peter Cole
Most abrasive: John Bouchard
Vanishing act (gone suddenly after this decade): John Stannard
Norman Clyde Award: Mike Hartrich
Fred Beckey Award: Ed Webster
Couple of the Decade: Barbara Devine and Kevin Bein

like Lyman and Bob Proudman. Before graduation, Wilcox was fully committed to climbing and looked around for a way to make a living that would enable him to climb a lot. That brought him to EMS and North Conway. Wilcox proved to be the right man in the right place at the right time. Combining practical business sense with a garrulous, friendly personality and a growing reputation as a very solid if rarely spectacular climber in all seasons, Wilcox walked in on the ground floor when north country climbing was beginning to grow, and he grew with it, as a person, as a climber, and as a businessman. During the 1970s he made EMS the hub of the north country climbing scene. When a dispute with top management caused him to leave EMS in 1979, he landed on his feet as president of the one significant rival store that had taken root in North Conway, International Mountain Equipment (IME). Quickly he built IME into the dominant technical climbing supplier for the region, forcing EMS to move toward general outdoor clothing and equipment. By the early 1970s and continuing into the 1980s Wilcox was indisputably the pivotal figure in North Conway climbing—"the guy who's pulled the scene together," according to Barber—a close friend of just about every climber of consequence, personally accessible and helpful to all, making all the right business moves to keep first EMS and then IME the prime source for north country climbers. At the same time he retained a boyish enthusiasm for climbing himself, performing ably both on local crags and expeditions from the Andes to the Himalayas.

In 1973 Lyman fell out with EMS management and was replaced by a man who became a second key figure, almost as important as Wilcox to the north country scene. Born and raised in England, Paul F. Ross was already a proficient rock climber when he came to the U.S. and took a job as instructor for Outward Bound at Maine's Hurricane Island in 1971. Hired by Lyman in 1973 and almost immediately succeeding him as Director of EMS's Climbing School, he moved aggressively to expand its operations. Eventually impatient with EMS's conservative marketing of that school, Ross left to found International Mountain Equipment in 1975. Never the businessman that Wilcox was, Ross did not enjoy running a store and was happy to hand over IME to Wilcox in 1979, continuing as head of its Climbing School and guide service. EMS kept up and later expanded its own school under Joseph Lentini.

Following the leadership of the youthful Wilcox and the veteran Ross, the North Conway climbing scene evolved its special character, poles apart from that of the Shawangunks. North Conway climbers basked in the resort atmosphere and embraced rather than spurned the commercial potential of the sport. First EMS, then IME were local gathering places for all the climbers. Professional guides employed by the two stores' Climbing Schools, and other schools that started in the 1980s, were the dominant figures. Climbing full time and training hard as well, the guides became the best climbers, put up most of the new routes, set the ethics and style, and served as role models for a rising generation of climbers, not only in North Conway but throughout New England. Their status led to something of a personality cult. There was an inner and an outer circle of top climbers, much admired and emulated. "They're definitely a club in North Conway," recalled one who was active there. Association with the stores put the guides in touch with all the latest developments in new climbing equipment, and Wilcox kept them and their legions well supplied. So the image of the North Conway climber featured shining new state-of-the-art racks, and a smart trendiness in outdoor clothing fashions as well. By the mid-1970s North Conway had evolved a major alternative personality for northeastern climbers, a world away from the Shawangunks.

The North Conway model was not simply different from the Shawangunks in institutional setting and personal style. The climbing itself moved in a different direction. These were the years when Cote, Streibert, and Barber were lifting the technical standards to 5.10 and 5.11. But an equally important change was being worked out by others, primarily Paul Ross.

When Ross arrived on the New England scene in 1971, he was thirty-three years old, a veteran of many years in the thriving, hectic-paced milieu of British rock climbing but new to New Hampshire. When he first saw the state's big cliffs, he could not believe how undeveloped they were. When climbers pointed out existing routes, he demanded incredulously: "You mean there's nothing between that and that?" Further inquiries satisfied him that neither direct aid nor bolt placement was taboo:

> When I came here and saw what they were doing on Cathedral, I said "oh well, anything goes." After that I didn't worry about whether to use a couple of bolts or not.

With delighted abandon and a variety of partners, Ross launched onto the blank walls of his adopted state. On Cannon in July 1971 he put up three long and intricate aid routes involving the full arsenal of aid techniques, including extensive bolting. In the same year he found the enormous south buttress of Whitehorse Ledge and nailed up its first big aid route, *The Eliminate*. In September 1971 he turned his attention to the North Conway area, establishing no fewer than nine new aid routes in the next eleven months, three on Whitehorse and six on Cathedral. These included some sensation-

"Creative and cunning."
British expatriate Paul
Ross was a major influence
on the pragmatic, oppor-
tunistic climbing style
adopted in New Hampshire.
At left he climbs Arete, *a*
climb made controversial by
the tactics used to achieve
the first ascent.

ally airy lines, including the central and most prominent feature on Cathedral, expressively called *The Prow.* Next he teamed with Henry Barber to pull off the first major "girdle" traverses of northeastern rock, girdling Cathedral in October 1972 and Cannon in August 1973.

Ross had a decisive impact on the tone of North Conway climbing. Recall that this was the era when Stannard and Wunsch were elevating Shawangunk free climbing to a purist ethic of absolutely no aid and not even pitons, much less bolts, to disfigure the rock. By contrast, Ross was, as one of his contemporaries mildly put it, "not guided by self-imposed constraints like Henry." Many of Ross's routes involved extensive direct aid, numerous bolts, and even long "bolt ladders" to surmount big blank stretches of wall, and little concern for style. In the very year that Stannard and his associates embarked on their campaign to eradicate aid from all Gunks climbs, Ross embarked on *his* campaign to establish a wealth of aid routes on north country rock.

The explanation for this divergence lies not only in the different personal codes of Stannard and Ross. The inherent difference between Shawangunk and White Mountain rock is a major factor. This difference is reflected both in the abundance of natural protection opportunities in Shawangunk conglomerate-—as contrasted with the elemental blankness of granite—and in the relatively small size and consequent lesser commitment required for Shawangunk routes, as contrasted with the sheer length and intimidating character of the big New Hampshire cliffs. The Gunks regulars might do several climbs a day and never be more than a rappel or two from the ground. Ross confronted climbs of an altogether different scale:

> When you have 500 feet of rock, you get up it that day to
> the best of your ability, with what style you can.

Ross's ethics and style were controversial. Stannard's sensibilities were outraged. Indeed most Shawangunks and many Boston and Connecticut climbers were incensed that such tactics should be flaunted at the height of the movement for environmental ethics. In North Conway, however, Ross was not only accepted but became a major influence on younger climbers. Until then north country climbing had seemed so faltering and amateurish, so far behind other areas. Here came a full-time, big-as-life professional climber, with years of experience on British rock—Ross preserved a thick Lancastrian accent that enhanced the image—moving with confidence and competence onto the biggest and blankest sections of New England granite. The rising generation was impressed. Indeed it is one of Ross's greatest coups that, while not really climbing at a technically high level even for his day, he was regarded then and is remembered now as one of the dominant climbers of his time—and he was. He was the consummate con artist, both in solving new climbing problems and in enhancing his own reputation in the process. "He'll find a creative and cunning way to get the job done," observed Kurt Winkler. The impact on the thinking of young North Conway climbers was incalculable. "He was the first adult," was the way John Bouchard, then a rising star, put it. (In 1975 Bouchard, though a brilliant free-climber, methodically hammered a long bolt ladder up a blank section of Cathedral Ledge, a line that one guidebook called "exceptionally contrived.") Only such an established and self-confident personality as Ross could have outweighed the influence of Henry Barber toward a purer ethic.

Ross was not alone in his style; nor were bolts the only controversial issue. In 1972 Joe Cote created a challenging face climb called *Ventilator*, originally rated 5.9, later 5.10, by first dropping a top-rope to rehearse the moves; then rappelling down to place three bolts for protection; and, only after all that, leading the climb. *Ventilator* may not have been the first route created in that style, but is was certainly not the last and was later cited as the precedent for such tactics. In the 1970s many of New Hampshire's 5.11s were established by prior inspection, cleaning, and sometimes even protection on rappel, including *Starfire* (1975), *Western Lady* (1977), *Arete* and *Kinesis* (1978), and *Budapest* (1979). Throughout the decade, the dominant North Conway climbers seldom hesitated to place bolts, on rappel if necessary, inspect and clean routes on rappel, and sometimes carry the "cleaning" process so far as to modify handholds. Cote cut down a hemlock that obscured a 5.8 crack called (with arboreal inaccuracy) *Pine Tree Eliminate*. John Bragg, a frequent figure at both Gunks and Cathedral, commented: "If someone did that at the Gunks, they'd be lynched."

All these tactics were controversial even in North Conway. After *Arete* was put in with extensive preparation on rappel, the whole range of issues came to a head and a more or less spontaneous gathering of all the leading climbers was called by an "Ethics Committee" of concerned climbers. It was held at Daisey's, a local pub. Impassioned pleas for a higher ethical standard were voiced by several local regulars. Their arguments were rebutted by the leading practitioners of the tactics at issue, who did not fail to point out that it was mainly 5.9 climbers who were telling the 5.11 leaders what they should and shouldn't do in pushing the standards. Tempers flared. No lasting consensus was achieved. Into the 1980s the ethics and style of north country climbing continued to be defined by whoever was at the leading edge, following a highly pragmatic perspective specifically geared to north country cliffs, climbing scene, and general life style—and contrasting sharply with the mode that prevailed at the Gunks during the same years.

Such peripheral issues aside, North Conway climbing exploded during the 1970s. As late as 1970 (after much of Cote's new route development) fewer than 100 rock climbs were known to exist in the White Mountains. In three years, 1971 to 1973, another 132 were added; in the next three years, 103 more; by the end of the decade, 178 more. With employment available at the climbing schools and stores, virtually full-time regulars crowded onto the North Conway crags. Boston climbers were encouraged by reports of many new routes and the general rise of their own standards—not to men-

Jim Dunn combined a unique personality and tremendous drive to become a leader in the north country in the 1970s. Here he is seen climbing on his Cathedral Ledge classic The Prow.

RICHARD AREY

tion the new Interstate Highway connections—and journeyed north in large numbers every weekend. Novices flocked into town to take advantage of guided climbing. At the head of the pack a score of extremely able climbers emerged, thoroughly at home leading 5.10 and an occasional 5.11. Nothing done was as technically demanding as the Gunks test pieces like *Kansas City* or *Supercrack* until the decade was almost over. But in other respects it was clear that the north country had emerged from its long years of quiet and had become a major rock climbing center.

On Cathedral the most exciting figure in these years was Jimmy Dunn. Fanatically dedicated to difficult free climbing, Dunn put in long hours on physical training and was willing to invest days at a time on endlessly repeated efforts to master a single difficult pitch. As an individual, Dunn was

Leaders of the Seventies. Jimmy Dunn (left) climbs Crack in the Woods.
Ed Webster (right) shown at Ragged Mountain.

complex and opaque, shy and sensitive, sometimes brilliant and attractive, other times moody and despondent. In good form, he was without equal as a free-climber in the north country (Barber excepted), though always regarded with a touch of skepticism by some because of his preference, on his hardest routes, for plenty of protection nearby, including bolts if needed. His best routes were and remain classics of the cliff: *The Possessed* (1975), a hard 5.11 when he did it, upgraded later when a key hold broke off; *The Beast* (1977), another 5.11 plus; and Cathedral's outstanding line, *The Prow* (1977), a 5.11 plus on which many able climbers had contributed heroic efforts but on which Dunn was the first to accomplish a complete free ascent from bottom to top. (John Bragg originally conceived the idea that Ross's giant aid route, *The Prow,* could be done free. Bragg freed the bottom pitch, in concert with three other North Conway climbers in 1973. In 1976 Rick Fleming and Mark Bon Signor freed the top pitch, whereupon, a month later, Bragg worked out the second and third pitches. Dunn then worked

for over a year to master the hardest moves of all on the fourth pitch and then put the whole thing together in one brilliant push on July 14, 1977.) Between 1975 and 1978 Dunn put in fifteen new routes at the 5.10 or harder level on Cathedral alone.

Even more prolific with new routes—and almost equal in difficulty and with even more pragmatic ethics and style—was Ed Webster. As open and direct as Dunn was indrawn and obscure, Webster candidly sought to establish his reputation by a relentless search for new routes. In 1975–1978 he topped Dunn with eighteen new 5.10 and higher routes on Cathedral—and added a thorough exploration of the Whitehorse cliff as well, especially its South Buttress. "Mr. New Route" was never held in as high esteem as Dunn by their New Hampshire peers. Yet his climbs included not merely quantity but some of exceptional quality and historic value, like the first free ascent of Arsenault's classic aid route, *The Pendulum* (1976); a magnificent amalgam of previously climbed pitches from other difficult routes forming the

S. PETER LEWIS

RICK WILCOX

Two unique personalities of the North Conway scene. George Hurley (above) was a veteran Colorado climber who brought an unmistakable touch of class to everything he climbed. Michael Hartrich (left) was reclusive, introspective, a hiker, backwoods explorer, and backcountry skier, as well as a front-rank rock and ice climber.

most sustained long climb on Cathedral, *Wild Women* (1979); and some of the prize 5.11s on Whitehorse's South Buttress.

While Dunn and Webster have been regarded as North Conway's dominant climbers of the middle and late 1970s, their style was not universally admired. Henry Barber and John Bragg, who were around North Conway between trips to far-flung ranges, were more respected both for style and sheer ability, though they did not play the new-route game with such fervor in New Hampshire. Others were highly esteemed among their peers at the time but much less well known to the outside world. These included several who had learned hard climbing on Connecticut traprock, like the genial and graceful Bryan Delaney and his brother Mark, and the high-spirited Doug Madara, who acquired a reputation for leads of great daring and style. Less flamboyant still, but acknowledged as a steady and cool performer at the top levels, was Peter Cole. An even lower profile was sustained by the reclusive, introspective Mike Hartrich, a hiker as well as a climber (unlike most of his peers), who may have explored more White Mountain backcountry than anyone since Darby Field first climbed Mount Washington in 1642. The legendary ice climber John Bouchard, who will loom large in chapter 21, was not admired for his style or ego-heavy personality but was immensely respected, on rock as on ice, for his strength, fearlessness, and a kind of defiant integrity of his own. Always in the background but still climbing well was the man who had really started the north country renaissance, though few of the new young tigers acknowledged their debt to him: Joe Cote. ∎

Reference Note

An especially effective description of the North Conway climbing scene may be found in the third part of Michael Macklin's three-part series "Fifty Years of Granite State Climbing, Part III—Into the Eighties," *Climbing*, July-August 1980, pp.19–29. (Cf. Thomas Starr King, *The White Hills*, Boston: Crosby, Nichols and Company, 1859, pp. 149–163.) The authors benefited from conversations with many climbers who have been a part of or keen observers of this scene as it has evolved since 1970. Special thanks are due to Rick Wilcox for arranging our meeting with many of these climbers.

20: Higher Standards throughout the Northeast: The 1970s

WHILE NORTH CONWAY'S stage glittered with all this attention, New Hampshire's other crown jewel of rock climbing, the big cliff at Cannon, pursued a separate and entirely different course. Far from the bright lights, the strip, the Climbing Schools, and the ambitious young-men-in-a-hurry, Cannon retained its character as a "serious cliff." Yet even here change found its way.

In the early 1970s the first Cannon "regulars" arrived, the first to haunt Franconia Notch every weekend and explore new routes systematically.

Cannon irregulars. A marked contrast with the North Conway elite, Cannon's "determinedly unfashionable" circle created their own style, suited to the climbing challenge of the East's highest unbroken cliff face.

Howard Peterson. Cannon's first "regular" and leader in a circle which thoroughly explored the potential of the vast granite wall in Franconia Notch. That's a bolt in his mouth.

COURTESY CHRIS ELLMS

These pioneers included several able climbers—John Porter, Roger Martin, David Tibbetts, Christopher Ellms—but the acknowledged leader of the pack was that determinedly unfashionable swain from Maine's potato-growing Aroostook County, Howard Peterson. A hard-living free spirit dressed in rags, never turning down a beer, Peterson cultivated a rough-tough image for the Cannon regulars, disdainful of the North Conway elite. Instead of loitering in the trendy climbing shops, the Cannon clan gathered at a dusty pullout known as Boise Rock (not the well-manicured asphalt-and-grass rest area built in the 1980s, but a much smaller rough and gravelly pullout right alongside the noise and exhaust fumes of the old Route 3 through Franconia Notch). Instead of the latest light-weight gadgets, their racks sagged with heavy strings of pitons. Instead of dashing up sunny roadside 5.11s, they dragged themselves up 5.9s—but all day long in all kinds of weather. "We didn't have the nice clothes that the North Conway crowd had," sneered Peterson. He and his coterie "believed themselves to be the sole bearers of the mountain spirit," recalled Webster. Another North Conway regular, Peter Cole, declared, "Howard hates EMS." A later Cannon devotee and preserver of the image that Peterson nurtured, Andy Tuthill, scoffed:

> Climb at Cathedral, and what do you look out at? Cars! Crowds! Condominiums! Climb at Cannon, and what's out there before you? The wild, the magnificent Franconia Ridge!

But image issues were secondary to good climbing. Peterson led a spurt of new-route development and authored Cannon's first published guidebook in 1972.

A trend that Peterson started and others quickly picked up was to climb one or two difficult pitches near the bottom, then rappel back down rather than continue the long way to the top. In 1972 Peterson and Tibbetts put in *Silly Putty,* a 5.7 on the north end, a lower-angled section which the Cannon regulars began calling "The Slabs." This joined the *Lakeview* route, leaving the option to future climbers of going on up that route or rappelling off. The following year, Peterson, Tibbetts, and Porter put up adjacent *Lyma Bean,* 5.8, with similar options. In 1974 more were put in, Peterson joined by Steve Schneider and Chris Ellms. These shorter climbs became very popular, such as *Falling Aspirations* (5.9) and *Sticky Fingers* (5.10). They added a dimension to Cannon climbing, removing the commitment of a long climb every time you left the ground. The old Cannon faithful were not happy: one who had known the big cliff well in the quiet days of the 1960s, Bob Hall, regretted the new trend:

> With the short (1, 2 pitch) climbs being put in, Cannon is taking on a more Gunks-like attitude. I am personally opposed to the short-route-ification [*sic*] of Cannon as it is a Mountaineering cliff, one of the few in the East and I would prefer it to remain that way.

But Hall, a realist and shrewd observer of the evolving climbing scene, was compelled to acknowledge that times were changing in the north country. The coming of the "regulars"—Cote and his followers at Cathedral and now even the Peterson gang at once-lordly Cannon—was transforming the sport in the 1970s. As Hall conceded: "If I lived fifteen minutes from Boise Rock instead of seven hours fifteen minutes, then perhaps my outlook would change."

Emblematic of these changes was the discovery, or rediscovery, of outlying cliffs. Cathedral, Whitehorse, and Cannon were the traditional cliffs of the north country, and they never lost their prominence. But in the shadows at the side of the spotlight, some formerly indistinct figures began to assume their own identity. The emergence of these once-obscure crags symbolizes the spread of modern rock climbing throughout the Northeast in the later 1970s.

In the early 1970s two little-known north country climbers, Dwight

Bradley and Tad Pfeffer, produced a slim document called "Obscure Crags Guide." It described in general terms (no specific route descriptions) a large number of little-visited north country cliffs. The authors grappled with the dilemma of those who, like themselves, treasured the adventure of exploring obscure crags. To tell the world is generously to share the treasure—but initiates the loss of the very qualities that make them treasured. Bradley and Pfeffer responded to this dilemma by avoiding publicity or wholesale distribution of their little guide, printing "only a few dozen copies," and expressing the hope that others to come would preserve the pristine character of these unspoiled places. During the next ten years, however, waves of well-known climbers washed over the lesser cliffs as well as the greater, and even these darker corners of Arcadia were brought into the glare of Filene's Basement. By 1982 a guidebook trotted out all the once-obscure crags and published full route descriptions.

Joe Cote led the exodus to smaller cliffs when his beloved Cathedral became too crowded. In 1971 he was often at White's Ledge; in 1972 he explored routes on Woodchuck Ledge with Roger Martin and Sundown Ledge with Dick Arey; in 1973–74, with Martin and Milt Camille, he developed the potential of Band M cliff; and in 1975 he and Mike Hartrich found good lines on the Rainbow Slabs. (The name of Band M cliff had a novel origin. One of its earliest explorers was Mike Hartrich; peering at a USGS topographical map and not noticing that an old Boston and Maine railroad line passed nearby, Hartrich hastily read off the letter "B and M" and christened the cliffs "Band M," a name that has stuck since.)

As at Cathedral, Cote's example inspired others. In the later 1970s the systematic development of these outlying crags opened up. In 1977–1978 Alain Comeau led a charge to new routes on the Frankenstein cliff. In 1979–1980 transplanted Coloradoan George Hurley mined possibilities on Humphrey's Ledge. In 1980–1981 John Bouchard almost single-handedly developed a collection of routes on a cliff between Cathedral and White-horse that he called The Guide's Wall. Others who were active on several of these cliffs during the 1970s included three who were known for a bolder style than most North Conway climbers: the restless anchorite Mike Hartrich; the ebullient and popular man-child Doug Madara; and the outstanding ice climber Kurt Winkler, who also shone on rock, a graduate of the AMC Trail Crew and its small but tough rock climbing cadre of the late 1960s. In the 1980s, several of these cliffs were still further worked over: White's Ledge by Hurley; Sundown by Hurley, Webster, Winkler, Hartrich, and Albert Dow; Band M by Webster, Hartrich, and Dow; the old 1920s favorite, Willard, and uncounted other obscure crags, by Todd Swain; and the Rainbow Slabs and an adjacent cliff known as The Painted Walls by Alain and Janot Comeau.

At cliffs all over the Northeast, the 1970s were a time when the high standards of modern free climbing permeated the region. But while the technical levels of the Shawangunks and Cathedral were emulated, the ethics and style of neither were necessarily accepted. In fact, most other climbing circles consciously rejected both the urban playground aura of New Paltz and the alpine resort atmosphere of North Conway. Different climbing milieus were established at different cliffs, according to the personal preferences of the leading climbers at each.

Katahdin rock had been sporadically raided since Helburn's climb of the Chimney in 1919—Underhill's parties of the 1920s, Hec Towle's Armadillo route of the 1930s, Arnold Wexler's party in the 1940s, some fine new routes on the Armadillo by Kruszyna, Reppy, and others during the 1950s, sorties by Hall and other Boston-based mountaineers in the 1960s. The finest route on Katahdin—a slender flake leading to a 5.7 crack up the very center of the Armadillo—was apparently first climbed during the early 1950s, but by whom is not known, regrettably. A bold party of relatively inexperienced RPI climbers with Peter Oliver and Carl Hendrickson in the lead climbed this line in 1951, possibly for its first ascent, though they were "under the impression we were climbing an established route." This uncertainty of route information was characteristic of the wild and primitive nature of Katahdin climbing right up through 1970. During the early 1970s a more modern approach was launched by University of Maine climbers, among whom Michael Opuda was outstanding. This approach was modern in the sense that they climbed regularly at the cliffs around Chimney Pond, introducing high technical standards, clean climbing ethics, and a relentless search for new routes in what had always been the Northeast's truly mountainlike setting. Opuda and the "boys from Bangor" climbed whatever obvious lines in the South Basin had been left undone by earlier Katahdinophiles. Next they began exploring the North Basin cliff but left this work incomplete when Opuda married and the old crowd broke up. A damper on Katahdin climbing was the poor relations between the regulation-conscious Baxter State Park management and the freedom-loving spirit of most climbers. Relationships between rangers and climbers deteriorated badly during the 1970s. However, the beginnings of change came in 1979 with the installation of Ranger Ben Townsend at Chimney Pond. As a technical climber himself, Townsend started a new surge of new-route exploration all over the mountain, encountering less official nervousness. Maine

Mount Desert idyll. The sea cliffs of Mount Desert provided their own special world. Here a climber tackles the premier route on Mount Desert.

S. PETER LEWIS

down-staters David Getchell and Peter McCartney were also active both in climbing and in working out smoother relationships with Baxter Park managers.

Mount Desert rock presented as sharp a contrast to Katahdin's as it is possible to conjure—short, clean cliffs at the edge of the sea in tourist-thronged Acadia National Park. Here too Opuda and the boys from Bangor arrived in the early 1970s, bringing new standards of difficulty. During the middle and later 1970s Mount Desert's first regulars began to develop routes of exceptional quality and to define a special character for Mount Desert climbing. Geoff Childs brought out a guidebook to the area in 1976; Tom Silocka became a park ranger; Jeff Butterfield and Caset Newman opened a climbing school and guide service in nearby Bar Harbor. Mount Desert climbers prized the unique ambiance of their seaside setting and sought to combine the pure ethics and style of the Shawangunks with the quiet and low profile of the old north country. When Webster arrived in 1980 and placed bolts to open up some new and difficult lines, the locals were horrified. Childs lamented:

No doubt, with popularity the present solitude will face the challenge of the blond-haired boys in white hospital pants and rugby shirts with their $8,000 vans, $400 racks . . . It is sad and disheartening to imagine the trail to the South Wall littered with magnesium carbonate [chalk] wrappers and beer cans.

Maine's lesser-known crags—the state is overrun with climbable cliffs— sought also to preserve their anonymity, with somewhat more success. Scattered widely across the state, little circles of local rock climbers found favorite cliffs and developed new routes, in some cases extensively. In most situations the locals avoided the new-route reporting rampant in New Hampshire, striving to maintain "a real pioneering spirit to get out and encounter the unknown and the uncertain." Still, the modern era of high standards had arrived: 5.10 routes were springing up all over the state, usually known only to the climbers who did them and a slender grapevine of others.

At Cannon the dominant climbers for the second half of the 1970s were the Peterson protégé Chris Ellms and the individualistic eccentric Andy Tuthill. An inseparable and untiring climbing team, Ellms and Tuthill matched their skills to the cliff they loved so much. They were by no means New Hampshire's top free-climbers. They bore no love for the sophistication of either New Paltz or North Conway. But they combined boldness and imagination with remarkable endurance plus a pragmatic resourcefulness that made them heirs to a tradition of Cannon climbers from Underhill and O'Brien (with their birch-stake pendulum on Old Cannon in 1928) through Whipple and Hall and Peterson. The size and seriousness of Cannon continued to dictate the ethics and style. Quoth Tuthill:

> It's a big cliff. Just climb. Just climb. I don't count it as aid unless I go on etriers.

Within this framework, Ellms and Tuthill established fifteen new routes on the big cliff between 1975 and 1978.

Around New Hampshire outside the White Mountains, standards rose apace. At Dartmouth a notable step forward came during the late 1970s with a talented circle of undergraduates, among whom Mark Sonenfeld was particularly gifted and regarded as one of the finest free-climbers in the region just before he left to pursue his climbing in the West. Down at Joe English, a new era of intensive difficult climbing was led by Boston AMC climbers Paul Nyland, Joe Landry, and Paul Duval at about the same time.

Over in Pawtuckaway State Park standards also rose, with some exception-ally talented locals from UNH (Steve Larson, Rick Fleming) and the city of Manchester (Mark Hudon, Paul Bossieneault).

In Vermont the state university at Burlington generated a growing cir-cle of climbers during the 1970s. This group was more remarkable for its high standards of ice climbing, but they also climbed rock most of the year. A roadside crag at Bolton was a favorite practice area. Smugglers Notch, Camel's Hump, the peaks near Lake Willoughby, Bristol Cliffs, and other more remote crags saw increasing activity at a modern technical level. As in Maine—in contrast with most of New Hampshire—the spirit was decidedly nonmodern in its avoidance of publicity and credit-taking. The name of one route by the Burlington boys expressed their attitude: *Who Cares Henry?*

Pok-o-moonshine in the Adirondacks witnessed one of the most re-markable manifestations of the spirit that sought to preserve the old north country quiet in an era of rapidly advancing technical standards. After John Turner's routes of the late 1950s, this fine cliff was little climbed for more than ten years. In the mid-1970s a small group of Plattsburgh locals began climbing extremely well—Gary Allan, Drew Allan, Pat Munn, Dave Hough, and Mark Meschinelli, with a somewhat older Geoff Smith as mentor and dominant influence. Inspired partly by visits from Gunks climbers like Williams and Goldstone but more by their own home-grown practice, this group began putting in 5.9s and 5.10s on their own. In 1977 New Hamp-shire visitor Jimmy Dunn teamed with Gary Allan to put in the area's first 5.11, *Firing Line.* Many fine routes followed, technically demanding, aestheti-cally impressive, and (with allowance for extensive gardening and even boulder-trundling on rappel) accomplished on the lead in a very pure style. But the locals rarely shared their cliff with outsiders, guarding its lack of no-toriety with "possessive passion." To such as Henry Barber, the attitude was inexplicable ("Some very strange people over there . . . Won't tell you any-thing," mumbled Barber). To those who deplored the carnival atmosphere of New Paltz and North Conway, however, the spirit was admired: an attempt to preserve a climbing environment of quiet, solitude, and commitment.

Elsewhere in the Adirondacks, technical standards lagged during most of the 1970s, save where outsiders made the long drive to explore one of the many cliffs of the Couchsachrage. In the mid-1970s Al Long and Al Rubin discovered previously little-known Moss Cliff and put in several long and committing routes, 5.9 and 5.10, in a remote wilderness setting. In the late 1970s first Henry Barber and later Jimmy Dunn developed very difficult routes in the Chapel Pond area. Gradually a local constituency emerged, attested by the opening of a climbing shop in Lake Placid in 1976 and sub-

Contrasting styles of the Seventies. Left: Pat Munn on the Adirondacks' big blank Pok-o-moonshine cliff. Right: Ken Nichols on the test piece Dol Guldur, *at one of Connecticut's tiny traprock outcrops.*

COURTESY KEN NICHOLS

COURTESY DON MELLOR

sequently a climbing school and guide service. In 1976 an updated guide-book appeared, though its sparseness showed that the area was still little developed. The later 1970s saw much more locally led activity, sparked by a new cast in which Don Mellor, Todd Eastman, Jim Cunningham, and Chuck Turner (no relation to John) were leading lights. Mellor's 1983 guidebook gave evidence that the modern age of climbing had finally arrived even here.

Southern New England cliffs provided a breeding ground for many north country climbers—the Delaneys from western Massachusetts via Connecticut, Ed Webster from Crow Hill, Doug Madara from Connecticut, many from the Boston area. But these small crags generated a significant climbing life of their own as well. Connecticut climbers continued to discover new cliffs, or rediscover the ones J. B. Gardner's generation had kept quiet about. Following the Reppy-Streibert tandem of the 1960s came a new crop of 1970s hard men, among whom Jim Adair, Mike Heintz, and Ken Nichols were particularly visionary in developing higher standards. In 1976 Nichols and Greg Newth were the first to lead a solid 5.11 in Connecticut. Later the same year Heintz and Tony Trocchi put in two weeeks of effort to complete *Dol Guldur* at East Peak, a 5.11 plus that stood as Connecticut's hardest climb for several years.

Thus, throughout the Northeast during the late 1970s, 5.11 represented the top of the technical standard, and a few climbers at just about every cliff reached that level. ∎

Reference Note

The evolution of rock climbing at lesser areas is poorly documented in print. Two exceptions are the areas furthest north and furthest south. For Maine, see Ben Townsend, "Katahdin Renaissance," *Summit,* May-June 1983, pp. 16–20; Geoffrey Childs' various writings on Mount Desert: his 1976 guidebook, *A Climber's Guide to Mount Desert Island* (no publication data); "By the Sea, By the Sea," *Climbing,* April 1977, pp. 30–32; and "Straight Up from Sea Level," *Yankee,* May 1977, pp. 152–157; and Todd Gregory, "The Maine Line," *Climbing,* June 1984, pp. 36–39. Connecticut climbing history is recounted in Al Rubin's historical essay in Ken Nichols, *Traprock: Rock Climbing in Central Connecticut.* A unique document is Tad Pfeffer and Dwight Bradley, *Obscure Crags Guide,* privately printed around 1973 and something of a collector's item. A copy is in the files for this book at Dartmouth College.

The Many Faces of Group Dynamics

WHEN WE BEGAN to interview old climbers for this history, we went to one at a time. But when we talked with Jim Gilchrist about whom we should see from the Burlington (Vermont) climbing set, he spontaneously offered to gather them all together for an informal pizza dinner. We could come along, meet them all at once, address our questions about Burlington climbing to the entire group, then sit back and take notes.

Thus was born the first of a series of group interviews—but, as it turned out, the results varied enormously.

As the time to meet the Burlington gang drew nigh, we didn't know what to expect. The only prominent name in the group was Steve Zachowski, who we knew had pioneered difficult first ascents with John Bouchard in Smugglers Notch and elsewhere. Now Bouchard is a world-class climber, brilliant intellect, keen observer, and otherwise a formidable presence—but he was well known to be an abrasive and difficult personality. Would Zachowski be the same? If so, he might be difficult to handle in front of his peers. Were the others like that too? Would these Vermonters be classically taciturn or distrustful of outsiders?

We needn't have worried. The Burlington boys were sweethearts, to a man. Zachowski turned out to be the mildest, most easy-going hard man you could imagine, just a low-key home-town boy from Burlington who (Bouchard had happily discovered) happened to perform brilliantly on rock and ice. The others were all articulate, good-natured, voluble (no taciturn Yankees here!), and obviously a close-knit coterie. They were well aware that their niche in climbing history was not large, but one sensed they were overmodest, hilariously self-deprecating about their own achievements.

In the group interview they were splendidly helpful to us, sparking each other on, bouncing recollections and opinions back and forth. We felt we gained a more complete, a better balanced picture of Burlington climbing as a result of the group dynamics. After pizza, we all walked over to Ben and Jerry's (the *original* Ben and Jerry's of Burlingon) for ice cream and pleasant chitchat.

Great! we thought. This is the way to learn about each climbing circle. Group interviews really work.

Our next target: North Conway.

Lo, the contrast between plain-spun Vermonterish Burlington and North Conway, fast-track resort center, the Aspen of the East, hothouse home to the hard-driving, leading-edge professional climbers, ambitious for attention, competitive as male dogs around a bitch in heat.

Through the good offices of that affable and durable guru of the North Conway scene, Rick Wilcox, we arranged a similar assembly at a classy North Conway pub. The leading climbers of New Hampshire originally all agreed to attend, but their gathering was reminiscent of one of those stormy councils of the rival chieftains brought together by Agamemnon, supposedly to fight the Trojans but largely to quarrel with each other.

Before we started, one of the climbers (Menelaus was it?) told us that Achilles was outside on the sidewalk but had decided maybe he wouldn't participate after all. Patroclus agreed to go out and talk nicely to him. At that, Achilles relented and agreed to come in, but once inside, as Homer might have put it:

> Black choler fill'd his breast that boil'd with ire
> And from his eyeballs flash'd the living fire.

So Achilles stormed out. Well, we'd try to interview him separately later. Then came word we had a phone call from the wily Odysseus, who was calling from home to tell us he couldn't attend the group gathering, but when we were through, why not come up to his house and spend the night? (In other words, get one version of history from the others assembled, then come up and note his corrections and amendments at the end of the evening.) We agreed but hoped there'd be no further defections from Agamemnon's council.

Once started, the council proceeded in a highly charged atmosphere, taut tension, suspicious glances. Agamemnon, Ajax, Menelaus, Nestor, et al. provided their divergent views of North Conway climbing lore. In contrast with the relaxed, neighborly Burlington gang, this was a high-level, high-performance competitive event, with an all-star cast that implicitly accepted their status as the best climbers in New England.

In truth, it was a productive session for our research. From among the eclectic personalities and their strongly individualized recollections, there emerged a vivid portrait of a most colorful, swift-changing, and tremendously vital and significant chapter in northeastern climbing history, a much more important one than Burlington's. We were grateful to the warring chieftains that they condescended to come together for our benefit and the historical record.

But what a change from Burlington!

We used the group interview technique on several other occasions. A dozen or so Boston climbers from the decade of the 1960s gave us a long and fascinating evening of reminiscences, from which a valuable picture of that time and place emerged. Dartmouth's current generation gave us a couple of hours' review of their special climbing world.

Twice Mohonk Preserve's Chief Ranger, Thom Scheuer, assembled leading Gunks climbers at his house for our benefit. The first time was tense and Greek chieftainlike. We learned a lot but laughed little. The group seemed inexplicably hostile to the project. But the second, enlivened and enlightened by the caustic wit and penetrating observations of Rosie Andrews, was a gem.

The surprises never ceased. In the mid-1980s, Shawangunks climbers told us that the people we really had to talk to were a group of kids who were climbing harder than anyone ever had in the Northeast, but using radical new methods, some of which their elders thoroughly disapproved. As elders ourselves, we fully expected to find these kids hard to take: probably brash, self-promoting, heedless of old values, and most likely somewhat hostile to being questioned by middle-aged has-beens writing a book, probably a dull one.

Finally we made the date: the kids asked us to meet them in a local bar. We feared the worst, picturing a dark, smoky tavern, our three interviewees sullenly nursing their drinks and reluctantly defending their new methods.

We could not have been more off the mark. The "bar" turned out to be a brightly lit ice cream bar. When we entered, the "kids" jumped up and down from their booth to attract our attention and welcome us. For the next three hours they eagerly plied us with their views on climbing, their enthusiasm, their verve, their good will, their delight that someone from the older generation would listen to (and take notes on!) their accomplishments as well as their view of where the future of climbing lay. The Great Debate over climbing ethics and style (chapter 26) contains some serious and possibly irreconcilable issues, but those three prophets of the new era, on that pleasant afternoon, played the role of good will ambassadors from a strange new world.

Thus the many faces of group dynamics. ∎

21: Revolution on Ice: 1969–1976

ERTAIN WATERSHED EVENTS are historically decisive: life on planet earth was one thing before and something fundamentally different after. Such was the flood during which Noah and his party made the first ascent of Ararat. Such also was the French Revolution, when Europe turned from the aristocracy to the bourgeois; the American Civil War, when America turned from agrarian to industrial; the coming of Babe Ruth, when baseball turned from defense to offense. But these are exceptions. Mostly change is evolutionary, slow. Dilapidation's processes, as Emily Dickinson said, are organized decays. But every once in awhile truly radical (by the roots!) change wrenches life from one image to something totally new.

Rock climbing has changed by evolution. The greatest names in northeastern rock—McCarthy, Stannard, Barber—have only inched a little higher over the giants on whose shoulders they figuratively stood. One decimal at a time: 5.8 . . . 5.9 . . . 5.10 . . . 5.11 . . .

But ice. What happened in the world of ice sometime around 1969 was revolution of Noachian, Napoleonic, Ruthian proportions.

As noted in chapter 12, northeastern ice climbing stagnated throughout the 1940s, 1950s, and 1960s. It was the Age of Huntington Ravine, step-chopping all the way, and solid but unspectacular performers like New York's securities analyst-cum-expeditioneer Boyd Everett.

In 1969, less than three months before he was killed on Dhaulagiri, Boyd Everett was one of a small group of New York and Connecticut climbers who journeyed northward to the Adirondacks' Chapel Pond for an unusual educational experience. In the role of teachers were the Pied Piper of American climbing equipment, Californian Yvon Chouinard, and the Gunks' prestigious rock climber, Jim McCarthy. With Everett as "students" were Ed Nester, Joe Burgeil, Julius Beede, and Johnny Waterman of the New York AMC and Jeff Lea and Frank Zahar of AMC's Connecticut Chapter (though the last two were soon to function more independently under the renegade Mud and Slush group).

On that sunny February weekend in 1969, Chouinard showed his students a new kind of ice ax. Shorter by one-third than the traditional ax, its most striking feature was a pick that drooped in a curving acute angle (rather than the usual straight 90 degrees) and was serrated with a row of teeth filed along the bottom edge. To go with the strange ax, Chouinard deployed a new hammer. The business end had the usual solid striking surface, but instead of tapering bluntly at the back of the head, it curved gracefully in a slender arc at the same acute angle as the pick of the ax and also bared sharp teeth on the underside. On their feet, Chouinard and McCarthy wore crampons with front points far sturdier and sharper than any the students had seen before.

With these new tools and a few words of explanation, Chouinard and McCarthy started up the Big Slab. But instead of cutting steps, they simply turned sideways, slammed all ten points of the soles of their crampons into the ice with toes pointing almost downhill, and, using the ax for balance, walked up. In about the time it would have taken to chop a good step or two, Chouinard was at the top of the first pitch and belaying McCarthy. When they reached steeper ice above, they employed an even more surprising tactic. Here Chouinard turned face into the ice, slammed his front points in and stood erect on his rigid front points and stiff boots. Swinging the ice ax directly over his head in one smooth arc, he drove the drooped pick straight into the ice. It sunk far enough so that the teeth on the lower edge bit well. As it landed, it quivered ever so slightly, indicating it was well seated. The hammer went in the same way with the other hand. With both tools firmly planted, Chouinard could commit most of his weight to these tools while he moved his feet up. Where the old right-angle picks would have popped out, the drooped picks held his weight securely. When he had stepped higher, he moved his tools higher, then stepped up again. In a small fraction of the time it would have taken to chop steps, he was over the steep bulge and belaying his partner. Below him the ice was smooth and steep, marked only by imperceptible nicks and chips instead of the old sight of alternating cavities for each foot and handhold.

Before the weekend was over, Chouinard and McCarthy had climbed not just the Big Slab but a route on the steep cliff 200 feet to the left that was well iced over that winter (as it was not to be again for almost ten years) and the steep gully across Chapel Pond, which came to be called Chouinard's Gully. On none of these routes did the leader cut a single step, save for a few stances for belays.

More important, Chouinard and McCarthy demonstrated the new techniques and loaned the new tools to the others. The revolution was set in motion. Boyd Everett called it "black magic." The younger climbers were convinced—in fact, their imaginations sparkled at the possibilities they saw ahead as they scampered up practice ice floes of 25 feet in seconds, where the most accomplished step-cutter could not have made steps at much better than one per minute.

The rest of that winter and the next, word spread fast. Lea and Zahar went back to Connecticut and within two weeks showed the new tools and techniques to four other Connecticut climbers. Ed Nester held similar seminars for New Yorkers, and some of his students became regular teachers of the new school at New York AMC weekends thereafter. McCarthy spread the word to some of the Vulgarians, among whom Pete Carmen and Claude Suhl became eager converts. Chouinard gave slide shows and demonstrations elsewhere in the Northeast. He soon produced a catalog that not only offered the new tools for sale but included a manual with photographs on how to use them. Even before the droop-pick ax was available commercially, however, climbers all over the region were altering their old axes by drooping the pick, filing teeth, and cutting the length of the shaft.

About one year after the Chapel Pond lessons, McCarthy walked up into Huntington Ravine and marched straight up Pinnacle Gully without cutting a single step. McCarthy used primarily ten-point (or French) technique rather than front points. He was followed by a generation-bridging quartet that included William Lowell Putnam III, Tenth Mountain Division hero and conqueror of Damnation Gully in 1943, and a very young Rick Wilcox, who showed his knack for being in the right place at the right time, as he would for the next two decades of north country climbing. Despite the party of five, McCarthy had them all up and down in fast time, while two-man parties ponderously chopped steps up the other routes all day long.

This February 1, 1970 stepless lead of Pinnacle Gully made reverberations around all the hitherto isolated climbing circles. "The rules of ice climbing were completely rewritten," observed Wilcox later. The effect was somewhat analogous to Stannard's 1969 ascent of *Foops* in opening everyone's eyes to the future. If Pinnacle, of all routes, could go without steps, there must indeed be black magic in the new techniques and tools. "An overnight sensation!" Ed Webster called it. An assessment of the stepless ascent of Pinnacle Gully by later climber S. Peter Lewis put it this way:

> From that time on, steep water ice would no longer pose the physical or psychological threat that it once had. The focus shifted suddenly from the limited to the limitless, and a vast untapped resource of ice fell under attack.

Initially the new tools and techniques simply made the old climbs easier. But the ultimate results transformed the speed, location, population, and social character of the sport of ice climbing.

The chief impact, of course, was that standards of difficulty soared. By the mid-1970s, the gullies of Huntington Ravine, for forty years the hardest climbs in the Northeast, came to be seen as moderate or even easy. People turned their attention to ice that had been unthinkable for the previous half century.

The new center of ice climbing. During the 1970s Frankenstein's ice cliffs replaced Huntington Ravine as the principal mecca for New England ice climbers. Left: George Hurley on the Streibert classic, Chia. *Right: John Tremblay on* Dracula, *one of John Bragg's notable breakthroughs to higher levels of difficulty.*

S. PETER LEWIS

S. PETER LEWIS

The second change was a shift in the geographical centers of climbing. New areas opened up all over the region. People still climbed at Huntington, Willey Slide, the Colden Dike, Race Brook, and Deep Notch, but mainly to introduce beginners or enjoy an easy-going weekend, or perhaps to appreciate the beauty of these areas. But the real action lay elsewhere—as we'll see in a minute.

Third, the speed of climbing greatly accelerated. The Huntington gullies, all-day expeditions before the revolution, were now the diversion of an hour or two. In 1971, two men, Ed Nester and John Bouchard, climbed Pinnacle Gully solo and unroped. By the late 1970s it was not uncommon to do all six gullies in a single day.

Fourth, because it was faster, the hardships were much reduced.

Fifth, because hardships were less, the popularity of ice climbing exploded. College-age climbers were especially attracted. The average age of the ice climber undoubtedly dropped sharply.

Sixth, with increased popularity came social acceptability on the outdoor scene. Where the old ice climbers with their long wooden ice axes and their baggy windpants had felt like social misfits, ice climbers of the new breed began to see themselves as admired hard men. Magazines reported new climbs. Soon a guidebook to New England ice climbs was published. Equipment suppliers, first following Chouinard, later blossoming out with innovations of others, vied for climbers' attention.

All of these effects fused to form a completely altered social scene in northeastern ice climbing. The "before" picture portrayed ice climbers as a small band of grizzled outcasts in battered old clothes and mouse boots— like Melville's whaling sailors at New Bedford, "a brown and brawny company, with bosky beards; an unshorn, shaggy set"—with ancient alpenstock-like axes and hinged ten-point crampons, holing up in the dark recesses of the Harvard Cabin, hidden away in obscure haunts like Race Brook or Deep Notch, or far off the mainstream in the Colden Dike. Came the revolution and suddenly ice climbers were a younger, more sociable crowd, flocking to easily accessible sunlit ice floes or congregating gregariously at overlit equipment stores and underlit bars in their spiffy bright-colored parkas and expensive mountaineering boots, loudly comparing the latest new tools that graced their holsters.

But away from the crowds, off at the lonely edge of the advancing standards, the top climbers of the new age began to open up the horizons. No longer did they look for sloping gullies with discernible belay points. The steepest and longest icicles were within the realm of at least conjecture— and gradually they were climbed.

One of the earliest converts to the new techniques was Sam Streibert, the patrician Yale rock climber who had pioneered at Ragged, Cannon, and Cathedral. In the winter of 1970, Streibert and his frequent climbing partners, Dennis Merritt and Al Rubin, went looking for new ice in Crawford Notch. Hitherto Willey Slide and occasional sorties to the easier gullies on Webster had comprised Crawford climbing. But way back in 1882 the AMC Snow-Shoe Section had noted as they passed through Crawford Notch:

> Stretching far up the sides of Willey and Frankenstein, were huge masses of sea-green translucent ice. . . . the white masses of the frozen cataracts and their long pendent icicles relieving the dark wall of rock.

Eighty-eight years later, Streibert and his partners saw Frankenstein's masses of sea-green translucent ice—and took their new tools and climbed them. Not a quarter mile from the road, in plain view, gleamed floe after floe, from 50 to 150 feet in height, a score of routes plainly discernible. Unclimbable to the step-choppers, these routes were ideal for the front-pointers: challenging but thoroughly feasible.

In 1970 they did several routes, the best of which was one done by Streibert and Merritt that became known as Frankenstein's *Standard*, a three-pitch groove significantly harder than Pinnacle Gully. In 1971 Streibert and Merritt added *Pegasus* and *Chia*, two magnificent two-pitch lines set in a captivating amphitheater of snow and ice. Rubin was also active that year in new-route development.

For several years, parties on Frankenstein were rare, but as the new generation of front-pointers grew in numbers and confidence, these cliffs perfectly suited their appetites. Close to the road, just steep enough to require the new techniques but with a variety of lines that lay well within the average new climber's capacity, they became the center of ice climbing in the late 1970s. After forty years' ascendency, Huntington Ravine was no longer the mecca of northeastern ice climbing—Frankenstein was.

Around the same time a group of young friends from Burlington, initially disciples of Dave Cass and Philip Koch, began to step up the standards at Smugglers Notch. Never fashionable or famous, the Burlington gang drooped their own axes, largely trained themselves by trial and error, and took a self-deprecating view of their own abilities, yet they established a local tradition of ice climbing at Smugglers that never made headlines but was always thoroughly respectable in relation to the gradually rising standard. In the 1970–1972 generation, the leaders were Bob Olsen, Chet Callahan,

Chuck Bond, Mark Carpenter, and one who went on to bigger things than most of the others, Al Long. In the winter of 1970 this gang began to employ the new techniques and tools to advantage, culminating in the classic *Elephant's Head Gully*, which Callahan, Olsen, and Bond first climbed. Over the next two winters they remained active, the hardest route being *Blind Faith* led by Olsen in 1972, with Bond and Long in support.

Over in New York state at the same period, 1970–1971, Ed Nester blossomed as the leading apostle of the new tools. Nester found new routes in the Chapel Pond area and Avalanche Pass in the Adirondacks, as well as closer to home on the Hudson Highlands' Storm King. Nester's routes were comparable in difficulty to Streibert's but never acquired the popularity of the Frankenstein gallery of climbs.

(While various rating systems have been invented for ice climbs, precise comparisons of difficulty are much more difficult for ice than for rock. For one thing, the ice changes quality from day to day, drastically altering the climbers' problem in climbing it. Therefore, this history will not use any formal rating system for ice.)

By the winter of 1972 the revolution had taken over. Almost literally no one climbed technical ice without a short droop-pick ax and an alpine hammer. Nester was using two hammers on steeper ice—no ax at all—and doing the moderate routes with only ax and the French technique—no front points. Almost no one cut steps. The new generation passed the word that one who would cut a step on northeastern ice would shoot a fox. More and more climbers were getting better and better with the new tools. Yet as with the advent of nylon rope to rock climbing, a pause took place before the implications of the new tools were fully realized. This pause, however, was short-lived.

One route and one man did more to change the perceptions of modern ice climbing than any others. Over on Cannon, in the shadowy void separating the Whitney-Gilman arête from the rest of the cliff, lay 600 vertical feet of ice and snow-plastered rock: the Black Dike. The sun never shone on this north-facing frozen maelstrom of malignancy. There in the gloom it sat: the ultimate dare for the new tools and techniques.

The best climbers had stared this opponent in the face—and withdrawn their bid. Hugo Stadtmuller had gone up to look at it and backed off. Little lion-hearted Jorge Urioste had weighed it and pronounced it suicidal. Chouinard and McCarthy would like to have pulled off the first ascent but never rose to the occasion. Cannon climber John Porter, the best winter climber of the Peterson crowd, considered it but didn't do it. In 1971 Chouinard wrote an article on the new techniques for the Sierra Club journal, *Ascent,* in which he described the Black Dike as "a black, filthy, horrendous icicle 600 feet high," adding a one-word sentence that rang with challenge: "Unclimbed."

Perhaps what deterred the good climbers who did *not* do the Black Dike was that they had all learned to ice climb in the step-chopping days and, for all their skill with the new tools and techniques, were still prisoners of old perceptions. In 1971 there came along a nineteen-year-old kid who had never cut a step and knew only the revolution.

> I didn't have to unlearn the fear of wobbly crampons skating out of their holds and taking a catastrophic fall because my ice axe and dagger were only good for balance and wouldn't hold my weight.

John Bouchard was by temperament a loner. Though a Burlington fixture in the previous winter, he seems never to have become part of the regular gang there. Brash to the point of arrogance, serious to the point of humorlessness, demanding of himself and his seconds, moody, Bouchard had qualities ill fitted for winning popularity contests but exceedingly well suited to contests of skill, strength, and daring. Henry Barber said of him:

> Bouchard had such energy and drive that occasionally he was hard to deal with, but he was also the only person besides Bragg you could really count on to push it out and get you up some of these difficult routes.

Rick Wilcox put it: "When it was really scary, [Bouchard] was at his best." Few northeastern mountaineers have ever matched his competitive drive and desire to excel.

On December 18, 1971, Bouchard had hoped to try the Black Dike with John Porter, but Porter had to work that day. So Bouchard took a rope and some pitons and headed up by himself, intending to investigate the route. At the first hard moves he found the rope jammed, so he dropped it and moved on up. Almost immediately he broke the pick off his hammer. He dropped one mitten. But by this time he was so high on the wall, he was committed. A 10-foot vertical pillar near the top, confronted in fading light, almost stopped him. Employing a variety of aid techniques in utter desperation, fighting down panic, he somehow clawed over it. Just before dark, he crawled to the top, having soloed by far the hardest route yet done in the Northeast. John Bouchard had seen the future and it worked.

New faces, new climbs. The climbs and the climbers that symbolized the radical break from ice climbing's past. Left: John Bouchard launches the second ascent of his land-mark Black Dike *on Cannon; right: John Bragg on the first ascent of* Repentance.

What Pinnacle Gully had been from 1931 to 1969, the Black Dike was to the 1970s. It became preeminently *the* climb to do. The following winter, harder routes began to be done, but the Black Dike remained the test piece of the new era, "a measuring stick for many aspiring climbers," Wilcox's guidebook called it. If other routes came to be harder, none had the sense of isolation and unforgiving meanness, the stupendous alpine setting. Bouchard's solo ascent of this "black, filthy horrendous icicle" must rank as one of the most celebrated and significant events in northeastern climbing. Looking back ten years later, Ed Webster appraised it thus:

RICK WILCOX

More than any other climb, Bouchard's solo seems an almost mythical ascent now, shrouded in mystery, clouded in
legend. I was just trying to think if there was a rock route
that had a corresponding mystique about it . . . but offhand
I can't think of one. I guess that's proof of the kind of "class
by itself" that the Black Dike is in.

The route was not repeated in 1972. The next winter saw two ascents,
the first party consisting of a sort of all-star cast of northeastern climbers,
Bouchard, Barber, Wilcox, and John Bragg, with Bragg drawing the difficult
leads; followed two weeks later by the Mud and Slush hard men, Jeff Lea,
Frank Zahar, and Rocky Keeler. Since Bouchard had been nearly out of control on his epic solo, the 1973 ascents, both done in good style, were accorded immense prestige and the seven climbers were represented as the
top of the new standard. There followed another lull in 1974; three or four
ascents came in 1975, including the first female ascent; and finally in 1976
the new generation fully arrived and the Black Dike began to be climbed
almost every weekend.

Meanwhile, back in the winter of 1973, the generation of whom
Bouchard was the prophet put on the first creative burst of new climbing.

Big John Bragg emerged as the leader in 1973. Bragg added a new
technique to the modern arsenal by affixing wristloops to his tools and
learning how to hang his full weight thereby, so as to relax the muscles of
hand and forearm. This was a key point, because it removed the necessity of
remaining basically in balance on the feet. Wristloops opened the way to the
purely vertical. It was almost as important an additional step as the drooped
pick of four years earlier.

With wristloops, a thorough mastery of the new tools and techniques,
plus the strength and calmness in extremity that characterized his rock
climbing (see chapter 15), Bragg moved into the forefront in 1973. Pace-
setting ascents in that year included his lead of the *Black Dike;* new routes at
Frankenstein, *Dracula* and *Smear,* which were a clear step harder than prior
routes there; and, most impressive of all, Cathedral's *Repentance.* The route
that had made history as a bold rock climb by Turner in 1959 thus re-
entered history as a pivotal ice climb of the new era fourteen years later.
Repentance was technically an advance over the *Black Dike.* It was the first
climb that probably could not have been done without wristloops. (Barber and
Chouinard did, but three years later—*not* a first ascent.) Thus it marked the
beginning of a higher standard that was not surpassed for several winters.

Leading new-breed ice climbers. Top to bottom: John Bouchard, John Bragg, Al Rubin.

S. PETER LEWIS

RICK WILCOX

KEN NICHOLS

"Ice which had been unthinkable." The intimidating verticality of Positive Think-ing *in the Adirondacks' Pok-o-moonshine, first climbed in 1975 by the strong team of Bouchard and Bragg.*

North Conway, burgeoning as an important rock climbing center in 1972 and 1973, now became a hotbed of ice climbing talent. Besides Bouchard and Bragg, Rick Wilcox was a steady presence, coolly seconding Bragg on *Repentance, Smear,* and the *Black Dike.* A. J. LaFleur followed Bragg on *Dracula* and was a bold innovator himself on other routes, including the prominent *Black Pudding Gully* on Humphrey's Ledge. Peter Cole emerged as a major figure on ice, a guiding influence for many of the younger climbers, and a coauthor, with Wilcox, of the first guidebook to New Hampshire ice, published in 1976. The far-ranging recluse, Michael Hartrich, was as respected on ice as on rock. Jeff Pheasant was a front-rank climber of that period who never received the acclaim his abilities merited. Bouchard remained at the top, collaborating with Wilcox on a new mixed route on Cannon in 1974, *Icarus;* joining Bragg on the Adirondacks' first major ice climb at the new standard in 1975, Pok-o-moonshine's *Positive Thinking* (another old Turner rock route of desperate reputation); and, with Burlington local Steve Zachowski, opening up a wide variety of difficult climbs in Smugglers Notch during the winter of 1974–1975, of which *Ragnarock* was considered the prize.

Standards rose elsewhere as well, and not just when Bouchard or other North Conway superstars traveled. In 1975 Al Long and Al Rubin began applying the new tools and techniques to the Adirondacks, doing a series of outstanding routes on the north face of Pitchoff Mountain. The hidden Dartmouth plum, Owl's Head in Oliverian Notch, was climbed in December 1974 as a winter rock route and first done on ice two winters later by Peter Kelemen and Rob Gilbert. Even lordly Katahdin was brought into the new era. John Porter, Geoff Wood, and David Isles did the first big route on the face above Chimney Pond in 1972; a year later Henry Barber and Dave Cilley went up the prominent ice line in the middle of that face; and in 1974 several major routes were done, some by a party in which Jorge Urioste and Mischa Kirk were the driving forces, and some by an AMC employee group under Bob Proudman.

Female ice climbers appeared as a discernible presence for the first time in the sport. In the early 1970s a few women did difficult routes primarily as seconds to strong male companions—e.g., Joan Nester, Ed's wife, and Joanne Selle, a friend of Jorge Urioste. In the winter of 1975–1976, Susan Coons was caretaker at the Harvard Cabin in Huntington Ravine and became a proficient ice climber in her own right. By the winter of 1975, as mentioned, women had been up the *Black Dike,* led the Big Slab at Chapel Pond, and participated in routes on Katahdin's big basin walls. In 1976 emerged several talented women in the new breed of winter climbers. Nancy Kerrebrock climbed the *Black Dike* that winter, seconded a first ascent on Cannon, *Lila,* and two winters later one at Lake Willoughby, the difficult *Renormalization,* while leading reasonably difficult (by the new standard) climbs in her own right. Karen Messer climbed the *Black Dike* in December

1976 and the following winter did *Repentance* and other extreme routes. Nevertheless, ice climbing remained much more a male preserve than rock climbing.

In some ways the big news of the middle 1970s was not made at the leading edge but down in the broad center of the sport. From the revolution in 1969 until about 1975, ice climbing was characterized by a few path-breakers exploring unknown frontiers—Bouchard, Bragg, and the few others mentioned hitherto. The majority employed the new tools more hesitantly, still sticking largely to the old locations: Huntington Ravine, Willey Slide, Chapel Pond.

The winter of 1976 was when the climbing community as a whole moved across the watershed. That was when the roster of bold leaders suddenly multiplied and the rank and file spilled into the new areas. That was when Frankenstein took over from Huntington as the most popular place to go. Cathedral ice now, rather than Willey Slide, was viewed as the most suitable beginners' area—beginners now started on front points right away. Even the staid old Boston AMC decreed, for the first time (and not without some grumbling from the old guard), that front-pointed crampons were mandatory for beginners in winter technical climbing. All over the region, vertical ice was explored by climbers who had mastered the new tools and techniques. The year 1976 was the first in which the *Black Dike* saw frequent ascents and the first year that several parties got up *Repentance*. The modern standard had finally been consolidated. The work begun by Chouinard and McCarthy on that sunny weekend at Chapel Pond in 1969 was complete. ∎

Reference Note

Written summaries of ice climbing history, with emphasis on postwar developments, include Rick Wilcox, "A Short History of New England Ice Climbing," a historical essay in his *An Ice Climber's Guide to Northern New England* (North Conway, NH: International Mountain Equipment, Inc., 1982); the equivalent essay in Don Mellor, *Climbing in the Adirondacks;* Wilcox, "A Brief History of Eastern Ice Climbing," *New England Outdoors,* January 1979, pp. 42–44; Ed Webster, "Ice in the Granite State," *Summit,* January-February 1981, pp. 9–10; and S. Peter Lewis, "Ice in the Granite State," *Climbing,* December 1983, pp. 14–18, 22–25. The authors also profited from conversations and correspondence with Henry Barber, John Bouchard, Kenn Boyd, John Bragg, Peter Cole, Clint Cummins, Jim Gilchrist, Bob Hall, Michael Hartrich, John Imbrie, Henry Kendall, Philip Koch, Bob Kruszyna, Jeff Lea, Al Long, Jim McCarthy, Bob Olsen, Bob Proudman, Rainsford Rouner, Al Rubin, Sam Streibert, Claude Suhl, Jorge Urioste, Jonathan Waterman, Rick Wilcox, Kurt Winkler, Michael Young, Steve Zachowski, and Frank Zahar.

22: Emergence of Climbing as a Popular Sport

AROUND 1980 OBSERVERS of the northeastern rock climbing scene wondered whether the days of glory had passed. Despite herculean efforts by Dunn, Webster, and others, not one of the north country's hottest young men seemed significantly better than Hot Henry Barber had been a full ten years before. Ten years is a long time in modern climbing chronology. Similarly at the Shawangunks, once at the forefront of American standards. Almost ten years elapsed before anything harder than *Supercrack* was climbed. The consensus appraisal was that California and Colorado climbers had left the Easterners behind. Reflecting on more than two decades of exciting events, Jim McCarthy dolefully concluded the Shawangunks were in:

> . . . a certain stasis right now. Until someone comes along with another leap of the imagination, the place is basically climbed out.

The concern was nationwide: as late as 1983 a think-piece in *Climbing* magazine asked "Has rock climbing peaked out?" and concluded:

> Nothing too significant has occurred in four years. . . . There has been no new thought, no changes in style, no radical departures from what the majority considers possible.

It seemed as if the long boom in rock climbing's popularity might subside; ethical questions seemed resolved, albeit differently at different cliffs; and standards of difficulty seemed stuck at 5.12, and even that level seemed barely attainable to the post-Barber generation.

On all these points, and others, the 1980s were full of surprises. Rock climbing was far from stagnating. Indeed, the quickening pace of events soon showed that the 1980s would be yet another period of creative intensity, bringing major changes in the sport.

"A broadly popular sport." The once-lonely crags, first explored in solitude by Robert Underhill and John Case, became crowded scenes of exuberant humanity as climbing became the pastime of a new generation. Above: Whitehorse Ledge, unclimbed during the 1920s, aswarm with climbers during the 1980s.

S. PETER LEWIS

The hiatus at the leading edge around 1980 had warped the perspectives of observers. Even that early, the sport as a whole (as distinct from the leading edge) was changing dynamically. Down below the top of the standard, climbing was emerging as a broadly popular sport. It was no longer the obscure pastime of a few eccentrics. Public visibility was signaled by frequent nationally televised programs covering rock climbing. At colleges young men and women all knew about climbing as a legitimately available athletic pursuit. Climbing equipment was universally recognized, widely available in stores, and something of an instant status symbol to be seen with. Summer camps, prep schools, and a new generation of specialized adventure programs featured "ropes courses" and visits to local crags for top-roping. "Properly practiced, rock climbing need not be high risk," reported the fashion-conscious magazine *Ultra Sport* in 1987. "At its best it is fun, safe, challenging, and very accessible."

The growing popularity of rock climbing during the early 1980s was a powerful force. It ran counter to the trend of the outdoor recreation boom, which largely peaked in 1975 and idled along on a plateau thereafter. Thus backpacking and hiking exploded between 1965 and 1975 but abruptly ceased to grow or even declined after 1975. But rock climbing simply kept going through the roof. The Mohonk Preserve, which had sold 790 seasonal buttons to Shawangunks climbers in the 1974–75 season, sold 1,225 eleven years later and estimated that day permit sales had risen even faster. Where two to three hundred cars had been counted on busy weekends in the 1970s, something close to five hundred could be counted in the 1980s. The trend was the same around North Conway. Where there had been one climbing school (EMS) in the early 1970s and a second (IME) after 1975, there were half a dozen by the mid-1980s, and the continual business of new clients inevitably meant many more climbers entering the sport each year. Perhaps even more striking was the change at the less well known cliffs throughout the region. Crags that had once seemed isolated and lonely now teemed with many parties each weekend.

It is interesting to observe that all this occurred even as the standards at the leading edge were stagnant. One might think that major growth would occur only during a period of attention-grabbing change at the frontiers of the sport. Yet the growth in climbing's popularity seemed only to quicken during the hiatus in standards around 1980.

Reflecting this growth in popular interest, leading climbers began to treat climbing as a professional calling, a full-time athletic career, not a weekend diversion.

Lynn Hill

THE EIGHTIES AT A GLANCE

Principal climbing event: the Great Debate on ethics and style
Climbs of the Decade:—rock: *Survival of the Fittest*
                                    —ice: *Promenade* (sure, done in the
                                    seventies, but way ahead of its time)
Hardest single climb: *Cybernetic Wall*
Boldest lead: *Yellow Crack* or *Stagefright*
Emblematic item of gear: Friends
Most important climber: Lynn Hill
Most colorful: Hugh Herr
Most prominent woman: Lynn Hill
Child prodigy: Jimmy Surette
**Still-active father figures (even though neither was forty until late in
    the decade):** Kevin Bein and Rick Wilcox
Brainiest: John Imbrie
Norman Clyde Award: Rich Romano
Most abrasive: Jeff Gruenberg
Fred Beckey Award: Todd Swain
Couple of the Decade: Alain and Janot Comeau
Person you'd most like to have climbed with: George Hurley

Henry Barber had been the first successful professional climber in the Northeast, but his combination of guiding, sales promotion for suppliers, lecture fees, writing, and photography had always seemed jerry-built and tenuous. By the mid-1980s a new generation of full-time climbers found the career more stable and predictable. Professional guiding broke down the barriers of amateur purity at the Shawangunks and became almost as accepted and prominent there as at North Conway—and at Mount Desert and at Chapel Pond and at Ragged Mountain. Public awareness of climbing created more opportunities. The lecture circuit was more lucrative. More magazines paid more money for articles and pictures. "Repping"—signing on to represent a major supplier to the many climbing stores around the region— was a regular source of employment.

With a career now available, leading climbers viewed themselves as professional athletes and trained and practiced accordingly. Training routines geared specifically to rock climbing were developed and publicized. Artificial climbing walls, climbing ladders, and other specialized training aids were marketed. Climbers became steady clientele of gymnasiums and fitness centers. Step-by-step routines were worked out to improve specific capabilities, like "lock-off" strength, stomach control, finger exercises. Routines were prepared for specific climbs. To express the difficulty of one extreme move, a 1980s climber declared: "The move seemed two winters in the gym away." *Climbing* magazine, emerging as the dominant American climbing journal, opened a regular monthly department devoted to "Training." Bouldering and even repeated "laps" on very difficult climbs were perceived as stepping stones to higher standards. One Gunks regular of the 1980s would do "laps" on *Supercrack,* with the intent of accustoming himself so thoroughly to 5.12 climbing that 5.13 might not seem so hard. North Conway climbers strung several ropes together and repeatedly top-roped *The Prow* for the same purpose ("the training breakthrough of the century," commented one observer). Some viewed constant climbing as the key to raising standards: "You gotta climb all the time if you want to be at the cutting edge." "You gotta be on the rock."

Technological improvements in climbing equipment arrived in profusion and had more impact on climbing standards and style than anything since the advent of nylon rope.

Throughout the postwar era, equipment modifications had made significant if little-noticed changes in the sport, but it was clear that the conquest of psychological barriers explained far more of the progress in standards of difficulty. The switch from steel to aluminum carabiners during the early 1960s and from rope to nylon slings in the mid-1960s materially re-

duced the weight of climbing racks and surely made leading less of a burden, and probably easier as well. In the late 1960s the development of the
stiff-soled "RR" boot made edging on small holds far more trustworthy. In
the early 1970s the use of gymnastic chalk, introduced in the Northeast by
Rich Goldstone during the mid-1960s, became slowly accepted by almost
the entire climbing population. Chalk remained moderately controversial
in that a small minority bitterly opposed and resented its use on aesthetic
and stylistic grounds. Nevertheless it was almost universally accepted during
the early 1970s and was regarded by some as providing a significant assist to
higher standards. The switch from pitons to nuts after 1970 was initially inspired by a host of motivations unrelated to technical difficulty but was soon
regarded as a factor in harder climbing, since nuts could be placed more
quickly and with just one hand. During the 1970s the fashion in boots
moved away from the stiff-soled RR, with its edging powers, to the highly
flexible ballet-slipperlike "EB," which had superior characteristics for
"smearing" on less well defined holds. In the middle and late 1970s wholesale adoption of mechanical belaying devices replaced the traditional hip
belay. A variety of sit-harnesses and leg loops replaced the old rope-around-
the-waist tie-in about the same time. These and the use of double-rope technique, which caught on rapidly about 1980, all acted to reduce the risks in
falling, thereby freeing the leader's mind from worries and providing further advantage in exploring upper limits of difficulty.

All these changes unquestionably assisted in the progress of technical
standards, but their contributions were modest compared with two developments that impacted the sport primarily in the 1980s (though their roots
can be traced back into the 1970s).

One was the introduction of radically improved protection devices.
These included much smaller nuts with superior strength, such as the line
of Pollock nuts. Until these came along, the smallest nuts were regarded as
unsafe for long falls. This meant that opportunities for difficult leads on
rock where only small placements could be found were correspondingly discouraged. Even more important was the development of a variety of sophisticated camming devices, culminating in the invention of the moveable-
parts "Friend." If nuts could be placed more quickly than pitons, Friends
could be placed still more quickly and with far less fiddling around. The difference on strenuous leads was enormous. On a crack climb like *Supercrack*,
the impact of Friends was so significant that climbers began to take note of
who had led *Supercrack* "before Friends" and who led it only after Friends
were available; the difference was almost like a difference in a full grade of
the climb. A leading climbing manual called Friends "the biggest technical

breakthrough since the nylon rope." Other improvements in protection involved ingenious new runners, with a series of attachments designed to release under progressively greater impact, thereby reducing the stress on the nut; and some extraordinarily complex arrangements for ensuring the stability of delicately placed hooks resting on minute holds, developed by Connecticut cragsman Ken Nichols, which the inventor conceded sometimes "tread a fine line between psychological and real protection."

The second development that drastically altered the ease of climbing was the advent of sticky-rubber boots. Beginning with the Spanish "Fires" (rhymes with "beer haze"), a succession of climbing boots hit the market that were basically like the EB but with a new material on the sole that had noticeably more adhesive qualities. The difference for climbers at any level of proficiency was to improve the ease of climbing, some said by a full grade or two. Fires were called "one of those quantum leaps in technology that occasionally set the equipment world on its ear."

Thus in the 1980s the sport that had so long seemed a lonely struggle between the rock and the inner resources of the climber now began to be increasingly encompassed with a formidable apparatus of technology. The 1930s climber Ron Gower had written:

> [Rock climbing] is so perfectly natural, there being no artificial aids except the rope. . . . In this respect rock-climbing runs close to tramping and swimming in its essential simplicity.

Fifty years later, what a change! Even in half that time the amount of required equipment—and its cost—had changed radically. A characteristic rack and assorted gear in 1962 seemed complicated, burdensome, and costly at the time. The complete outfit—rope, rack, boots, hammer and holster, work gloves for belaying—cost approximately $130. The corresponding expenditure for 1987's outfit—no hammer, holster, or gloves, but two ropes, a vastly expanded rack, sticky-boots, belaying and tie-in devices, chalk, plus guidebook (nonexistent in 1962)—cost somewhere very close to $900. Inflation was but a small part of the change; according to the standard measures, $130 in 1962 was equivalent to $488 in 1987. The rest was added or improved function—plus just plain cost.

(Cost comparisons vary widely according to what is perceived as a characteristic rack and outfit for each time period. Our computations could certainly be disputed but are intended to be as fair as we could make them.

The data are as follows: For 1962, one 120-foot goldline rope, $22; twelve pitons ranging in price from $.75 to $1.50, totaling $15; twenty-two carabiners at $2, totaling $44; sling material, $10; boots, $14; hammer, $8; holster, $2; work gloves, $5; no specialized gear for tying in, belaying, or rappelling, no chalk, and no guidebook. Total for 1962: $130. For 1987, two 165-foot perlon ropes, $176; rack of six RP nuts ($33.75), six wired stoppers ($29.40), two tricams ($18.45), two wired bliss ($70), and five Friends ($187.50), totaling $329.10; nut remover, $9; five sewn slings and five quick-draws plus keular cord, totaling $43.75; twenty-six carabiners at $5.50, totaling $143; boots, $86; tie-in harness, $49.50; belay plate and associated carabiner, $15.75; chalk bag, chalk, and associated toy carabiners, $18.64; guidebook, $20; no hammer, holster, or gloves. Total for 1987: $890.24. While some leaders might dispense with some items on these lists, others might wish for additional items.)

Even at the Shawangunks technical breakthroughs beyond 5.11 were virtually unknown throughout the late 1970s. This is assuredly not to say that extremely difficult climbing was not going on—just that no one rose above the splendor of Bragg's *Kansas City,* Wunsch's *Supercrack,* and Stannard's many classics. To the top Gunks climbers of the late 1970s, the 5.12s climbed by Bragg, Wunsch, and Stannard in 1973–1974 (chapter 15) seemed superhuman achievements. Cowed by the luster of these demigods, the lesser mortals almost despaired of doing their own FFAs ("first free ascents") at that standard and focused their ambitions on what they called FHAs ("first human ascents") of the Bragg-Wunsch-Stannard classics.

Despite this seemly reverence for their predecessors, the top Gunks climbers of the late 1970s were in fact climbing very well. Technically, the hardest climbing of the region still lay on those escarpments overlooking the Hudson valley. Several more or less distinct circles evolved, with no formal division and much crossing over; one group led by Russ Raffa and Mike Sawicky; a second and larger brigade in which Kevin Bein, Mark Robinson, and Sandy Stewart were prominent; the Rezucha brothers; and one cat that walked by himself, Rich Romano. All these were putting in hard 5.11s during the late 1970s but for the most part were unable to break through to 5.12s.

Besides climbing well, these various circles climbed with a remarkable divergence of style, exemplified by some of their more conspicuous artisans. As examples of contrasting styles, consider Raffa, Bein, and Romano.

Russ Raffa represented the established Gunks devotion to the purest ethics and style. He was the closest thing to an heir to the Stannardian

Mayor of the Shawangunks. The popular, influential "grand master of 'Beta'," Kevin Bein. Below on Open Cockpit.

DICK WILLIAMS

HARVEY ARNOLD

mantle. Stylishly modern in his attention to the latest trends in equipment and clothing but resolutely traditional in *climbing* style, Raffa believed in leading from the ground up, placing protection on the lead, disdaining all aid, no bolts, no pitons, "letting style stand in the way of achievement if necessary," as Barber had remarked of Stannard and Wunsch. In an era of very difficult climbing, Raffa's pure style called for extraordinary mental toughness and cool self-discipline, executing 5.11 moves well above chancy protection. His leads of the late 1970s and those of the handful of like-minded others were uncommonly bold.

Bein's circle was equally pure on ethics but far more casual about style. Mastery of difficulty was the main point. They would congregate in a sociable group around the base of a 5.11 or 5.12 pitch and siege it all day, taking turns on the rope, coaching each other effusively, sometimes leading, sometimes top-roping, and often doing something in between ("Leading is a relative thing," mused Bein). Their pursuit of the purely difficult with little regard for style was an important precursor of controversial approaches during the mid-1980s.

Kevin Bein himself was a pivotal figure, a Shawangunk institution by the 1970s. He had started as a thirteen-year-old Wunderkind with the New York Appies in the early 1960s. Taking his cue from Rich Goldstone, he had applied himself assiduously to exercise, bouldering, and climbing, climbing, climbing. By the late 1960s he developed awesome upper-body strength and technical skills that nearly matched his mentor's, especially as a boulderer and top-roper. In 1973 he and Barbara Devine moved to New Paltz and became everyday climbers, the center of the most prominent circle of Gunks regulars, Kevin hailed as "Mayor of the Shawangunks." For twenty long years—from the age of McCarthy right to the late 1980s!—Bein was always just one short step behind the very top of the Gunks standard. He was never quite the pace-setter, but he continued to move up right behind those that were. It was a feat of durability and dedication without parallel in northeastern climbing.

Bein and his wide circle of friends and followers considerably relaxed the tight view of ethics and style set by Stannard and his elite. Kevin Bein was an extrovert for whom climbing was not a lonely challenge but a social activity, not a grueling ordeal but a kaleidoscope of delights, best enjoyed with a voluble throng of friends. He loved to tell climbing stories and delighted in move-by-move accounts of each route. "The grand master of 'Beta,'" he was called. Said Steve Wunsch: "Kevin probably helped more people up more climbs than anyone alive."

Prophets of the future. Two leading ground-breakers of the 1980s: Russ Raffa (left) and Rich Romano.

Bein's philosophy of climbing was accepted by a large and happy circle at the Shawangunks. The purpose was for everyone to do the most difficult move they could possibly master, after repeated practice and plenty of help from their friends. The old values of grit and commitment were not rejected, but they took a back seat to sociability and the pursuit of the purely difficult. This reasoning was to be carried a step further by the next generation. (However much the pursuit of difficulty may have blurred Bein's perception of style, it should not be construed that he was blind to the aesthetics of climbing or the natural beauty of his beloved Gunks. When a visiting hotshot climbed *Kansas City*, Bein greeted him later with: "Oh, that's a beautiful climb. How'd you like it?" The hotshot shrugged: "It wasn't really hard." Bein, angered, responded: "That's not what I asked you.")

Romano was possibly the most individualistic personality yet to come along at the top levels of this individualistic sport. A young, moody redhead, sporadically employed as a male nurse, Romano was something of a misfit even in the tolerant social scene of climbers. He devoted himself to climbing with indefatigable single-mindedness, literally living at the cliffs (sleeping under overhangs) for weeks at a time. Avoiding the limelight, he shunned the crowds and popular places in favor of the Gunks' tallest cliff, Millbrook, plus other obscure corners of the ridge where few others even knew there were cliffs. He never reported his accomplishments. At first regarded as "kind of strange," he acquired growing respect as it gradually dawned on his peers that somewhere out there he was climbing with brilliant ability and impeccable style. His 5.11s in the late 1970s and occasional 5.12 in the early 1980s were highly valued for their commitment and integrity. "A tough little customer," an admiring McCarthy called him.

Thus as the 1970s drew to a close, the entire Northeast had reached the modern age of hard free climbing. The conservative tradition was buried and forgotten. So much exciting progress had been made during the decade that rock climbers could only wonder what lay in store for the 1980s. ∎

Reference Note

The best printed source for 1980s developments is the preeminent American climber's magazine, *Climbing*. Good perspective on changing standards, equipment, and style may be gleaned by following the evolution of that magazine's reporting, advertisements, and underlying focus and style. Ultimately the best source is, of course, the climbers themselves.

23: Restoring Parity: The Reemergence of Women in the 1980s

O NE OF THE most striking changes which occurred in northeastern rock climbing during the 1980s was the emergence of women. More accurately, it was the reemergence of women after a long period of uncharacteristic subordination.

In the early days of the sport—the 1920s right up through the 1940s—everyone normally climbed all of the routes. Most of the pioneering leaders were men, but among the general population of climbers, women were very nearly as prominent and as proficient as their male compatriots. In the 1920s, there were Miriam O'Brien (later Underhill), Margaret Helburn, Elizabeth Knowlton, Florence Peabody, Marjorie Hurd, and Jessie White-head—as representative a group of 1920s climbers as any list of half a dozen men of that era. During the 1930s the great athlete Betty Woolsey was a favorite partner of Case, Wiessner, and House. Boston's Thelma Bonney and Red McDonald, New York's Marguerite Schnellbacher and Helen Fair were among the more prominent in prewar circles.

Probably the most gifted of those who started during the 1930s was Maria Leiper (later Millar). She was a born climber: before she discovered rock cliffs, she had alarmed family and friends on water towers, churches, hotel balconies, slow freight trains, houses, and trees. Leiper led the harder established routes of the late 1930s and established (with Wiessner) a superb 5.6 Shawangunks route that bears her name.

During the 1940s came Bonnie Prudden. Attractive and unconventional, aggressive and competitive, Prudden climbed fully as well as the men of her generation. Teamed mostly with her mentor and close friend, Hans Kraus, she helped put in thirty first ascents between 1946 and 1955, including the long and exposed *Hans's Puss, Dry Martini, Something Interesting,* and *Bonnie's Roof* (on which she led the ceiling using a sling for aid).

Jan Conn was a part of northeastern climbing only briefly—mainly on the amazing 1945 ascent of *Conncourse* on Cannon cliff. She, not Herb, led the harder pitches.

Up to the 1950s, outstanding women leaders were familiar figures in northeastern climbing: Appie leader Krist Raubenheimer; Ann Church;

Pioneers of the 1950s. Left: Bonnie Prudden on Layback. *Right: Krist Rauben-heimer on* Broken Sling.

Appie-turned-Vulgarian Dorothy Hirschland; and Ruth Tallan, whom Maria Leiper Millar remembered as the one with the most natural grace and skill of them all. In the Adirondacks, the first rock climbing guide was authored by the remarkable Trudy Healy.

But then came a strange lapse in the standards of women climbers. From somewhere around 1960 to somewhere around 1980, women did not climb at anything like the male standards of the day. At the Shawangunks women were on 51 percent of the first ascent parties on routes done between 1940 and 1950; on 29 percent of those done from 1951 to 1959; and on just 5 percent of those done during the period 1960 to 1970. There were "good" women climbers during the 1960s—Patty Crowther, Cherry Austin Merritt, Gerd Thuestad, Muriel Mayo, and others—but the best were not close to the best men in performance. Throughout the climbing population in general it became accepted that women were not expected to manage as difficult climbing as their male friends. This was a switch from the expectations of the 1930s and 1940s, a pronounced relapse. By 1980 it became accepted as the norm; the old days of Thelma Bonney and Maria Millar were forgotten, buried, not known to have even existed.

The Northeast seemed particularly backward in this regard, as California and Colorado women were climbing much better in the 1960s and early 1970s. The situation was self-reinforcing: with no women climbing hard climbs, new women climbers had no role models, no evidence that they should expect to climb as well as their male friends. In a sport where psychology counts so heavily, this was a vicious cycle to break.

Why this diminuendo? At the very start of the movement toward women's rights and "liberation," when women moved strongly toward greater economic, political, and social equality, why should they fall back in the field of climbing? Some of the possible reasons seem insufficient explanation:

1. During the McCarthy-Stannard era much Shawangunk climbing focused on gigantic overhangs at a previously unexplored standard of difficulty. Women and men alike accepted the hypothesis that greater male upper-body strength uniquely qualified that sex to dominate in this new aspect of climbing.

2. The spirit of climbing seemed to become more competitive after 1960. Possibly competitiveness is a more characteristic male trait? Vera Watson, New York AMC climber of those times, later killed on the all-women's expedition to Annapurna, commented that when climbing with women alone she found "more of a feeling of camaraderie, less competitiveness."

3. The dominant leaders of the pre-1960 period—the Appies and especially Hans Kraus and Fritz Wiessner—personally liked to climb with women, and Kraus at least was happy to share leads with them. By contrast the Vulgarians who emerged as dominant after 1960 cultivated a male dominant world.

Whatever the reasons, the long twilight lasted nearly twenty years. Not until the late 1970s did the first leader of real change emerge. Hers is a story worth noting, as she overcame major social and psychological barriers and paved the way for the women who restored parity to the world of climbing during the 1980s.

In 1970 Kevin Bein took his girlfriend on her first climb, *Northern Pillar,* the classic Shawangunks 5.2. She panicked, froze, cried, wanted to go down, then refused to go down, finally was dragged to the top, terrified and resolved never to climb again. But the idea of overcoming her fear took hold, and she returned to the cliffs for another try. Barbara Devine came to stay.

Two years later she accompanied Bein to Yosemite and did her first 5.8s. In 1973 Bein and Devine (now married) moved to New Paltz and became probably the most constant presences at the cliffs, climbing "literally every day," training intensively, bouldering hard, striving constantly to improve their standards. Tall and thin, Devine developed a phenomenal strength-to-weight ratio when she took up serious training. By 1974 she led *Retribution,* probably the first female lead of 5.10 in northeastern climbing. That was just the beginning. By 1976 she had done *Foops* and *Persistent,* Stannard's old test-piece 5.11s. In 1977 she did *Kansas City* (5.12) and such desperate 5.11s as *Open Cockpit, To Have or Have Not,* and *Wasp Stop.*

Devine was moving fast: her first 5.10 came thirteen years after McCarthy's; her first 5.11 nine years after Stannard's; her first 5.12 four years after Bragg's. After a three-year exile when she and Bein moved to the Needles in South Dakota, she was back at the Gunks and, in July 1983, did the first female ascent of *Supercrack,* plus other 5.12s of that day.

Like her husband, Devine was always subjected to an undercurrent of whispers about poor style—willingness to accept a top-rope and preplaced protection, lengthy sieging, and a preference for nearby protection on leads. For sheer technical virtuosity, however, there was no denying that she was far and away the outstanding woman climber in the Northeast during the 1970s.

Barbara Devine had a signal effect on the climate for other women climbers. At last a role model! If such a slender form could do monster 5.11 overhangs like *Foops,* clearly masculine upper-body strength was no prerequisite to 5.8.

The message was slow in gaining acceptance, but gradually more Gunks women began leading 5.8 and following 5.10 during the late 1970s. By about 1980 one of the Gunks regulars, Iza Koponicka, a graceful five feet two inches and 108 pounds, was leading 5.9s and the odd 5.10. Others like Laura Chaiten and Annie O'Neill were not far back. O'Neill seconded Ivan Rezucha on a great many first ascents at a demanding level during the years around 1980.

Trend-setters of the 1980s. From left: Barbara Devine (on Foops*), Rosie Andrews, Lynn Hill, Alison Osius (below right).*

HARVEY ARNOLD

DICK WILLIAMS

Before 1980, north country climbing had fewer able women climbers. Perhaps the politics of a tourist town and of the state of New Hampshire were less conducive to women breaking out of traditional roles, or perhaps the North Conway guide circle was something of a male "club." The best female climbing in New Hampshire in the late 1970s tended to be by "girl-friends" of strong males. Some of these women climbed very well, but not with the independent leading authority of Devine or Koponicka. These included Susan Patenaude (Ed Webster's friend), Ann DeBurro (Bryan Delaney's), Janot Comeau (Alain's wife), and Karin Winkler (Kurt's).

The next woman with an independent impact on female climbing was Rosie Andrews. Coming up through the Hurricane Island Outward Bound program, Andrews began to lead consistently in the 5.10 range by 1980, then moved up into the world of 5.11 in 1981. She became the second really prominent presence in the perceptions of other women in the Northeast.

Where Devine's career had always been closely linked to Bein's, Andrews appeared to stand much more on her own. She broke into the exclusive male circle of North Conway guides in 1982, wrote an avidly devoured landmark article on women climbers for *Mountain* in 1984, and in 1985 settled in the New Paltz area as a full-fledged professional climber. In 1981 she had stunned the Gunks community by leading a crux 5.12 move on a first ascent of *Point Blank* with Russ Raffa. Though Raffa ultimately first led the entire climb, word got around about Andrews leading that one desperate move.

Andrews led a growing movement toward more independent self-contained women climbers in the early 1980s. In the north country Alison Osius emerged as another who consistently led 5.11, occasionally 5.12. Others not quite in that league, but not far behind, included Connecticut's Nancy Emro, Vermont's Wendy White, and New Hampshire's Helen Curcio. At the Gunks it was now commonplace to see all-women teams comfortably handling 5.9 and 5.10 routes. Even within the Boston AMC—once a stronghold of the conservative tradition—women like Craigen Bowen and Beverly Boynton led 5.10 with authority and style.

Though cited here as exceptional "women climbers," these women of the 1980s were beginning to think of themselves as simply "climbers." The distinction was significant. Andrews, Osius, Curcio, and others vehemently disclaimed special recognition as women and sought simply to be accepted as climbers. Their example spread. Osius insisted, after a first free ascent of Cannon's *Labyrinth Wall,* with three pitches at 5.11 and six at 5.10, wherein she shared the lead with Neil Cannon: "There's no intrinsic reason why women can't climb as well as men. So we shouldn't get congratulated for lesser accomplishments." Andrews argued:

> In reality, the margin separating the best male and female climbers today is already fairly slim. Setting a separate, lower standard only encourages women to expect less of themselves than their abilities allow. Accomplishments should be measured in relation to the sport, not one's gender, and women should not expect public praise for doing routes done by men ten years ago.

In 1983 a twenty-one-year-old slight, slender, attractive California woman came east. Lynn Hill had been a gymnast, swimmer, and hiker from childhood. Gifted with uncommon strength but even more flexibility and grace, she took to rock climbing with ease. Before she left California, she had climbed 5.12. But when she arrived in the Northeast, her climbing activity level, physical fitness, competitive instincts, and mental attitude came together to make her a top-flight climber.

Not a top-flight woman climber; simply a top-flight climber. In 1983 she was one of four Gunks climbers to master the region's first 5.13, *Vandals*. In 1984, making one of her few trips to North Conway to sample local test pieces, she took on *Tourist Treat,* "a problem that had been stumping local climbers for years." She led it on sight, with but one fall, perhaps the most difficult first ascent in the north country at the time. In the same year, back at the Gunks, she led the first ascents of *Organic Iron* (5.12 plus) and the original aid line on *Yellow Crack* (5.12 plus with scant protection), the latter called by Russ Raffa, himself a 5.12 leader with a reputation for boldness: "the best lead I've ever seen in my life." When the 1986 guidebook was published, the cover photo unselfconsciously showed Lynn Hill leading *Open Cockpit.* That long-time observer of the Gunks scene, Kevin Bein, pronounced her, in 1986: "the best climber in the Gunks now." Most observers declined to set any one of the seven or eight top 1980s climbers ahead of the rest, but the point was clear that no man was climbing significantly better than Lynn Hill.

Women had caught up. Actually, only this one woman. The general level of female climbing was still well below males'. But clearly barriers had been removed, and it appeared unlikely that another "dark ages" could return. The new outlook owed much to the path-breaking by Devine,

Andrews, Osius, and Hill, but the real story written in the 1980s was by the anonymous multitude of women who climbed well and independently, perceiving themselves once again in the mainstream of northeastern climbing. ■

Reference Note

An early assessment of the decline in women's climbing standards during the 1960s was Laura Waterman, "When Women Were Women at the Shawangunks," *Off Belay*, February 1979, pp. 8–12. An updated and expanded account appeared as part of an anthology, *Rock and Roses: An Anthology of Mountaineering Essays, By Some of the Best Climbers of the World*, Mikel Vause, ed. (Mountain N' Air Books, La Crescenta, Calif., 1990). The authors acknowledge with appreciation the willingness of Mountain N' Air Books to have the foregoing chapter closely follow the account in *Rock and Roses*. The landmark article on the reemergence of women during the late 1970s to early 1980s was Rosie Andrews, "No Spare Rib: The Advent of Hard Women Rock Climbers," *Mountain* 97, May-June 1984, pp. 22–29. See also David Roberts, "Alison Osius: Rock and Other Hard Places," *Outside*, August 1985, pp. 51–52. Lynn Hill has been a popular subject for media pieces; see, for example, John Steiger, "Lynn Hill," *Climbing*, August 1987, pp. 48–57; and Trip Gabriel, "Cliffhanger," *The New York Times Magazine*, December 31, 1989, pp. 20–25, 44–45. The August 1987 issue of *Climbing* was devoted largely to the renaissance of women's climbing. Besides the article on Hill, see especially Sallie Greenwood, "Frame of Reference: A Historical Perspective," pp. 44–46, and several short profiles—of Rosie Andrews by Alison Osius (pp. 93–95), of Barbara Devine by Susan Rogers (p. 102), and of Alison Osius by Susan Rogers (p. 104). The authors also were assisted by much conversation and correspondence with contemporary climbers, both women and men.

Can Women Lead on Ice?
Learning by the process of default

Exhilaration—is within—
There can no Outer Wine
So royally intoxicate
As that diviner Brand
The Soul achieves—Herself—
Emily Dickinson

BACK AROUND TWENTY, twenty-five years ago when I started climbing no women were leading hard climbs. None that I heard about anyway. I know for sure that no women back then were leading at the top of the day's standard. Certainly not at the Gunks, which is where I learned to climb.

It hadn't always been this way, as you know by now, reader, if you've read the chapters about women's accomplishments on rock in the 1940s and 1950s. But by the time I came along, long gone were Maria Millar, Bonnie Prudden, Krist Raubenheimer. They were just names in the guidebook, not anyone I knew. The day of Barbara Devine, Rosie Andrews, Lynn Hill was far in the future, not doing me any good right then.

As for ice, I had never heard of a woman in the Northeast leading ice at all. Very, very few even followed it. On many occasions Guy and I went to Chapel Pond and Huntington Ravine, and I can scarcely ever recall another woman going to the top of the Big Slab or staying at the Harvard Cabin. Lonely times.

I just tell you these bare facts to set the scene for what follows. The word "role model" was not in our vocabulary then. I would have given a lot for some strong ice woman to look up to. Such a one would have had a big influence on me and shortcutted my stumbling path in quest of leading on ice myself. But, then, if such a creature had existed, the tale I'm about to tell would not have happened in quite the same way.

I started climbing ice in 1970, just missing the torturous step-chopping age and just in time to grasp Chouinard's revolutionary first-generation drooped picks.

Every weekend, leaving Friday after work, Guy (who wasn't yet my husband) and I drove four wintry hours up to the Adirondacks. We routinely set up our tent on Chapel Pond, securing it with deadly old Marwa ice screws (nicknamed "the coat hanger" because they were as effective as coat hangers at catching falls, as was proved by Dan Doody and Craig Merrihue on a sad day in Pinnacle Gully. That's why we used these screws for attaching our tent to the ice on Chapel Pond, *not* for climbing). We would pound them in with our new Chouinard Alpine Hammers and be comfortably settled in our sleeping bags before midnight.

The next day's early light might reveal four or five other tents on the pond's solid surface. We were all ice climbers from the New York area who during the warm months climbed rock together at the Gunks. All of us had speeded through Friday night to be in the right position to use well those bounteous floes around Chapel Pond.

I didn't pay much attention to the fact that I was about the only woman interested in climbing ice—regularly, that is. Some of the women I knew from the Gunks might come for a weekend or two but didn't stay. It was nothing new for me. In those days there were always more men than women at climbing areas. Anyway, as a kid I had grown up playing with the boys.

I climbed with Guy and he always led. I became expert at removing ice screws. If you take out enough protection over a long period of time you have also learned (without knowing it) how to put it in. It's like learning how to cook: you don't actually have to help your mother get dinner every night to know how, when it's your turn, to get dinner yourself.

I was interested in learning to lead, but the opportunity never came up. We were both just having so much fun the way things were.

One Saturday we decided to climb a lovely route called Roaring Brook Falls, which is four pitches. There were Guy, our nephew Dane, another fellow named Ed, and me. Guy was the only one of us who led and he started up. Suddenly there was a strange rattly, whirry sound. We all quickly looked up not knowing what to expect and Ed, who was belaying, got bonked by a large, white, round-faced alarm clock—the type you set on the bedside table at night—which Guy carried in his shirt so as to be sure it would keep going in cold weather. The clock's career as a timepiece ended on the ice at our feet and Dane intoned: "My, how time flies."

That was the first event.

Guy brought us all up to the belay and took off again. Next, we heard up above a funny scuffling, a sort of yelp, and then, "Oh damn! I've sheered off my crampon points." Our leader improvised and reached the next belay.

That was the second event.

WILLIAM THOMAS

Women at the front. Author Laura Waterman leading Huntington Ravine's classic Pinnacle Gully during the 1970s.

Back in those days we were in love with the romance of climbing. We'd read the great masters of Alpine lore: Geoffrey Winthrop Young, Leslie Stephens, Whymper, and Mummery and would sprinkle their stories into our conversation. One of our favorite lines when we were in a tough place was: "And Vedenz was then sent forward with the rope." Vedenz was, apparently, a guide, or maybe only a porter, who was constantly getting the British gentleman climbers out of trouble.

Now, at this critical moment with our leader sidelined, I thought: my chance to be Vedenz! Guy thought so too, since he handed me the rack and said it was up to me to lead the last two pitches.

That was the beginning of leading ice for me: the breakthrough. Next came consolidation.

Not long after the Roaring Brook Falls incident, we made the even longer drive up to New Hampshire's White Mountains. We wanted to climb the famous Willey Slide, which we knew to be low-angle and not terribly hard (harder then than it is now, though, of course!). Though easy, it has many pitches and all of the belays are out on the ice, anchored by ice screws, no sturdy trees to quickly throw a sling around.

We were a party of three: Guy, me, and our good friend Lou. Lou didn't lead, so Guy and I agreed we'd flip and put Lou in the middle, which was fine with him.

At the base of the long wide floe—it looked to me like several acres of perfect ice!—we begin gearing up. Crampons first. Lou and I are crouched, tightening straps, when we become aware of frantic movement next to us. Guy is up to his elbows burrowing in his pack, pitching things out. Useless gear is strewn in a heap on the snow, disorganized. His eyes are wide. I'm hearing an inarticulate gurgle, which sounds like a person strangling. Guy had forgotten his crampons.

This was the third event.

His loss, that day, was my gain. As Lou and I moved steadily up Willey's thick floes we caught glimpses of Guy, poor thing, pacing up and down the old railroad line that ran through the notch below. He had dwindled to doll size when I finally reached the top.

Those two incidents—the one at Chapel Pond, the other on Willey Slide—completely removed our mental block about my leading. The next time we were in Huntington Ravine, Guy handed *me* the rack and I led *him* up Pinnacle Gully.

In the 1990s this tale probably rings pathetic, a woman of limited vision, a man so domineering as to surrender the lead only when physically handicapped. I don't see it that way. To me it tells less about us—remember, I saw almost no other women on the ice at all—and more about the ways of history, the changing vision of expected roles, slowly evolving perceptions of possibilities. Perhaps the message is in the eye of the beholder. ∎

24: 5.13 and Beyond

A S WE DESCRIBED in the start of chapter 22, the year 1980 saw northeastern climbers questioning where the future of the sport lay. Nothing significantly harder had been achieved since Bragg's *Kansas City* and Wunsch's *Supercrack*. Indeed, few routes even that hard had been done since Wunsch and Stannard had ceased pushing the standards in 1974.

In the final years of the decade of the 1970s, 5.12 was very tentatively approached for the first time since *Supercrack*. John Bragg, author of *Kansas*

Rick Fleming. "Quiet and unassuming," Fleming seemed to elude the North Conway limelight. Yet his routes of the early 1980s broke new ground in difficulty on north country rock.

City in 1973 and now a superstar in the international mixed climbing arena, returned to the Gunks in 1978 and 1979 to put in three major new 5.12s, including the classic *Gravity's Rainbow.* Mark Robinson and Mike Sawicky took the aid out of *Happiness Is a 110° Wall* in 1979, becoming the first of the post-Stannardians to reach the realm of 5.12 on their own.

In 1978 the north country finally saw its first 5.12, but to the chagrin of North Conway regulars, it was an "outsider" who cracked the barrier. Actually, Mark Hudon was a southern New Hampshire boy, but in the mid-1970s he had gone West with the frank object of becoming America's best rock climber. Through full-time climbing, he very nearly reached that goal. In 1978 he returned to the Northeast and breezed through most of the hardest climbs in the region, including Wunsch's *Supercrack* (its fourth ascent). At the same time Jimmy Dunn had devoted one of his long sieges to attempting to free *White Eye,* one of Arsenault's splendid aid routes. Hudon opened eyes by whirling up *White Eye* free and pronouncing it the only 5.12 he had found in New Hampshire. "It looked like he was flying," sighed an awestruck Webster.

It was more than two years before one of the North Conway regulars contributed a bona fide home-grown 5.12. This was on October 10, 1980, when the quiet and unassuming Rick Fleming showed that he had reached the top rank in the state as a free-climber with his lead of *Heather,* also on Cathedral. Another year passed before Whitehorse's first 5.12, *Wonder Wall,* climbed by Ed Webster and Russ Clune.

But these impressive achievements of 1978 to 1980 still failed to advance the standards over the Stannard-Bragg-Wunsch-Barber era of the first half of the 1970s. Had climbing really reached a dead end? Was further progress in difficulty possible? Had the species as climber reached the limit?

In the opening years of the decade of the 1980s, a growing number of talented individuals began to inch the limits slowly toward a new breakthrough. At the Gunks, Russ Raffa began leading very serious 5.12s, with *Point Blank* and *Project X* in 1981 and others in the next three years. Rich Romano came along with *Nectar Vector* and *Infinite Space,* also in 1981. New faces arrived at the Gunks and moved into this level as well: Hugh Herr beginning (at age seventeen!) with *Sticky Bun Power* in 1981; Russ Clune with *Drop Zone* in 1982; Jeff Gruenberg and Jack Meleski with the roof on *Manifest Destiny* in 1983; and Lynn Hill with *Organic Iron* and *Yellow Crack* in 1984. Even the veteran Kevin Bein got in the act with *Dark Side of the Moon* in 1984.

In New Hampshire, Rick Fleming continued at the forefront, though his modest demeanor, thoroughly uncharacteristic of most modern rock stars, generated far less recognition than his talent deserved. The more

Hugh Herr. A route of unbelievable difficulty and daring was Stagefright *on Cathedral, first climbed by the remarkable Hugh Herr—and rarely repeated.*

S. PETER LEWIS

aggressive Neil Cannon also forged to the fore among north country climbers, doing all the hardest routes in 1981 and 1982 and putting in still harder ones in 1983 and 1984. His *Reconciliation* in October 1983 was regarded by some as a distinct step harder than Fleming's *Heather*. North Conway did not have the star-studded galaxy of superstars at the forefront that the Shawangunks did, but they were pushing closer. Still, local pride was pained in the summer of 1984 over a "last great problem" at Cathedral, *Tourist Treat* (5.12): the best North Conway locals had worked for a long time to master this crack system, all to no avail, when Lynn Hill blew into town one summer day and waltzed up on her second try. In the following summer, Hugh Herr overwhelmed the locals with an incredibly daring, unprotected lead of *Stagefright* (5.12+). "Hughie really put it on the line on that one," marveled EMS's Lentini. Webster called it "a bold statement of dedication and excellence."

Elsewhere, standards lagged below those of the Gunks and North Conway. The most remarkable top climber not associated with either of those two traditional top centers was probably Connecticut's Ken Nichols. Older than most of the other superstars, a Vietnam veteran, Nichols was a person of fierce principles, abrasive candor, and phenomenal dedication to the sport of climbing and to the merits of his chosen locale, the short traprock cliffs of central Connecticut. Devoting himself to a systematically exhaustive and meticulously recorded exploration of every climbable rock in the area, Nichols authored a unique 479-page, handsomely hardback guidebook detailing 1,318 climbs. A walking Guiness Book of Records, Nichols also churned out—and again meticulously recorded—a personal streak of 654 consecutive days of climbing and a lifetime total that surpassed 20,000 climbs by 1991. Never avoiding controversy if he could find it, Nichols championed an uncompromising free-climbing, ground-up, antibolt ethic.

COURTESY DICK WILLIAMS

Lynn Hill. A major breakthrough in northeastern standards of difficulty was the Shawangunks' Vandals, first climbed through a combined effort by four of the key climbers of the time: Jeff Gruenberg, Jack Meleski, Russ Clune, and—shown here at the crux—Lynn Hill.

"The preservation of the rock is far more important than individual climbers," he contended. "Climbers come and go, but the rock remains forever." His zeal for this principle sometimes embroiled him in bitter battles (sometimes close to physical blows) with others who failed to live by his creed.

With all these exceptional qualities, Nichols was also a superb free-climber whose accomplishments on Connecticut rock, albeit on small cliffs, were close to the same league as his contemporaries in New York and New Hampshire. Determined never to overrate his climbs, he claimed Connecticut's first 5.12 only with *Chain Reaction* in 1985, but several earlier routes might have been awarded that rating by less exacting appraisers.

As the diversity of these names suggests, no one shot ahead of the rest; there was a crowd at the front. "The aura of the big name is gone," it was observed. Raffa's boldness was admired, Gruenberg's relentless dedication, Hill's raw talent, Clune's aggressiveness, Nichols' persistence, Bein's affable durability, Cannon's performance on big cliffs. Hugh Herr was unquestionably the most unusual of the top climbers: in the winter of 1982 an ice climbing misadventure cost him both legs due to frostbite, yet he returned as a double amputee not just to climbing but to the very top levels. But other than Herr's unique saga and the fact that Hill was a woman, the names tended to blend together, no superstar shining above the rest. The situation bore out Andy Warhol's prediction: "In the future everybody will be famous for fifteen minutes."

In the spring of 1983 Gruenberg and Meleski spotted a possible line through a large Shawangunk roof but saw no way to protect the bottom moves. To decrease the hazard of a ground fall they cleared the nearby area of boulders and scree, calling themselves Vandals for so doing. Later in the year Gruenberg and Clune began working on the lower face leading to that roof, but even their superb talents were unable to master the moves. Invited to give a try, Lynn Hill "walked through" this section, got in some protection, and began work on the roof. When she was stopped, Gruenberg and Clune took over and inch by inch began to work out the roof. Later Hugh Herr joined the effort. Finally one day in the fall, Gruenberg and Herr made the first full ascents, each doing it on the lead. Shortly thereafter Hill and Clune also led it. *Vandals* was the first climb in the Northeast to be given the rating of 5.13. As harder routes were done in the late 1980s, that rating was sometimes questioned. In 1983, though, it was clear that *Vandals* represented a breakthrough.

It is symptomatic of the heroless new era that, while posterity vividly recalls *Foops, Kansas City,* and *Supercrack* as each the inspirational vision of one

Jim Surette. The youthful Surette was the first north country climber who regularly climbed at a standard of difficulty comparable to that attained at the Shawangunks. He is shown at left on his landmark Liquid Sky.

S. PETER LEWIS

man, remaining unattainable by others for a decent interval, *Vandals* was a group effort and was led by four different individuals in quick succession.

For fewer than three years *Vandals* remained the hardest climb in the Northeast. Forces were gathering at the Gunks for a serious assault on 5.13. Jeff Gruenberg was training with fanaticism that put all previous regimens in the shade, getting up in the dark to run, working out for hours, climbing every day, virtually starving himself to reduce excess body weight to a minimum. Jack Meleski was keeping pace as Gruenberg's most frequent climbing partner. Russ Clune was climbing all over the world at a whirlwind pace but still maintaining the Gunks as his home base. Hill was better than ever. So was Herr. Eager new faces surfaced: three young New Paltz college climbers—"the kids," as other 5.12 climbers called them—who reveled in the joy of extreme climbing and who acknowledged no limits to their emerging powers, Al Diamond, Jordan Mills, and little (five-foot-four-inch) Scott Franklin. As Hill commented: "The vision is being expanded."

In the fall of 1985, Franklin led his *Survival of the Fittest,* a significantly more difficult climb than *Vandals.* Adding luster to this achievement was the fact that Franklin led the route from the ground up, placing protection on the lead, a standard of performance increasingly being abandoned by others. In 1986 the 5.13 barrier crumpled. Gruenberg and Meleski freed a variation on that quintessential Shawangunk overhang (or enduring series of overhangs), *Twilight Zone,* and established another climb almost as hard, *Clairvoyance.* Clune put up *Thunderdome.* Diamond mastered *Pumping Pygmies.* Franklin was back with *Love Muscle* and *Cybernetic Wall,* the latter probably the most difficult of all that generation of climbs. The consolidation of 5.13 had begun, and "the kids" were openly talking 5.14.

In 1985 the career of a north country original burst into full bloom, and with him came 5.13 to New Hampshire. Jim Surette, a slightly built, quiet North Conway native, emerged as a 5.12 climber at age fifteen. In October 1985 Surette became the first to free the original aid line of Cathedral's *Cerberus,* a difficult 5.12. He was also the first North Conway climber to repeat Hill's *Tourist Treat* (causing the frustrated established climbers of the area to scoff that this must be a climb for only women and children). Finally in 1986 Surette brought New Hampshire climbing fully into the 5.13 standard with his ascent of *Liquid Sky.* By this time, though still in high school, he was accepted as unquestionably the best climber in the area. Not until a visit from Franklin in 1987 was anything harder than Surette's best routes done; that was when Franklin did a variation off *The Prow* known as *The Edge of the World.* (In the jargon of the technical stratosphere, *Liquid Sky* was called 5.13c, Franklin's route was exalted to 5.13d.)

While extreme performance on the cutting edge was limited largely to the Shawangunks and Cathedral, higher standards were established all over the region. New generations of dedicated climbers sprang up in the north country of the Adirondacks (especially around Chapel Pond) and of Maine, around the cities of Boston and Manchester and Hartford and Burlington, and everywhere that rock was to be climbed. The sport enjoyed boom years throughout the Northeast.

An additional measure of the advance in standards, a sort of sideshow, was the progress in free soloing. Unroped climbing had a long history back to Underhill and Whitney, but during the years of the conservative tradition it fell into extreme disfavor. During the 1960s Vulgarians, IOCAns, and even an occasional Appie (notably Chuck Loucks) solo climbed in the intermediate range of difficulty (5.5 to 5.6) but were secretive about it, so severe was the disapprobation attached to the solitary art. Occasionally someone soloed something really hard—e.g., Dick Williams doing *Maria Direct* during the early 1960s—but these were exceptions. The overwhelming proportion of all this early soloing was on climbs well within the soloist's control.

Henry Barber was the first to flaunt his willingness to solo difficult climbs. Barber astonished his contemporaries with on-sight solos of climbs very nearly at the top of his ability. It was one more tactic Barber employed to demonstrate his unrivaled confidence and mental control.

Cannon climber Andy Tuthill was a quiet but remarkable soloist, once soloing a complete girdle traverse of the Cannon cliff in one day, and on the following day soloing up *Moby Grape*, down *Old Cannon*, up *Sam's Swan Song*, down *Cannonade*, and up the *Whitney-Gilman*.

In 1985 a different phase of soloing enjoyed a brief but giddy moment on the Shawangunk stage: solos of the very hardest routes by the very best climbers, but only after such thorough rehearsing that every move was totally mastered (or "wired"). In this mode Gruenberg amazed his friends by soloing *Foops* and *Yellow Wall*, while Clune topped that with *Open Cockpit* and *Supercrack*. Jimmy Surette showed they could do it in the north country too, with *Airation* (5.11). Finally Franklin topped them all in 1986 by soloing *Survival of the Fittest*, claiming to be the first American to have soloed a consensus 5.13.

The fad lasted little more than a year, to the great relief of both onlookers and participants. "Someone was going to get hurt," admitted Clune. Nevertheless, elsewhere in the country, the soloing of difficult climbs remained a ticket to fame and thus continued to attract adherents.

The continuing advance of standards at the 5.13 level in the late 1980s—as well as the conquest of 5.14—is a development for future historians to record and appraise with greater balance and perspective than is possible for those of us who are too close to it in time. History requires a waiting period, some distance from which to view such towering achievements.

But one point is clear: the "stasis" that McCarthy observed in 1980 was gone, swept away in a tide of brilliant personal accomplishments by a remarkable new cadre of top climbers. The 1980s showed that new worlds were still there to conquer. Humanity acknowledged no limits. The tradition handed down from Robert Underhill and Fritz Wiessner, through John Turner and Jim McCarthy, and on through John Stannard and Henry Barber, was finding deserving successors. There was still excitement and spirit at the leading edge. It was, and is, and always will be, a great world. ∎

Reference Note

The progress into 5.13 and beyond is chronicled in new-route reports in the climbing press. The authors are indebted to many currently active climbers for illuminating discussions of 1980s trends.

25: Lake Willoughby and the Quandary of Northeastern Ice during the 1980s

I CE CLIMBING PURSUED a completely different pace of change from that of rock climbing after 1976. As we saw, rock climbing standards ground to a dead halt for the latter half of the 1970s, then surged ahead with excitement during the mid-1980s. Ice reversed that pattern. During the winters of the late 1970s, technical standards on ice soared until the longest and steepest ice in the Northeast had all been climbed. That left a problem for the 1980s ice climber: where to go from there? At the end of the 1980s' decade, that question remained essentially unanswered.

During this period, as before, the technology of ice climbing equipment played a role in change. During the middle 1970s, technical developments in equipment presaged further breakthroughs at the top of the standard. New tools were introduced that represented advances over the Chouinard ax and hammer. From Scotland's Hamish ("The Terror of Glencoe") MacInnes came a blunt, ugly, sharp-nosed weapon called the Terrordactyl, the pick of which was not curved but hooked at a sharply acute angle. The Terrordactyl was used on the *Black Dike* in 1975 and was widely adopted in the late 1970s. Shortly thereafter a straight, tubular ice pick was introduced, the best known called the Hummingbird. Displacing less ice, tubular picks were placed with greater ease and seemed to represent a radical breakthrough. However, they did not take over the field as originally predicted. Still newer pick designs were introduced. Finally the diversity of choices was formally recognized by the development of shafts with interchangeable picks, enabling climbers to deploy curved picks, straight Terrordactyl-like designs, or tubular ones according to their preference and specific ice conditions anticipated each day. Other technical developments of major importance were improved ice screws capable of one-handed placements and ratchet devices for more convenient placement and removal of screws. Traditional crampons soon had competition from a variety of products, among which a flat platform known as a Footfang became widely used.

Partly as a result of these technical developments, but perhaps more because it was time for another leap of the imagination, the winter of 1977

Lake Willoughby discovered. Michael Hartrich on the first ascent of the first major route at the new mecca of extreme ice climbing: Lake Willoughby's Twenty Below Zero Gully.

HENRY BARBER

brought a new advance in ice climbing standards. As so often with break-throughs, it took new faces to soar beyond what the Bouchard-Bragg generation had accomplished. In this case a new scene was involved as well.

"Away up in northern Vermont," wrote M. F. Sweetser in 1892, "two great mountains rise above the wooded plains of Westmore, holding in the gap between them the celebrated Willoughby Lake." The mountain on the east side of this lake Sweetser identified as "the rocky spine which is variously known as Mount Annanance, or Willoughby, or Pisgah," and its "crumbling cliffs" plunged several hundred feet to a talus slope on the edge of the lake. Well to the north of more popular vacation spots, Lake Willoughby was never precisely overrun in summer. In winter it was desolate. One resident of a nearby hamlet said it could get so cold "the mercury crawled under the porch." The lakeside cliffs in winter, reported Sweetser, became a stark and lonely scene, "as unvisited as the heart of Greenland."

In January 1974 Henry Barber and Al Rubin drove north for some ice climbing but found parties already on the routes they had intended. So they drove further north and over to Vermont, where Rubin had heard rumors of fabulous ice cliffs at Lake Willoughby. Al Long and other Burlington climbers had been there, had been thoroughly impressed, but had done no major routes. Others must have seen the ice cliffs but not believed them relevant to climbing. When Barber and Rubin came around the bend of the twisting road, up in country that till then had little association with climbers and climbing, they could scarcely believe their eyes. For a good half mile on the right side of the road, a continuous cliff several hundred feet high fairly dazzled with gleaming clear water ice. Floe after floe, giant icicles, huge pillars, wreaths of delicate glass lacework, all of dizzying verticality, confronted them. And all "as unvisited as the heart of Greenland." That day they stared incredulous before retreating across the frozen lake to a somewhat milder ice slope on Mount Hor, which they climbed that Saturday. That night they returned to warm haunts in North Conway and met Mike Hartrich, letting him in on their secret and inviting him to come along next day. On that cold Sunday morning, Barber led a remarkable three-pitch route of a difficulty matching anything yet done in the Northeast. Because of the weather, they called it *Twenty Below Zero Gully*, a play on Scotland's premier ice climb, *Zero Gully*. But what was most significant was that on either side of them gleamed a dozen routes harder yet.

A handful of brave spirits visited Lake Willoughby over the next two winters. They climbed routes on the edges of the main face, routes that would have rated as major achievements anywhere else but that shrunk to lesser significance in the presence of the huge towers of ice in the central portion of the cliff. The best of these winters-of-1975-and-1976 routes was *Shaker Heights*, an impressive route climbed by Harvard's Ken Andrasko and Chris Field in 1975. These two did a second ascent of Barber's route, ignorant of his earlier ascent and therefore dealing with all the psychological barriers of a first ascent. They also made bold attempts on the steeper zone, sometimes getting two pitches up but never completing a big route. Boston AMC climbers Ernie Richards and John Shelton were also trying the giant icicles, also getting well up but never reaching the clifftop. Susan Coons was along on some of the Andrasko-Field trips, performing well but, like the others, not quite making the big breakthrough. A group of talented Burlington ice climbers, then roaring up the hard routes at Smugglers Notch, came over to see the new area and went away defeated—"we were basically overwhelmed," one recalled.

A prophet of the new verticality on ice, Rainsford Rouner, shown here with Mark Richey on their 1976 line, The Senator *on Humphrey's Ledge, combined boldness and unexcelled skill.*

HENRY BARBER

Two new climbing teams were the ones who had the vision to elevate modern ice climbing to the challenge of Lake Willoughby.

The first was a brace of brothers, Rainsford and Timothy Rouner. As a high school graduate marking time before getting into Harvard, Rainsford Rouner worked at EMS in the winter of 1974–1975, met Peter Cole, and took to ice climbing with flair. Rouner developed an aggressive style, using two axes and attacking the ice with power and confidence. He also adopted the prevailing ethic of the day: that ice was not the purist's arena that rock was, so "anything goes" in the way of style. By the winter of 1976 Rouner was as good as anyone on the North Conway scene, putting in such formidable routes as *Lila* on Cannon, *Drop Line* on Frankenstein, *The Senator* on Humphrey's, and the elegant *Myth of Sisyphus* on Whitehorse (avoiding the final and steepest bulge on the last). During this winter Rouner did two routes that reached greater difficulty than any yet done, the first significant breakthroughs since Bragg's *Repentance* of three years before. One was the bold, long, exposed, committing mixed route, *Omega* on Cannon, on which Bouchard was his partner. The other was a controversial ascent of *Remission* on Cathedral, climbed with Peter Cole and the younger Rouner, Tim. The latter route was controversial because they openly resorted to etriers to surmount the steepest final section. Bragg had been up the route as far as that top bulge but had backed off rather than resort to aid. However, there was no denying that by the winter of 1976 the Rouners were as hot on ice as anyone around.

Early the following winter the Rouner brothers arrived at Lake Willoughby. Over four days in December they worked on one of the steepest and highest pillars of icicles, the kind of unrelieved verticality only to be found at "the Lake." They finally won. *The Last Gentleman* was a clear advance over any pure ice route in New England. A week later Rainsford, joined by Peter Cole, began work on one even harder. In two days they completed *Promenade*. Five years later Wilcox's comprehensive guidebook to New England ice climbs called it "probably the hardest pure water ice in New England." The next month, with yet another partner, Chip Lee, Rouner put in *The Glass Menagerie*, third of his outstanding routes on the littoral cliffs of Pisgah.

During the same winter, two other climbers arrived at Lake Willoughby, climbing at very nearly the same level. In the winter of 1975 Harvard student John Imbrie began climbing ice under the tutelage of Andrasko and Field. The following winter he showed ice climbing slides to aspiring freshman climbers, among whom one took a special interest: Clint Cummins. In the winter of 1976 Imbrie improved his standards radically, while Cummins put in a most remarkable first year on ice. Cummins' fast start was a classic case of one who was not held back by old conceptions of what was possible and who accepted the new standards of 1976 as a baseboard on which to stand right away—and from which to spring. On his second weekend on ice. Cummins did most of the gullies in Huntington Ravine, soloing Pinnacle. On his third weekend he led Streibert's *Chia* at Frankenstein. Before the winter was over he led the *Black Dike,* the first time he roped up with Imbrie.

The next winter—the same one when the Rouners were active at Lake Willoughby—Cummins and Imbrie joined the attack there. Cummins' style was in marked contrast to Rainsford Rouner's. Where Rouner assaulted the ice with two axes and an explosion of power, the slender and lanky Cummins was light and deft in his approach, employing smaller tools to hook into the ice with just enough purchase. Imbrie, watching the two, was struck with the contrast: Rouner "all muscles and blast away," Cummins "much more delicate." Yet in the winter of 1977, Cummins and Imbrie put in several routes on Willoughby's cliff, one of which, *Mindbender,* was probably as difficult as any of Rouner's save *Promenade.* The following winter their *Called on Account of Rains* was in the same class. In February 1978 they journeyed far to the north to a little-known cliff on Maine's Kineo and put in a route of the same standard.

With the classic climbs of Lake Willoughby in 1977 and 1978, the final phase of the ice revolution that had begun with Chouinard in 1969 was basically completed. There simply was no place physically to excel Lake Willoughby's ice, nowhere further for the standards to go. As ice historian S. Peter Lewis put it, "nowhere else in the East will one find an area more blessed with truly vertical ice." During the late 1970s and 1980s, therefore, the story of ice climbing was primarily one of consolidation, the spreading of the gospel throughout the Northeast, and perfection of style.

The standards established by the Rouners and Cummins and Imbrie became more widely emulated. Lake Willoughby climbing did not become quite as commonplace as Huntington's had been in the 1960s or Frankenstein's in the 1970s, but nevertheless several parties could be found there every good winter weekend, climbing routes that had been unthinkable before the revolution. To the post-Rouner generation, Willoughby was "the Lake," as Huntington had been "the Ravine." Even the Boston AMC scheduled trips there in the late 1980s.

To a generation that regarded "the Lake" as a playground, the "old" classics of New Hampshire—i.e., those first done only as far back in ancient times as 1973—were romps comparatively. The *Black Dike* and *Repentance* were now often climbed, even by relative newcomers following guides. On Frankenstein, beginners were hauled up Streibert's once-awesome routes. This area had grown so popular that one visiting western climber marveled: "The crowds were nothing short of amazing." Climbers routinely soloed the Huntington gullies and Willey Slide. To be sure, parties could still be found roping up and having minor epics on the old classics, but the post-1976 standards became widely accepted by hosts of new climbers.

The new standards spread throughout the region, as they had on rock during the late 1970s. The Adirondacks, a land shimmering with vertical ice in the High Peaks every winter, developed a talented local community of front-pointers, with the tireless Al Jolley at the forefront. In Smugglers Notch a third generation of Burlington gang—this time including Bouchard's partner of 1975, Steve Zachowski, as well as Dave Marvin, Jim Gilchrist, Michael Young, Tom Schwarm, and D. J. Bouyea—made Smugglers Notch and other Vermont ice a regular scene for climbing at the standards of the day. A small squad of Mainers, among whom the David Getchells (father and son) and Geoff Heath were prominent, developed a series of ice cliffs in the Camden Hills. In the 1980s more good climbers made the annual trek to Katahdin and climbed long and technically modern routes in that most magnificent setting. Even in lower New England, ice was sought and, in cold spells, found suitable for the modern tools and techniques. By the mid-1980s enough "natural crags, roadcuts, gorges, and quarries" had been found in Massachusetts, for example, to produce a full-page write-up for *Climbing* magazine. The modern age of ice climbing had permeated every piece of frozen verticality in the Northeast.

With nothing physically bigger than the classic cliffs at "the Lake," where could the 1980s ice climbers take the sport? As we have seen on both rock and ice, climbing is inherently dynamic. Each generation stands on the shoulders of its predecessors to lift the standards. By 1980 there were climbers ready to step up from where Rouner and Cummins and Imbrie had left off. But where could they go? For pure ice, there simply were no routes in New England longer and harder than *Promenade*.

Partly they wedged routes in next to the Rouner classics that were just as long and scary, like *Reign of Terror*, put in by Matt Peer and Tom Dickey in 1981. Partly they found ice of just as much unrelieved verticality though of shorter overall length, like Kurt Winkler's *Nomad Crack* on Cathedral Ledge or *The Geographic Factor*, a series of airy pillars on Rattlesnake Mountain in the Baker River Valley. Partly they exported the new standards to the remoter basins of Katahdin so as to combine pure difficulty with a more de-

Kurt Winkler. Perhaps New England's top performer on ice during the first half of the 1980s, Winkler climbed the hardest routes in an impeccable style. Right: on The Eagle's Gift.

JOSEPH LENTINI

manding alpine setting, as in Dave Getchell Jr.'s *Black Fly* in the North Basin. Some went further north to Quebec and found still higher vertical ice there than even in Lake Willoughby, but that lies outside the scope of this history.

But another solution to the question of where to go after *Promenade* was found in a closer attention to style than had been hitherto enforced on ice. Unlike rock climbing, ice had always been more ambiguous on the question of style. Conceptually, the use of tools made all ice climbing a form of aid climbing. Yet there were obvious degrees along the free-aid continuum if you wanted to look for them.

Some who climbed at the leading edge during the early 1970s tried to apply a stylistic standard almost as pure as the Gunks rock climbing ethic. Henry Barber felt that even hanging from wristloops was a form of aid, that climbers should simply grip their tools harder and keep their weight on their feet more. Some early ascents of the *Black Dike* were done in that style, but rarely if ever after 1975. John Bragg, who introduced wristloops without qualms, nevertheless tried to keep style as clean as possible beyond that point. Resting on an ice screw was "a different ball game" to Bragg. So was hanging from a tool while putting in protection—and, Bragg added, "Anyway, I never trusted the tool well enough to hang on it!" Others who acquired a reputation for a very high stylistic purity on significant routes were Al Long and Mike Hartrich. As we saw, Bragg declined to complete *Remission* with flawed form, losing the first ascent to the Rouners, who went on etriers for the final moves. But neither Bragg nor anyone else was prepared to take on the awesome verticality of Willoughby with purer style.

The breakthroughs of the 1977 generation, the Rouners and Cummins and Imbrie, were associated with acceptance of resting on protection, hanging on tools while placing ice screws, and in some cases long sieging with ropes left in place or even outright aid with etriers. On the extremes on which they were launched, ethical niceties seemed absurd. Chouinard once quoted a Scottish climber as describing a route as "a line too cold for ethics." Declared Imbrie: "Free ice climbing is something for guidebook editors, not for climbers." This milder ethic was widely accepted during the late 1970s, though various distinctions were honored. In 1979 western ice guru Jeff Lowe instructed his generation to loop an elbow through the wrist-loop while placing screws, but cautioned that actually tying in at the waist while doing so was "too much like aid." These tactics were one reason why harder climbs were done, but their impact should not be exaggerated so far as to detract from the achievements of the 1977 generation. Nor did that generation make a travesty of ethics. Imbrie felt "there was never any climb that I couldn't have done without resting."

Nevertheless, it was in this realm that some of the 1980s ice climbers sought to raise standards—not by harder climbs, since none were available, but by completing the hardest climbs in pure style. Brian Becker and Chris Hassig were early leaders in this movement. They claimed "first free ascents" of such late 1970s classics as *Promenade* (Becker), *Remission* (Hassig), and others. Gradually Kurt Winkler emerged as leader and spokesman for this school of ice climbing. Quiet and courteous, but with an inner core of grit, Winkler thus capped a long and varied climbing career—having started as a disciple of Bob Proudman's on the AMC Trail Crew in the late 1960s, slowly but steadily advanced to the front rank of north country rock climbers during the late 1970s, and become indisputably the top all-around ice climber in the region during the early 1980s.

The ultimate in pure style was to free-solo such routes. By the mid-1980s such high-standard ice men as Randy Rackliffe and Craig Reasoner were setting heads wagging by soloing such routes as *The Last Gentleman* (Rackliffe) and *Drop Line* (Reasoner).

Another answer to where to go after the Lake was found in combining a series of extreme climbs in a single day, like knocking off several of the big

Lake Willoughby routes in quick succession. Bouchard and Rackliffe pulled off the ultimate in this kind of stunt by a one-day tour de force in which they climbed *Promenade* at Lake Willoughby, *Black Dike* at Cannon, and *Remission* at Cathedral, with some speedy highway driving from place to place between climbs. The pair also did *Whitney-Gilman, Black Dike,* and *Sam's Swan Song* on Cannon in a single winter's day. Andy Tuthill and Steve Larson put together the *Black Dike, Repentance,* Frankenstein's *Standard,* and the old classic *Pinnacle* in a single day's outing.

JOSEPH LENTINI   S. PETER LEWIS

John Tremblay. During the second half of the 1980s, no one undertook bolder, more improbable lines up the thinnest veneers of ice over rock than Tremblay. "He thrives on insecurity," it was said. Left: at Pitcher Falls. Right: at Frankenstein.

Where to go after the Lake, indeed? The question was still unanswered, as neither more-of-the-same nor purer style inspired the kind of respect and awe commanded by the breakthroughs of the 1970s by Bouchard, Bragg, Rouner, and Cummins.

The closest thing to a genuine breakthrough during the 1980s came in the scary realm of very steep, very thin ice, mixed with stretches of rock or snow—or whatever the desperate leader could find to defy gravity. Such was the quality of Winkler's hardest route in 1984, *The Eagle's Gift* on Eagle Cliff in Glen, seconded by Alex Behr and Joe Lentini.

The grand master of this new dimension in ice was John Tremblay. In December 1986 he astounded the climbing community by climbing absolutely every hard route in New Hampshire before the first of the year, many of them in barely climbable condition. He climbed on twenty-four of thirty-one days that December. "He thrives on insecurity," reported *Climbing* magazine. When Tremblay tiptoed up a route on Iron Mountain, often with each tool finding just enough ice to get one tooth in, one observer called it "one and a half grades harder" than the crux on the hardest previous climbs. His follower on that route, Dave Rose, said: "There wasn't one place where you could take the weight off your arms . . . following it was substantially harder than leading anything on *Remission.*"

Thus, on ice as on rock, the climbers of the 1980s continued to strive for even higher standards. No matter that there was nothing higher or steeper than *Promenade* or *Remission.* Climbers would find thin smears, or seek purer style, or do several hard routes a day. The tough cold sport of Whittlesey and Scoville on the Pinnacle Gully in 1930 continued to advance over fifty years later. ∎

Reference Note

The development of ice climbing at Lake Willoughby is traced in Clint Cummins and John Z. Imbrie, "Lake Willoughby Ice Climbing," *Harvard Mountaineering*, September 1979, pp. 40–64; and S. Peter Lewis, "Hard Water Ice Climbing at Lake Willoughby," *Climbing*, December 1984, pp. 18–20. For another view, see Craig Reasoner, "In the Deep Freeze: A Commentary on North American Waterfall Ice," *Climbing*, December 1986, p. 52.

Education in Verticality—a Short
Comedy or Farce in Four Scenes

The date: February 7, 1981.

The scene: Lake Willoughby, Vermont, which lies roughly three million miles north of anywhere warm.

Dramatis personae: (1) Mike Young, an ice climber of considerable attainments; (2) one of the authors, of considerably fewer attainments, if indeed any at all.

Dramatis personae.
Left: Michael Young.
Right: Author Guy
Waterman.

The occasion: Research for this book. The authors felt that at least one of them should have personally experienced the exotic pleasures of climbing the most extreme ice routes in the northeast. Young, a close friend and superb climber, has agreed to take one of the authors up one of the infamous Lake Willoughby climbs. Each of the authors nominated the other for this honor, but eventually one was condemned—er, chosen. Such are the requirements of field research for writing a climbing history. It beats writing a history of capital punishment.

Scene 1. The two climbers are roping up at the base of more than 300 feet of almost dead-vertical hard-frozen water ice. Wind whistles mournfully through the leafless trees in the woods below. Spindrift races fitfully across the cold surface of the ice.

Waterman (throwing out the rope, while looking up fearfully at the towering ramparts of frost): Say, Mike, does anybody actually fall on this stuff? I mean, do these ice screws really hold a dead-vertical drop like you could take on this?

Young (abstractedly, while lacing on crampons): Oh, sure, the modern ice screw is really quite reliable. People fall a lot. No problem.

(A few minutes pass in silence, the two climbers busied with their preparations.)

Waterman (lacing on crampons, but evidently an idea having occurred while observing that Young weighs approximately fifty-one pounds more than Waterman, and will be leading, of course): Uh, Mike . . . do you ever fall?

Young (absorbed with sorting hardware): Huh? Oh, fall? Me? Yes. Funny thing, actually. Every season I seem to take two leader falls. Never more than two. No matter how much I climb, or how little, I always seem to manage to take two falls, and only two. Every winter. Isn't that funny?

Waterman (hastily): Yes, yes, funny . . .

(A few more minutes pass in silence.)

Waterman (a bit more softly): Uh, say, Mike . . . have you taken any falls this winter?

Young (to the point): One.

Waterman (barely audible): Oh.

Curtain.

Scene 2. The second pitch. Young has executed a flawless lead of the second pitch and is now belaying at a point two-thirds of the way up the ice. Waterman is attempting to follow. Starts to fall. Actually, let's skip this scene. If you like, we could tell you about the first pitch, which went very smoothly.

Curtain (quick!).

Scene 3. Top of the second pitch, and showing the ice a bit above that point as well. Both climbers have tied in there. Waterman is wearily handing the rack to Young, who seems unwearied in spite of the strenuous weight lifting he has just completed, having hauled a weight scarcely fifty-one pounds lighter than his body weight up most of the second pitch.

Young (with enthusiasm that Waterman finds hard to take): Wasn't that a great pitch, though?

Waterman (smiling weakly): Yep, wonderful!

Young (gesturing upward): This next part's a whole lot easier. You won't have any trouble. It's really nice climbing. You'll love it.

Waterman: Yeah, wonderful!

(Waterman puts Young on belay. Young leads up about 10 feet.)

Young: This is lousy ice. It doesn't take the tools well at all. (Pause.) I don't think it would take ice screws either. Just flakes off.

(A further pause. Young has moved up another 5 feet.)

Young (falling): Falling!

Curtain.

Scene 4. Top of the second pitch, but showing also the ice a bit *below,* rather than above the belay point. Young now appears approximately 35 feet below the spot where he appeared at the end of the previous scene. He is in a horizontal position, face up, not significantly touching the ice, swaying gently in the air, rather like a piece of scaffolding against the side of a sheer glass skyscraper. The rope, taught as a piano wire, runs from his harness up to the waist of Waterman, who is holding on for dear life.

Young (shaking his head slowly): Two.

Curtain. ∎

26: Climbing at the Crossroads: Ethics and Style Questions for the 1990s

Very likely the Native Americans who climbed on Plymouth Rock were incensed when the first Puritan scrambled up the back in his buckled sticky-boots to peer down and inspect the route from above before climbing it. Arguments over ethics and style have enlivened climbing from its earliest days.

There was a brief period in the early 1970s when each climbing area seemed to have reached consensus on ethics and style. At the Shawangunks, Stannardian purity reigned, pitons and bolts were excommunicated, clean climbing prevailed, and ground-up leading was the only acceptable route to a first ascent—though multiple falls were stylistically valid and chalk found instant acceptance. In North Conway bolts and pitons were still standard practice and prior inspection and gardening suffered little shame. Other independent fiefdoms selected their own ethics and style. Mount Desert and Connecticut inclined to puritanism, while Boston happily top-roped and publicized everything at the same time that Adirondacks regulars suppressed information on their cliffs and Cannon's inner circle frowned on chalk. Ethical and stylistic issues were debated between areas, but within each local group there was an unforced unity of thinking.

During the later 1970s this happy harmony began to be disturbed by discordant notes. The north country's 1978–1979 debate over such controversial routes as *Arete* led to the celebrated airing of viewpoints at Daisey's, where speeches were intoned, steam was released, Jimmy Dunn stormed out, but nothing was lastingly resolved. In Connecticut Ken Nichols' rigorous insistence on leading-from-the-ground and no-bolts was meeting resistance from a counterethic of top-roping and bolting for protection. Caustic charges were aired in the letters columns of the climbing press. The Gunks were not immune—witness a controversial article in *Climbing* by Mark Robinson in 1979 headed "Pox in Vulgaria: The Profit of Impurism," in which the author deplored:

> . . . a loss in style for a gain in difficulty, and a loss in style for the sake of making a name.

318

But it was not until the mid-1980s that northeastern climbing—indeed climbing everywhere—witnessed a major escalation of ethical and stylistic controversy.

A key factor was the stylistic influence of France. Until the 1980s the French were known principally for their 1950 ascent of Annapurna and the grande alpinisme of Gaston Rebuffat. As rock climbers they were not distinguished.

Hidden away in the anonymity of their deep gorges, which few foreigners had heard of, a new generation of French rock climbers embarked on a radical departure from old ethics and style. The frankly avowed purpose was to master the highest possible level of pure difficulty with complete disregard for how success was achieved. Oversimplified, the French method involved three steps. The first was to dangle from a top-rope and rehearse each individual move as often as necessary until a long sequence of extremely difficult moves was mastered. If necessary, the artificial creation or improvement of one or two holds, by use of hammer or drill, was accepted if it would open up a route otherwise impossible. The second step, once all the moves were thoroughly rehearsed and mastered, was to preplace all necessary protection, also with the aid of the top-rope. The final step was to start at the bottom and lead this route, if possible with no falls.

This was clearly a break from the ethics and style of England or Germany, to say nothing of Stannard or Barber. It perceived rock climbing as purely a gymnastic exercise, with no element of adventure or risk.

For a while the French gymnasts labored away virtually unknown to the rest of the world. But during the 1980s it gradually dawned on climbers elsewhere that the French had passed them all in sheer technical virtuosity. With little warning, the French suddenly moved into the forefront of world climbing.

Americans were especially impressed. French climbers visiting the U.S. in 1985 handled American 5.13s with ease. They reported that their tactics had produced dozens of climbs in France more difficult than any in this country.

By 1985 and 1986 a small but growing band of American climbers adopted the French methods, openly ignoring traditional ethics and style in pursuit of major breakthroughs in technical difficulty. Nationally, California's Todd Skinner, Colorado's Christian Griffiths, and Oregon's Alan Watts were among the most prominent. Emerging as an articulate spokesman for the new approach, Griffiths asserted that, abroad and in the U.S., rock climbing had become "the sole pursuit of physical difficulty." Pointing to the incredible difficulties being mastered, he demanded: "With such extremes, who wants to worry about anything else?" The old ideals of style and commitment were irrelevant to Griffiths' view:

> It isn't a question of bravery. It bears no resemblance to the pursuits of Goretex and pile clad mountaineers. The German climber, the French climber and even now the British climber at the top end doesn't want to worry about dying or even having his mind clogged by speculation of which one of fifteen number one RP's are going to hold should he fall off.

In the Northeast, partly due to the French influence (especially a late 1985 visit to the Gunks by Patrick Edlinger) and partly to a home-grown impatience to master more difficulty, elements of the new approach were employed in creating early Shawangunks 5.13s like the Gruenberg variation on *Twilight Zone*, *Thunderdome*, and *Pumping Pygmies*—and in assaulting the fortress of 5.14. Among the tactics used were repeated rehearsals on toprope before leading; placement of bolts on rappel; and even modification of holds and, in one case, cutting a tree—the action that but five years earlier Bragg had declared would lead to lynching at the Shawangunks.

If such tactics gained acceptance at the Shawangunks, they ran rampant elsewhere. Jim Surette's *Liquid Sky* on Cathedral Ledge was an outstanding fruit of the new techniques. North country jargon rang with the new terminology of hang-dogging, red-pointing, and Beta. Because of its origins, the style was sometimes called "Euro-dogging."

The revolutionaries openly avowed their break with the past. Their goal, said the Gunks' Al Diamond, was "difficulty in the execution of moves," with "whatever it takes to achieve them. Risk and adventure have taken a back seat." The adventure in small-crag rock climbing, argued Scott Franklin, "was contrived to begin with." The name of the game now was what Russ Clune called "the quest for technical difficulty at the cutting edge." Said Diamond: "I look on myself as a high-angle gymnast." Added Jordie Mills: "We work our routes like gymnastic routines."

The new generation felt that all the choice lines on which natural protection was obtainable had been done by Stannard's generation. What remained for them were the steep overhanging walls, with just enough for holds but not enough for protection—climbs not unlike the French limestone climbs. (They called their new approach a "Limestone Ethic.") "If you tell us 'no bolts,'" argued Diamond, "you're telling us no new routes. . . . We can only do *Supercrack* so many times." They placed bolts—not indiscriminately, but with careful consideration of where and how many were needed—so as to make possible the outstanding climbs of the 5.13 to 5.14 era. The old no-bolts ethics, "the kids" claimed, would relegate their generation to twenty years of top-roping. They were not to be denied.

A couple of new developments issued from the new approach. One was the increasing acceptance and prestige of indoor artificial climbing walls. Indoor practice areas had been created during the 1970s. But in the latter half of the 1980s large-scale climbing walls sprang up in college gymnasiums and fitness centers. Furthermore, some climbers began to accept such contrivances as fully as valid an arena for their sport as the great outdoors, with all its bugs, temperature extremes, rain and snow, not to mention the difficulty of rigging top-ropes, with consequent risk of injury.

Closely related to the growing acceptance of artificial climbing walls was the open avowal of competition. The modernists took the view that, after all, the top climbers had always viewed each other competitively. Why not legitimize competition? Bring it out of the closet! So, beginning in Europe, scheduled climbing competitions were arranged, either on carefully inspected outdoor cliffs or inside on gymnasium walls. In either case, space for a large audience soon became essential: climbing competition suddenly leaped into the limelight as a media event and an instant route to glory and fame.

In America, organized climbing competitions received a major boost in June 1988 with the well-publicized International Sport Climbing Championships at Snowbird, Utah, in which France's Patrick Edlinger won the men's division and Catherine Destivelle beat out Lynn Hill in the women's.

The pages of *Climbing* magazine began regular reporting of the results of competitions on both sides of the Atlantic. Much like tennis or golf tournaments, the top winners and their "scores" would appear in boxes, and readers eagerly looked for who was winning and which Americans were placing well in head-to-head contests with French, Germans, and Brits. The only American who consistently did well was Lynn Hill, who could be counted on to finish first or second in the women's division of almost any competition she entered; rivalries between her and two or three top French and Italian women attracted much media attention.

Northeastern climbing traditionalists were outraged. "It's not climbing anymore," growled old Gunks Vulgarian Dave Craft, "it's gymnastics." The traditionalists deeply resented a few individuals "changing the rules" and destroying the hard-won consensus that had made the Gunks so admired for its ethics and style. Even the one-time pragmatic 5.11 pioneer Ed Webster disliked where he saw the new school heading:

The discipline of rock climbing is fast approaching an evolutionary dead end, a stagnant morass of historically unre-
deeming, topo-mapped, pre-rehearsed, pre-bolted, 5.12s
and 5.13s.

Those who were strongly rooted in the 1970s ethics rejected the claim that
difficulty was a sufficient objective of its own. They argued that there had
always been and always must be something more to climbing. They also
pointed out, with pride, that the Stannard-Wunsch-Bragg-Barber circle in
the early 1970s simultaneously raised *both* the technical standard *and* the
purity of ethics and style. The sense of commitment and adventure, the
"fine mental control" of leading from the ground up into unknown terrain
was what climbing was all about, said the traditionalists. The modernists,
they charged, were failing to grasp the essential metaphor of climbing.
Warned Henry Barber: "These people are missing some of the adventure,
and some of the struggle of climbing." In a response to Griffiths' arguments,
fellow Coloradoan Mark Wilford declared:

> The possibility of dire consequences, should we fail, has
> traditionally evoked great excitement in climbers. . . .
> Knowing the moves are possible and that all the protection
> is safely in place eliminates almost every aspect of tradi-
> tional climbing save the physical act.

One interesting irony was that, but a quarter century earlier, the radicals of climbing had insisted on infusing climbing with a sense of adventure
and danger that the conservative tradition had virtually suppressed. Now in
the mid-1980s Wilford and others were invoking adventure and risk as the
"traditional" values, in the face of radicals who called for eliminating danger
from climbing.

The tension between these two ways of thinking heated up during the
late 1980s. The letters columns of the climbing press became filled with
emotional, abusive, and ultimately futile attacks. Periodic local disputes
flared in which modernists would bolt a new route, traditionalists would
chop or bash the bolts, and occasional fisticuffs would ensue.

One dramatic result was the action taken by the land managers at the
Shawangunks. Charged with the responsibility of the environmental protection of the Shawangunk ridge—and egged on by traditionalists, a strong
force at the Gunks—the Mohonk Preserve called a series of meetings with

climbers and then promulgated a policy expressly forbidding new bolts, alteration of the rock, or tree-cutting on Shawangunk cliffs. A strong majority of Gunks climbers supported this policy. The modernists deplored it—and went looking elsewhere for blank walls on which to place bolts and establish routes of incredible difficulty.

North country climbers also continued to debate the ethical and stylistic issues. When several new routes were "created" (principally at the relatively obscure Sundown ledges) by means of chipping the rock, gluing holds, and fixing bolts with "modular" holds attached, north country traditional climbers protested and called a meeting of climbers to air local viewpoints. An overwhelming majority expressed disappointment and outrage at such tactics. The traditionalists hoped that this articulated consensus would prevent proliferation of the censured methods.

It is not the function of this history to evaluate which view was right or wrong, but to record that in the 1980s northeastern rock climbing was caught in a storm of controversy. An American Alpine Club meeting in late 1986 scheduled a panel discussion, the title of which perfectly expressed the issue: "The Great Debate: Is 5.14 Worth It?" During the last half of the 1980s, that question was not answered to everyone's satisfaction. But as New Hampshire climber S. Peter Lewis reported in a note in *Climbing* in late 1987: "Everyone seems to stay happy as long as they can keep yelling at each other."

Which way would northeastern climbing go during the 1990s? One possibility emerged, which optimists hailed as a possible happy outcome of the debate. Perhaps the deliberate competitive gymnastics of Euro-dogging would drive most such climbing into indoor gymnasium walls and a few specialized climbing areas like Oregon's Smith Rocks. Then the big mountain settings and smaller bastions of traditionalism like the Gunks would remain for those who sought outdoor adventure of the old flavor. "I think that there are two sports," said one proponent of the new school, the talented Italian climber Luisa Jovane:

> One is climbing and putting in protection, the other is just
> climbing. Putting in protection is a skill that some find to
> be demanding and exciting, but I'm not interested in it.

A two-track course might divide climbing and make it possible for each school of thought to have its own locales, undisturbed by the other. The gymnasts could then develop their skills on their indoor walls, while the traditionalists could enjoy old values in the magnificent outdoor setting of the mountain world.

As the 1990s began to unfold, climbing remained hesitating at the crossroads. Which way would the sport turn? To many climbers, absorbed in their own views, the answer seemed clear. To the historian, recognizing the difficulties of judging events without the perspective of many years, the answer was far from clear.

All that can be said with confidence is that the impulse to climb remained irresistible. Verticality remains, and the human spirit continues to respond to its call. The mountains remain. Further, in this evolving world, change is inevitable—and yet enduring values retain a strong hold on humankind. Out of the tension of these powerful influences, the future of climbing will bring exciting new chapters. ∎

Reference Note

A full account of the "great debate" on ethics and style in 1986 is Pat Ament, "Futurism and Nostalgia—The American Alpine Club Meeting, December 1986," *The Climbing Art*, December 1986, pp. 14–22. Both the letters columns and the current new-route reports in the regular climbing press include the airing of many viewpoints on all sides of the issues in the debate. The authors are indebted to the Mohonk Preserve for access to memoranda and reports covering that organization's deliberations regarding climbing practices on the Preserve land in the Shawangunks.

Index

Harvard, 10
Harvard Cabin (Huntington Ravine), 83, 91, 258
Harvard Mountaineering Club: beginnings, 112;
ice climbing, 83–84, 149, 307–308; 1930s, 38–39,
112; 1950s, 145–146; 1960s, 206; 1970s, 194
Hassig, Chris, 311
Hatch, Rick, 221
Hathaway, Mel, 10
Hawk, The, 173
Healy, Trudy, vii, 206, 283
Heath, Geoff, 309
Heather, 296
Hedgehog, Mount, 35
Heintz, Mike, 249
Helburn, Margaret: in the Alps, 18; in Boston area,
16, 18, 21, 282; ice climbing, 73; at Katahdin,
17, 35, 73
Helburn, Willard: in the Alps, 17–18; in Boston
area, 18, 21; ice climbing, 73, 84; at Katahdin,
17, 35, 73; on north country rock, 35; reputa-
tion, 29
Henderson, Ken: in the Alps, 18, 22–23; in Boston
area, 22, 102; ethics and style, 54, 60, 63; films by,
81; as mentor, 84, 102, 112; on north country
rock, 34–35, 37–38, 41; reputation, 29, 135;
solo climbing, 63
Hendricks, Steve, 221
Hendrickson, Carl, 244
Hendrickson, Esther, 166
Herr, Hugh, 273, 296–300
Higginson, T. W., 17
High Corner, 159
High Exposure: first ascent, 121–123; reputation,
128, 129, 142, 191; Wiessner on, 100
Hill, Lynn: as beginner, 289; in competition climb-
ing, 321; on north country rock, 289, 297; rep-
utation, 273, 289, 299; at Shawangunks, 289,
296, 299, 300; views on difficult climbing, 127,
300; as worldwide climber, 321
Hirschland, Dick, 141
Hirschland, Dorothy, 283
Hirtle, Bert, 142
Holden, John, 22, 35, 74
Holden, Roger, 73
Hor, Mount, 305
Horseman, The, 121
Hough, Dave, 247
House, William P., 81, 96, 99, 112
Houston, Charles, 78–79, 83, 112
Howe, Walter, 77, 103–106, 142
Howell, W. T., 9–10, 15
Howorth, Beckett, 98, 109, 118, 124
Hudon, Mark, 247, 296
Hudson, John, 178, 183
Hudson Highlands: first climbs, 22–23; ice
climbing, 260; New York AMC on, 23, 35,
95–96, 107–109, 117, 119, 124; New York in-
dependents on, 113–115; nineteenth century,
9–12; Underhill on, 35; Wiessner on, 95–96;
World War II closure of, 124
Hughes, Charles Evans, 15
Hummingbird, 303
Humphrey's Ledge, 96, 243, 267, 307

Huntington Ravine: early ascents (rock), 11, 18,
32–35, 41–52; early ascents (ice), 67–68; major
first ascents (ice), 74–86, 87–93; 1960s, 148–153;
1970s, 255–258, 309
Hurd, Jack, 18–20, 74–75, 102
Hurd, Marjorie, 18–20, 34–35, 102, 107, 282
Hurley, George, 179, 243, 273
Hyjek, Michael, 149, 159

Icarus, 267
Ice-axes, 128, 229, 253–256, 260, 264, 303
Ice hammers, 254–255, 260
Imbrie, John, 273, 307–311
Indian Head, 16, 63, 99
Indians. *See* Native Americans
Indoor climbing, 272, 321
Infinite Space, 296
Ingalls, Moses, 3
Intercollegiate Outing Clubs of America (IOCA):
conservative tradition and, 155–157; 1950s,
146–147, 155–157; 1960s, 186, 217; 1970s, 194;
solo climbing, 301
International Business Machines (IBM), 134,
194, 200
International Mountain Equipment (IME), 230
Intimidation, 214, 218
Inverted Layback, 174
Iron Mountain, 313
Isles, Dave, 149, 267

Jacob's Ladder, 175–176
Jacobus, Phil, 170, 175
Jaffe, Morrie, 194
Jane, 192, 223
Jervis, Steve, 135
Joe English Hill: 1916 ascent, 13–14; 1920s, 18,
112; 1950s, 142, 209; 1970s, 246
John Hudson Boulder Problem, 178
Jolley, Al, 309
Jones, Chris, 127, 200
Jovane, Luisa, 323

Ka-Na-Da-Hi, 113–115
Kaaterskill Falls, 6–7
Kama Sutra, 190
Kansas City, 190, 192, 280, 285
Katahdin: Chimney ascents, 17, 73, 150, 192; ice
climbing, 73, 150, 267, 309–310; 1920s, 35,
38–39, 112; 1930s, 106–107, 164–167; 1940s,
206–207; 1950s, 144, 165–169, 244–245; 1960s,
207; 1970s, 244–245, 267; 1980s, 309–310;
reputation, 77
Kauffman, Andrew, 81, 84, 112
Keeler, Rocky, 264
Keleman, Peter, 267
Kelsey, Joe, 158
Kellner, Wayne, 162
Kendall, Henry, 149, 153, 156
Kenesis, 234
Kenmore Square, 223–224
Kennedy, Owen, 73
Ken's Crack, 141
Kenway, Lester, 166